Springer Series in Healthcare Management and Innovation

The Springer Series in Healthcare Management and Innovation presents a curated collection of research monographs, contributed volumes, and professional titles that illuminate emerging theories, empirical studies, practical applications, strategic frameworks, and real-world case studies in healthcare. Each volume addresses a broad spectrum of topics in healthcare management and innovation, including—but not limited to—leadership, financial management, ethics and corporate social responsibility (CSR), human resource management, managed care, workforce and patient diversity, research and development (R&D) of medical technologies, organizational strategy and planning, and healthcare information systems.

By bridging the gap between theory and practice, this series serves as an essential resource for academics, researchers, scholars, and practitioners. It equips readers with the insights and competencies needed to navigate and lead effectively in the dynamic and evolving landscape of healthcare.

Alessandra Ricciardelli • Lorenzo Mercurio
Editors

Building Innovation in Ageing and Health Policy

Interdisciplinary Management Mechanisms and Strategies

Springer

Editors
Alessandra Ricciardelli
Department of Economics, Statistics
and Business
Universitas Mercatorum
Rome, Italy

Lorenzo Mercurio
Department of Public Health
University of Naples Federico II
Naples, Italy

ISSN 3091-3810 ISSN 3091-3829 (electronic)
Springer Series in Healthcare Management and Innovation
ISBN 978-3-032-09162-8 ISBN 978-3-032-09163-5 (eBook)
https://doi.org/10.1007/978-3-032-09163-5

This Springer imprint is published by the registered company Springer Nature Switzerland AG
The registered company address is: Gewerbestrasse 11, 6330 Cham, Switzerland

Foreword

Growing older is a privilege—one that we must cherish. Yet, longevity alone is not the goal. What truly matters is the quality of those additional years. We aspire not merely to extend life, but to enhance it. To ensure that our later years are marked by vitality, independence, and meaningful engagement with the world around us.

This is why the European Commission is committed to increasing not just life expectancy, but the number of healthy, active years we live. Our approach is holistic, recognising that there is no single solution to the complex challenge of healthy ageing.

One of the most powerful strategies is to start early. We often hear that health is wealth. Well, much like investing in a retirement fund, taking care of one's health from a young age pays dividends later in life. Avoiding major risks such as smoking, maintaining a nutritious diet, and staying up-to-date with vaccinations are foundational steps that can significantly influence long-term well-being.

Prevention remains at the heart of healthy ageing. This is why the European Commission is championing a preventative approach. For instance, about 40% of cancer cases in the EU are preventable. The Commission therefore put forward recommendations to support Member States in their efforts to prevent cancer through vaccination, as part of Europe's Beating Cancer Plan. Vaccination, quite simply, is the main tool for primary prevention of disease and one of the most cost-effective public health measures available. With Europe's Beating Cancer Plan, we have also earmarked EUR 4 billion for cancer prevention, detection, and care.

Our '*Healthier Together—EU non-communicable diseases*' initiative supports EU Member States in identifying and implementing effective policies against key health challenges. This initiative covers a broad spectrum of health issues, from diabetes to mental health, as well as looking more broadly at health determinants such as physical activity and nutrition. It is backed by close to 300 million euro of funding through the EU4Health programme, with the aim of improving citizens' health and well-being—whatever age they are. With this goal in mind, the Commission intends to present a Cardiovascular Plan in the coming year—a comprehensive, life-long approach plan that addresses critical risk factors to heart health. The Plan will harness the potential of technology for both prevention and treatment, to deal with the leading cause of premature death in the EU—cardiovascular diseases.

At international level, this is also an important year when it comes to tackling non-communicable diseases and improving public health. The UN General

Assembly is set to adopt a political declaration on non-communicable diseases in September, setting the direction for future action around the world. The EU is actively engaged in this global discussion and ready to lead by example.

Digital technologies also hold great promise. When accessible and user-friendly, they can help older adults stay connected, manage their health, and combat loneliness. From appointment reminders to monitoring vital signs, digital tools can empower seniors to take charge of their well-being. The European Health Data Space will mean that older Europeans, even if they choose to retire in another EU Member State, will have digital health records that their new GPs will be able to access and utilise.

As life expectancy continues to rise, our collective responsibility does too. We must ensure that these additional years are not only lived—but lived well. By fostering environments where older adults feel valued, supported, informed—and of course healthy—we can help make the golden years truly golden.

DG Health and Food Safety (SANTE)
Bruxelles, Belgium

Sandra Gallina

Contents

Processes of Innovation

New Horizons for Health and Care: From Digital Innovation and Ageing to Integrated Systems: Organizational Challenges and Opportunities

Alessandra Ricciardelli and Lorenzo Mercurio

1 Introduction

Health systems across the globe are undergoing a profound transformation, driven by the intersecting forces of population ageing, the rise of chronic conditions, and the rapid digitalization of care. These changes are not merely technological or epidemiological, they are fundamentally organizational. Traditional healthcare models, largely designed around acute, hospital-based care, are increasingly misaligned with the complex, continuous, and socially embedded nature of contemporary health needs. As populations live longer but often with multiple chronic conditions, and as digital tools redefine how care is accessed and delivered, health systems must evolve in structure, governance, and culture to remain effective, equitable, and resilient (Ferlie & Shortell, 2001).

From an organizational standpoint, this shift demands a rethinking of institutional boundaries and professional roles. Healthcare organizations can no longer function as isolated, hierarchical entities focused narrowly on service delivery. Instead, they are becoming nodes within larger, adaptive ecosystems that include public administrations, technology companies, academic institutions, civil society actors, and patient communities (Best et al., 2012). Within these ecosystems, the capacity to generate value increasingly depends on the ability to coordinate across sectors, share knowledge, manage complexity, and respond to local contexts. This

A. Ricciardelli (✉)
Department of Economics, Statistics and Business, Universitas Mercatorum, Rome, Italy
e-mail: alessandra.ricciardelli@unimercatorum.it

L. Mercurio
Department of Public Health, University of Naples Federico II, Naples, Italy
e-mail: lorenzo.mercurio@unina.it

A. Ricciardelli, L. Mercurio (eds.), *Building Innovation in Ageing and Health Policy*, Springer Series in Healthcare Management and Innovation,
https://doi.org/10.1007/978-3-032-09163-5_1

requires new organizational capabilities, including participatory governance, cross-disciplinary leadership, integrated data systems, and continuous learning mechanisms (Denis et al., 2015).

At the same time, health organizations face mounting pressures to demonstrate legitimacy and public trust. In an era marked by heightened citizen expectations, social inequalities, and institutional volatility, trust has become a strategic asset. It is shaped not only by clinical outcomes or efficiency metrics, but by how transparently systems operate, how fairly they allocate resources, and how meaningfully they engage with diverse populations (Gillespie & Reader, 2018). Crossing these tensions requires an ethical and inclusive approach to innovation, one that focuses on rights, equity, and intergenerational responsibility, rather than on cost containment or technological determinism.

This chapter argues that demographic and digital transitions in health must be understood as organizational challenges that require integrated, system-wide responses. It adopts a cross-cutting analytical perspective, grounded in contemporary organizational theory, to explore how health systems can adapt to the structural demands of ageing and the opportunities and risks of digital transformation.

Drawing on international case studies, theoretical insights, and recent policy developments, the chapter examines how health organizations are reconfiguring their practices, partnerships, and governance models in response to these converging imperatives.

Ultimately, the goal is not simply to highlight problems or propose isolated solutions, but to trace an emerging horizon of health and care, one in which organizations evolve to be more inclusive, adaptive, and relational. By focusing on structural adaptation, institutional design, and the social dynamics of change, the chapter aims to contribute to a deeper understanding of what it takes to build sustainable, person-centered health systems in an ageing and digital society.

1.1 From Lethal to Chronic: A Paradigm Shift in Organizational Design

Over the past two decades, advances in biomedical science and therapeutic innovation have transformed the landscape of healthcare by converting numerous acute, fatal diseases into chronic conditions. This shift is emblematic of a broader epidemiological transition: one that moves health systems from focusing on crisis intervention to the long-term management of complex, slowly progressing illnesses. Chronic conditions such as diabetes, cardiovascular diseases, cancer, and chronic obstructive pulmonary disease (COPD) have now become the dominant burden on health systems globally (WHO, 2020). While this evolution marks a scientific achievement of historic proportions, it also places sustained and multidimensional pressure on healthcare organizations. These institutions must now be reconfigured to deliver ongoing, coordinated, multidisciplinary care to diverse patient populations with complex medical, psychological, and social needs (Ham & Curry, 2011).

Legacy health systems, designed for episodic care and built around acute hospital interventions, are fundamentally misaligned with the logic of chronicity. The structural features of many healthcare organizations still reflect an industrial-era model of care delivery, emphasizing standardization, throughput, and specialization. This configuration, while effective for high-intensity, short-duration interventions (e.g., surgeries or trauma care), proves insufficient when addressing diseases that require continuous engagement, behavioral adaptation, and relational support over years or even decades (Christensen et al., 2009). Such systems frequently prioritize volume over value, reactive over proactive intervention, and institutional metrics over patient-centered outcomes.

The Chronic Care Model (CCM) proposed by Wagner et al. (2001) was a foundational attempt to systematize an alternative vision for managing chronic disease. It highlighted six key elements necessary for effective chronic care: self-management support, decision support, delivery system design, clinical information systems, health system organization, and community linkages. However, the practical uptake of this model has been slow and uneven, particularly in settings where organizational silos, fragmented payment mechanisms, and hierarchical professional cultures persist (Nolte & McKee, 2008). Many organizations continue to underinvest in preventive care and care coordination, resulting in avoidable hospitalizations, poor treatment adherence, and patient dissatisfaction.

From an organizational theory perspective, chronicity challenges the prevailing bureaucratic and mechanistic models of healthcare management. Scholars such as Mintzberg (1993) have long noted that professional organizations (like hospitals) tend to operate in compartmentalized ways, with loosely coupled units and fragmented authority structures. Chronic care, by contrast, demands a high degree of integration, relational coordination, and team-based collaboration. Gittell's (2009) work on "relational coordination" emphasizes the importance of shared goals, mutual respect, and timely communication among interdependent actors. These elements are not simply soft skills, they are core organizational capabilities that drive performance in complex care environments.

Health systems must therefore invest in redesigning their core structures, processes, and cultures to support integrated chronic care. This includes aligning incentives for collaboration across primary care, specialty care, and social services; implementing interoperable electronic health records (EHRs) to enable seamless information sharing; and standardizing care pathways that support early detection, patient activation, and shared decision-making.

Organizations such as Kaiser Permanente and the Veterans Health Administration in the United States have demonstrated that such integrated models can produce better outcomes and lower costs, but only when supported by robust institutional frameworks, clear accountability, and sustained leadership commitment (Shortell et al., 2015).

Leadership is a crucial lever in this transformation. Traditional command-and-control approaches are often ill-suited to managing the complexity and uncertainty of chronic care. Instead, leadership must be understood as a distributed and adaptive function that mobilizes diverse stakeholders around shared values and evolving goals (Heifetz & Linsky, 2002).

Clinical leadership, particularly from nurses, general practitioners, and case managers, plays an essential role in bridging silos, facilitating team learning, and anchoring patient relationships. Moreover, leadership must extend beyond individuals to include processes, cultures, and decision-making protocols that are inclusive and reflexive.

Adaptive organizations are those capable of learning and innovating in response to internal feedback and external shifts. This aligns with the concept of the "learning health system," in which real-time data, patient experiences, and organizational performance indicators are systematically analyzed to guide continuous improvement (Friedman et al., 2017).

Tools such as rapid-cycle evaluation, Plan-Do-Study-Act (PDSA) cycles, and service design workshops support the development of organizational learning cultures. Such tools are particularly valuable in chronic care contexts, where patient pathways often cross multiple services and jurisdictions, requiring iterative coordination and responsive adaptation.

The shift to chronic care also demands a profound transformation in patient-provider relationships. Chronic disease management is fundamentally different from acute care in that it relies heavily on patient engagement, lifestyle changes, and psychosocial support.

This requires a redefinition of professional roles and boundaries. Organizations must invest in training that enhances health professionals' competencies in motivational interviewing, health coaching, and culturally sensitive communication. Moreover, they must foster organizational climates that support empathy, trust, and partnership with patients and families (Bodenheimer et al., 2002).

In parallel, digital health technologies offer promising tools to support chronic care management, through remote monitoring, decision support systems, and patient portals. However, their impact is contingent on organizational capacity for implementation. Technology is not a panacea; it must be embedded in workflows, aligned with professional values, and governed by ethical safeguards. Organizations must develop digital readiness at multiple levels, including strategic alignment, workforce training, and infrastructure development (Greenhalgh et al., 2017). Poorly implemented digital tools can create new burdens, amplify inequities, or erode trust.

Equity is an additional and pressing concern in chronic care delivery. Research shows that socially disadvantaged groups experience higher rates of chronic conditions and poorer access to coordinated care (Marmot et al., 2010). Organizations must proactively address social determinants of health through partnerships with community-based organizations, use of population health data to identify disparities, and culturally tailored interventions. This may involve establishing health equity taskforces, collecting race and ethnicity data, and adopting community participatory approaches to service design.

Hence, the transition from acute to chronic care is not just a shift in medical needs—it is a fundamental reordering of how healthcare organizations must think, act, and collaborate. It challenges established models of authority, financing, service delivery, and professional identity. The organizations best positioned to meet the needs of patients with chronic diseases will be those that are flexible, collaborative, and mission-driven; that see patients as partners; and that invest in systems, people, and technologies that support continuous, coordinated, and compassionate care.

1.2 Ageing Populations: Organizational Adaptation in a Demographic Shift

The ageing of populations represents one of the most significant and accelerated demographic transitions of the twenty-first century. According to projections by the World Health Organization (WHO, 2015), by 2050, over 2 billion people, more than 20% of the global population, will be aged 60 or older. This seismic shift is reshaping the health needs of societies at a structural level.

Ageing is not merely an issue of longevity; it brings with it a rise in chronic diseases, cognitive decline, frailty, and complex psychosocial needs. Health systems that were originally designed for acute, episodic care now face the imperative of supporting long-term, integrated, and personalized care trajectories. This transformation is not only clinical or epidemiological, it is fundamentally organizational, requiring a rethinking of institutional roles, workflows, and strategic orientations (Ham et al., 2012).

Healthcare institutions are often ill-equipped to manage the intricate and evolving care needs of older adults. Traditional hospital-based models tend to prioritize acute episodes, marginalizing the continuity and coordination necessary for managing multimorbidity, functional limitations, and social vulnerability. Integrated geriatric services are sparse, and transitions between hospital, community, and home care are frequently disjointed, leading to fragmented service delivery, duplicative diagnostics, and medication-related complications (Kodner & Kyriacou, 2000).

This fragmentation is exacerbated by rigid administrative boundaries between health and social care sectors, a lack of interoperable digital infrastructures, and professional cultures that still undervalue geriatrics and community medicine (Briggs et al., 2018).

From an organizational design perspective, ageing necessitates the adoption of new models of service delivery, governance, and professional collaboration. The WHO's concept of "age-friendly health systems" (WHO, 2017) advocates for care models that preserve autonomy, dignity, and participation throughout the ageing process.

Operationalizing this vision requires redistributing resources toward primary and community-based care, establishing interdisciplinary geriatric assessment teams, and creating mechanisms for joint decision-making that include older persons and their caregivers. Organizations must also adopt integrated care pathways that facilitate seamless transitions across services, grounded in shared electronic records, unified case management, and performance metrics oriented toward long-term functionality and quality of life (Valentijn et al., 2013).

At the same time, health systems are experiencing a parallel demographic shift within their own workforces. In many countries, a significant portion of healthcare professionals are nearing retirement age, placing additional strain on institutional capacity.

Organizations must manage dual human resource challenges: retaining and supporting ageing employees, through ergonomic interventions, flexible work arrangements, and lifelong learning, and preparing the next generation of health workers with the competencies needed to care for older adults effectively (Ilmarinen, 2006; Stone, 2020). This includes not only clinical knowledge but also soft skills such as empathy, communication, and cultural competence.

Organizational adaptability is essential. Institutions must foster cultures of continuous learning and innovation, embedding tools such as quality improvement collaboratives, communities of practice, and cross-sectoral learning networks into everyday routines (Martin et al., 2015; Bate & Robert, 2007). These learning mechanisms enhance reflexivity, allowing organizations to respond dynamically to emerging needs, evidence, and demographic shifts. Moreover, involving older adults themselves in the co-design of services is key to ensuring that systems remain attuned to lived experience and avoid technocratic or ageist biases.

Finally, reframing ageing not as a burden but as an opportunity for organizational renewal is a critical cultural shift. It challenges the deficit-oriented narratives that dominate public discourse and instead positions longevity as a societal achievement that calls for investment in person-centered, rights-based, and community-rooted forms of care. From this perspective, organizations are not simply service providers, they are platforms for social solidarity, human dignity, and intergenerational justice.

1.3 Sustainability, Rights, and Digital Leverage: A Strategic Organizational Balancing Act

Health systems today face a pivotal moment due to the fact that the combination of an ageing population, the rising incidence of chronic diseases, growing citizen expectations, and persistent workforce shortages place pressure on institutional capacity and fiscal viability.

This complex convergence of demographic and economic factors raises urgent questions about the sustainability of healthcare provision in both high-income and resource-constrained settings. However, sustainability must not be interpreted narrowly as cost containment or operational efficiency. Rather, it must be conceived as a multidimensional goal that integrates economic responsibility with the ethical protection of individual rights, social equity, environmental awareness, and intergenerational justice (Saltman et al., 2011; WHO, 2015).

From an organizational perspective, this broader interpretation of sustainability requires health systems to engage in strategic rethinking of their mission, governance structures, and operational models. Hospitals, primary care networks, and public health institutions are increasingly tasked with balancing seemingly conflicting imperatives: providing equitable access to quality care while ensuring financial resilience and fostering innovation.

This balancing act demands not only technical solutions but also deep cultural and organizational transformation (Mintzberg, 1996; Porter & Lee, 2013).

Digital technologies have emerged as central tools in this transformation. They are often presented as the key to reconciling limited resources with rising demand by increasing efficiency, enabling preventive care, and extending reach to underserved populations.

Technologies such as telemedicine, remote patient monitoring, clinical decision support systems, and electronic health records have demonstrated potential to reduce administrative burden, prevent unnecessary hospitalizations, and improve coordination across care teams (Greenhalgh et al., 2017). However, the realization of these benefits is not automatic. The organizational conditions in which digital tools are introduced matter profoundly.

If health organizations lack a supportive culture, clearly defined processes, and adequate governance mechanisms, the implementation of digital technologies can introduce new forms of fragmentation, complexity, and inequity.

Inadequate training, poor change management, and the absence of meaningful staff engagement often lead to low adoption rates or even outright resistance.

For instance, clinicians may distrust algorithmic decision-making tools if they perceive them as opaque or inconsistent with professional judgment. Patients may opt out of digital health platforms if they do not feel adequately informed about privacy implications or if they lack digital literacy.

These challenges highlight the fact that technology alone cannot transform care delivery unless it is embedded within a broader organizational commitment to ethical innovation and inclusive practice (Lupton, 2014).

Organizational strategy must therefore embrace digital transformation not as an auxiliary feature but as a core dimension of mission, structure, and identity.

This shift involves articulating clear values that govern digital development and deployment, including privacy, fairness, transparency, and accessibility. As Van Dijck and Poell (2016) argue, digital health systems must be shaped not only by market logic or technical functionality but by democratic accountability and public interest. This implies that digital governance frameworks should include mechanisms for stakeholder participation, rights-based design, and oversight of algorithmic decision-making processes.

Specifically, organizations need to build internal capacities for algorithmic literacy and data ethics. Leadership teams must ensure that digital applications comply with national and international legal frameworks such as the General Data Protection Regulation (GDPR) and that informed consent procedures are meaningful rather than symbolic.

Governance should extend to cybersecurity, risk assessment, and procurement, especially when partnering with external technology providers or adopting artificial intelligence-based solutions. Without these safeguards, digital innovation may compromise the very trust and equity that sustainability demands.

Moreover, a sustainable digital transformation requires rethinking the relationship between technology and organizational culture. As Llewellyn et al. (2014) emphasize, health systems must undergo a cultural shift to fully embrace the potential of digitalization.

This means moving from reactive to anticipatory care models, where early intervention and patient engagement take precedence over episodic crisis management. It also requires a transition from siloed expertise to interprofessional collaboration, and from static bureaucratic procedures to iterative learning cycles informed by real-time data and feedback.

Learning health systems exemplify this orientation. These are organizations that continuously collect and analyze data on performance, outcomes, and user experience in order to inform service improvement and innovation.

Learning systems value experimentation, adaptive leadership, and participatory governance, recognizing that knowledge is co-produced among professionals, patients, and communities (Friedman et al., 2017). In such environments, digital tools become enablers of empowerment and inclusion, rather than drivers of control and standardization.

Yet, sustainability also requires a critical awareness of unintended consequences. The increasing reliance on digital technologies must not widen existing disparities in health access and quality. For example, rural populations, older adults, individuals with disabilities, and people from low-income backgrounds often face digital exclusion due to infrastructural, educational, or linguistic barriers. Organizations must actively address these vulnerabilities through inclusive design, targeted outreach, and multichannel service provision. Digital equity should be monitored as a strategic indicator, just as clinical effectiveness or financial performance is today.

Another dimension of sustainability relates to the environmental impact of healthcare and digitalization. Data centers, electronic devices, and telehealth systems consume energy and generate electronic waste. Sustainable organizations must consider their ecological footprint and integrate environmental responsibility into procurement, infrastructure design, and technology use. This aligns with the emerging concept of "green health systems," which link clinical care, organizational governance, and planetary health (Karliner et al., 2020).

Therefore, the sustainable integration of digital technologies into healthcare organizations is a complex, strategic task that extends far beyond the acquisition of new tools. It requires visionary leadership, inclusive governance, robust infrastructure, and a deep commitment to human rights and social equity. Organizations that thrive in this environment will be those capable of aligning technological capability with ethical responsibility and social purpose. They will not only adapt to demographic and fiscal pressures but will also help shape a more just, inclusive, and resilient future for health systems.

1.4 Data Governance and Policy-Making: Organizational Intelligence and Accountability

Health data is increasingly recognized as one of the most valuable assets within contemporary health systems. It is a resource with the potential to radically transform clinical care, public health planning, research, and operational efficiency. When leveraged effectively, health data can support predictive analytics, guide precision medicine, enable risk stratification, and facilitate population health management. It can also provide feedback for quality improvement, inform resource allocation, and support system-level accountability. However, data is not neutral. Its value is highly contingent upon how it is collected, processed, interpreted, and governed within organizational settings (Cresswell et al., 2022).

The mere existence of vast amounts of health data does not guarantee improvement. Rather, the ability of organizations to convert raw data into meaningful action relies on a complex interplay of infrastructure, culture, leadership, and regulatory compliance. Too often, health systems have invested heavily in data acquisition technologies while neglecting the human and organizational frameworks required to manage and govern data responsibly. This has resulted in information overload, inconsistent data quality, limited interoperability, and—most critically—erosion of trust among patients and providers.

Organizational governance of data goes beyond ensuring compliance with external legal frameworks. While the General Data Protection Regulation (GDPR) offers an essential baseline for data privacy and protection in the European context, it does not provide a roadmap for internal organizational decision-making. Effective data governance requires institutions to define clear policies on data access, usage rights, retention periods, and secondary uses.

These policies must be supported by role-specific responsibilities and mechanisms for oversight and audit. As Vayena et al. (2018) argue, governance should address both legal and ethical dimensions, especially in contexts involving algorithmic decision-making, automated risk prediction, and machine learning.

Data governance also involves the creation of institutional roles and structures such as data protection officers, ethics boards, information governance committees, and data stewardship teams. These structures must be empowered to intervene, question, and shape data-related decisions.

They serve not only a compliance function but also a strategic one, helping organizations navigate ethical dilemmas, reputational risks, and the political consequences of data misuse. Importantly, these governance bodies must be embedded within the broader institutional architecture and connected to both clinical and administrative leadership, not siloed as technical or legal appendages.

Cultural dimensions are equally important. Data cultures vary widely across health organizations. In some institutions, data is viewed primarily as an administrative tool for reporting and reimbursement, while in others, it is treated as a dynamic asset for learning and improvement.

Developing a mature data culture requires active leadership engagement, investments in data literacy across the workforce, and the articulation of shared values that promote transparency, accountability, and collaboration. For example, fostering an environment where frontline professionals feel safe to question data quality or propose improvements can be a powerful driver of change.

Transparency plays a central role in cultivating trust in data use. When patients, professionals, and the public understand how data is collected, who has access to it, and how it is used to improve care, they are more likely to support digital innovation and data sharing.

Transparency is not simply a matter of publishing privacy policies or technical documentation. It involves active communication, public engagement, and participatory design processes that respect the concerns and perspectives of users. As Greenhalgh et al. (2022) suggest, designing digital platforms with users—not merely for them, enhances usability, legitimacy, and long-term sustainability.

Participatory data governance involves co-design and co-production approaches that bring together clinicians, managers, patients, IT developers, and policymakers. These collaborative methods enable the alignment of technological design with real-world practices, workflows, and expectations. For example, in the context of electronic health records (EHRs), involving clinical teams in interface design and data entry protocols can reduce administrative burden and improve clinical relevance. Similarly, engaging patients in decisions about consent models and data access mechanisms can strengthen ethical foundations and increase user satisfaction.

Organizational readiness for participatory governance varies considerably as it requires a shift away from technocratic decision-making toward deliberative, inclusive, and dialogical practices. Institutions must create spaces for dialogue, reflection, and joint problem-solving, which may include data ethics forums, citizen juries, and interdisciplinary working groups.

These participatory mechanisms are not simply procedural add-ons; they are essential components of a democratic and socially responsive data strategy.

The example of Italy's national telemedicine initiative, for instance, coordinated by Agenas in collaboration with regional health authorities such as Lombardy and Apulia, highlights both the promise and the complexity of data integration.

The initiative aims to create a unified telemedicine infrastructure that supports remote consultations, home monitoring, and continuity of care across settings. Technically, this requires interoperability between regional electronic health records, secure authentication mechanisms, and standardization of data formats. But organizationally, the challenge is even greater: ensuring that the data generated through telemedicine is governed transparently, used responsibly, and made accessible to both clinicians and patients in ways that enhance care without compromising privacy or increasing inequality.

Governance mechanisms must ensure that digital tools deployed through national programs adhere to principles such as privacy by design and equity by default. This includes conducting regular Data Protection Impact Assessments (DPIAs), establishing feedback channels for users, and monitoring for potential biases or exclusions in algorithmic systems. For instance, if a remote monitoring system disproportionately flags male patients for intervention due to biased training data, governance bodies must have the capacity to detect and correct this imbalance.

Furthermore, equity considerations must be embedded into data governance from the outset. Without deliberate planning, digital tools can entrench existing disparities by excluding populations with limited access to devices, connectivity, or digital literacy.

Organizations must assess the differential impact of digital innovations across demographic groups and create adaptive strategies that ensure no population is left behind. This may include offering alternative, non-digital options, investing in digital literacy programs, or establishing community-based data access points.

Another important aspect is the integration of data governance into broader organizational strategy. Data strategy cannot be developed in isolation from clinical strategy, human resources, finance, and operations. It must be integrated into board-level discussions and long-term planning, with clear alignment between data goals and institutional missions.

Only through this integration can data governance support organizational resilience, innovation, and public trust.

Health data, therefore, although representing a cornerstone of twenty-first-century healthcare systems, its value and legitimacy depend not only on technical capacity but also on organizational intelligence, ethical sensitivity, and participatory governance.

Institutions must move beyond minimal legal compliance toward proactive stewardship, shared decision-making, and continuous learning. Those organizations that succeed in establishing inclusive, transparent, and accountable data governance structures will not only harness the full potential of digital transformation but also reinforce their legitimacy, improve patient outcomes, and build sustainable, people-centered health systems.

1.5 One Health and Global Governance

The COVID-19 pandemic and the accelerating consequences of climate change have brought into sharp focus the deeply interconnected and systemic nature of contemporary health threats. These threats do not respect borders, institutions, or disciplinary silos.

They manifest across multiple domains, including human, animal, environmental, and social systems, and have cascading impacts on economies, infrastructures, and public trust.

As a result, traditional models of health governance that rely on siloed expertise, sector-specific responses, and national-level jurisdiction have proven insufficient. In this context, the One Health approach has emerged as a crucial framework for addressing the complexity, scale, and uncertainty of emerging global health risks, as highlighted by Kickbusch and colleagues in 2021.

The One Health paradigm proposes an integrated approach to health that explicitly recognizes the interdependence of human health, animal health, and the health of ecosystems. It calls for holistic thinking and collaborative action across sectors that have historically operated in isolation.

While originally conceived as a strategy to manage zoonotic diseases and antimicrobial resistance, One Health has grown into a broader conceptual and operational framework capable of guiding responses to pandemics, biodiversity loss, environmental degradation, and food system disruption. It emphasizes coordination, co-learning, and co-governance among a diverse set of actors, including ministries of health and agriculture, environmental agencies, academic institutions, and civil society organizations.

From an organizational perspective, adopting the One Health approach demands more than technical coordination or inter-agency cooperation. It entails a profound transformation in governance structures, institutional culture, and managerial capabilities.

Health organizations must not only collaborate with veterinary and environmental institutions, but must also rethink their own organizational boundaries, decision-making logics, and strategic objectives. This involves a shift from institution-centric models of control to systems-oriented models of collaboration, where shared goals, mutual accountability, and distributed leadership become central, as discussed by Ahrne and Brunsson in 2005.

One of the most ambitious proposals emerging from this paradigm is the idea of establishing an Intergovernmental Panel for One Health, known as IPOH, inspired by the Intergovernmental Panel on Climate Change, or IPCC.

The IPOH would serve as a global meta-organizational structure tasked with synthesizing scientific evidence, forecasting systemic risks, and coordinating multilateral responses to global health challenges. Its primary function would be to provide authoritative assessments that inform national and international policy while fostering collaboration across disciplines and sectors.

However, establishing such an institution raises important questions of legitimacy, authority, and coordination. The involvement of multiple stakeholders with divergent interests, unequal resources, and varied governance capacities presents a formidable challenge to institutional coherence and operational effectiveness, as noted by Buse and Harmer in 2007.

The complexity of building such global governance structures lies not only in the technical and financial challenges but also in the organizational design choices that must be made.

Issues of representation, decision-making rules, resource allocation, and accountability mechanisms must be carefully negotiated to ensure that the resulting body is both inclusive and effective. Moreover, such a body must be adaptive enough to respond to emerging evidence, flexible in its modes of engagement, and transparent in its communication strategies.

These are not merely matters of policy, but core organizational design challenges that affect legitimacy, authority, and trust.

At the national and regional levels, implementing the One Health framework requires the development of intersectoral governance mechanisms that can operate across traditional ministerial and institutional boundaries.

Ministries of health must work closely with ministries of environment, agriculture, and education, while also engaging with local governments, community-based organizations, and private sector actors. This intersectoral coordination requires health organizations to build new competencies in collaborative governance, including conflict resolution, joint strategic planning, shared financing, and multi-stakeholder evaluation.

Leadership must evolve to embrace what scholars call boundary-spanning practices, which involve the ability to operate across institutional domains, manage competing logics, and align diverse interests around shared public value goals, as proposed by Williams in 2002 and Emerson and colleagues in 2012.

Organizational capabilities for adaptive governance are critical in this context. Adaptive governance refers to the ability of institutions to respond flexibly and reflexively to changing conditions, uncertainties, and stakeholder demands.

It involves creating structures that support decentralized decision-making, foster iterative learning, and enable cross-sectoral dialogue. In the context of One Health, this means designing governance architectures that are capable of adjusting to new scientific insights, evolving threats, and sociopolitical dynamics. It also requires a commitment to continuous organizational learning, which can be supported by mechanisms such as joint simulation exercises, scenario planning, and shared performance metrics.

Importantly, One Health implementation is not solely about creating new institutions or mandates. It is also about reimagining existing organizations and networks as platforms for collective action. Hospitals, universities, public health departments, veterinary agencies, and environmental regulators must work together not only through formal agreements but also through deeply embedded collaborative practices.

These include shared information systems, co-managed programs, interprofessional education, and regular joint training. Such collaboration relies on building relational trust, cultivating shared language and values, and developing institutional memory that supports ongoing partnership rather than episodic cooperation.

Health organizations must also embrace a new ethos of responsibility, one that recognizes the ethical and social dimensions of planetary interdependence. In this view, global health is not only a matter of preventing disease but also of promoting ecological stewardship, social justice, and human solidarity. Organizations that operate within this ethos prioritize equity, transparency, and resilience in their governance strategies.

They measure success not solely by efficiency or outputs, but by their contribution to long-term system integrity and collective well-being.

The shift toward One Health thinking also has profound implications for how organizations measure and evaluate success. Traditional performance metrics such as hospital readmission rates or vaccination coverage may need to be supplemented with indicators that capture environmental sustainability, intersectoral collaboration, and community engagement.

Evaluation frameworks must be multidimensional, integrating qualitative and quantitative data, and must reflect the complexity of working across domains and disciplines. Learning-oriented evaluation, rather than accountability-driven audit, becomes essential for navigating the uncertainties and interdependencies that define the One Health landscape.

The One Health paradigm represents a necessary and urgent response to the interconnected health threats of the twenty-first century. However, its implementation is not merely a scientific or technical task, it is a deeply organizational challenge.

It requires rethinking governance at every level, from local institutions to global bodies. It demands that organizations become more open, more flexible, and more collaborative, capable of acting locally while contributing to global systems of care, resilience, and sustainability. Only through such systemic and inclusive organizational transformation can the promise of One Health be fully realized in practice.

1.6 Structural Conflicts and the Organizational Role of Prevention

Healthcare organizations routinely operate across, and are shaped by, the boundaries of multiple, often competing, institutional logics. These include the medical logic, which prioritizes clinical autonomy, diagnostic accuracy, and evidence-based care, the managerial logic, which emphasizes cost-efficiency, performance metrics, and accountability, the political logic, which introduces electoral imperatives and public scrutiny, and the civic logic, which is grounded in the principles of equity, inclusion, and community responsiveness.

As Waring and Currie (2009) have observed, these different logics are not always compatible, and their intersection often gives rise to structural tensions within organizations, particularly around issues such as access to care, resource distribution, and accountability for outcomes.

In this fragmented landscape, prevention and health promotion have historically been marginalized within organizational priorities. Although there is a robust and growing evidence base that supports the cost-effectiveness and long-term benefits of preventive interventions, these services continue to receive less attention and fewer resources compared to acute care.

This marginalization is not a consequence of scientific uncertainty or professional resistance. Rather, it reflects deeper institutional biases that favor short-term, tangible results, such as hospital admissions, procedural volumes, or mortality reductions, over the more diffuse and long-term gains associated with public health efforts (Bailey et al., 2017).

To shift toward a prevention-oriented model, health organizations must undertake a profound organizational transformation. This transformation involves more than integrating a few public health programs into hospital workflows.

It demands a reconfiguration of organizational priorities, governance arrangements, incentive structures, and performance management systems. Prevention must be embedded as a strategic objective, supported by leadership at the highest levels, and operationalized through concrete changes in how resources are allocated, how outcomes are measured, and how teams are structured and incentivized.

One of the first steps toward embedding prevention into organizational life is the creation of dedicated units or departments focused on population health.

These units serve as hubs for designing, implementing, and evaluating preventive interventions across communities, and they facilitate partnerships with external actors, such as schools, employers, and urban planners. By institutionalizing population health functions, organizations signal that prevention is not peripheral but core to their mission. These units also play a critical role in linking clinical data with social and environmental data to identify risk patterns, forecast demand, and target interventions more effectively.

Equally important is the integration of preventive indicators into performance dashboards. Most health organizations track outputs such as patient throughput, emergency department wait times, or surgical success rates. However, few systematically monitor rates of physical activity in the population, levels of childhood immunization in underserved neighborhoods, or the availability of healthy food in hospital cafeterias.

Embedding such indicators into routine organizational reporting systems creates visibility for preventive outcomes and allows them to be managed and improved in the same way as traditional clinical metrics. Moreover, tying executive compensation or departmental incentives to improvements in these indicators can help align organizational behavior with public health goals (Berwick et al., 2008).

Another essential lever is the reengineering of financial flows to reward long-term outcomes rather than short-term outputs. Many current payment systems reimburse activities such as admissions, procedures, and consultations, which can unintentionally create perverse incentives to treat illness rather than prevent it.

Transitioning to value-based payment models, where organizations are rewarded for maintaining health and reducing avoidable utilization, can drive investment in upstream interventions. Capitation, bundled payments, and shared savings arrangements offer promising mechanisms to encourage preventive care, especially when paired with accountability measures that ensure quality and equity are not compromised.

Beyond internal reorganization, prevention cannot succeed without robust inter-organizational collaboration. Health promotion often requires interventions outside the clinical environment, in spaces where people live, learn, work, and play. Collaborations with educational institutions can support programs on nutrition, mental health, and sexual education.

Partnerships with transportation agencies can foster walkability and reduce exposure to pollution. Engagement with housing authorities can mitigate the health risks of overcrowded or unsafe living conditions. Such collaborations are inherently complex, requiring the alignment of different professional cultures, timelines, and success criteria. However, when governed effectively, they can extend the reach of prevention far beyond the walls of the hospital or clinic.

Organizational development literature underscores the importance of internal cultures in enabling or hindering change. Successful prevention strategies often emerge in organizations that have cultivated cultures of learning, experimentation, and responsiveness.

These are environments where staff are encouraged to challenge the status quo, where feedback is valued and acted upon, and where innovation is supported rather than penalized. Developing such cultures involves investments in leadership development, change management training, and knowledge-sharing infrastructure.

It also requires psychological safety, where employees feel confident raising concerns or proposing new ideas without fear of retribution or dismissal.

This vision aligns with the model of the "learning health system" as described by Friedman et al. (2017). In a learning health system, data from real-world practice is continuously collected, analyzed, and used to refine care delivery. Feedback loops allow organizations to test interventions rapidly, learn from failures, and scale successful practices.

For prevention, this model is particularly powerful. It allows organizations to track the impact of public health initiatives in real time, adjust interventions based on population feedback, and disseminate successful models across departments or facilities. Learning health systems also facilitate collaboration between clinical and nonclinical staff, recognizing that effective prevention depends as much on communication, trust, and community engagement as it does on biomedical knowledge.

Community responsiveness is another cornerstone of prevention-oriented organizations. Health systems must not only deliver services to populations but must also listen to them, involve them in decision-making, and adapt to their needs and preferences.

Community engagement strategies, such as citizen advisory boards, participatory budgeting, and community health worker programs, allow organizations to better understand local determinants of health and co-produce solutions that are culturally appropriate and locally relevant. When people see their needs and voices reflected in organizational action, trust increases, and participation in preventive programs becomes more likely.

Transforming healthcare organizations into engines of prevention is not a marginal reform, but a systemic endeavor that touches every aspect of organizational life.

It involves rethinking what constitutes success, redesigning how services are funded and delivered, and reshaping how organizations relate to their staff, their partners, and their communities. The rewards of this transformation are profound: healthier populations, reduced disparities, lower long-term costs, and more resilient health systems.

Yet achieving these outcomes requires courage, vision, and persistence. It requires leadership that sees prevention not as an ancillary task but as a strategic imperative. And it requires organizations that are willing to evolve, to learn, and to act in partnership with the communities they serve.

1.7 Chronicity and Complexity: Coordinating for Continuity

Chronic conditions, such as diabetes, cardiovascular disease, chronic respiratory illnesses, and musculoskeletal disorders, have become the leading causes of mortality and morbidity globally. While these diseases are traditionally understood through a biomedical lens, focusing on their physiological and pathological mechanisms, their management is equally, if not more, a matter of organizational design. Chronic illnesses unfold over time, often interacting with social, psychological, and economic factors.

As such, they demand forms of care that go far beyond episodic medical intervention. They require sustained engagement with patients, cross-functional collaboration among professionals, and adaptive decision-making structures that can respond to fluctuating health states, comorbidities, and psychosocial dynamics (Valentijn et al., 2013).

At the heart of the organizational challenge is the concept of continuity. Chronic care cannot be reduced to a sequence of clinical encounters. It must be conceived as a process that ensures informational, relational, and managerial coherence over extended periods.

This means that care providers must have access to the same data, share a common understanding of patient goals, and operate within systems that reward long-term outcomes rather than short-term efficiencies. However, the current reality in many health systems remains one of fragmentation. Different providers work in silos, patients are forced to repeat their histories at every visit, and communication breakdowns lead to duplicated tests, medication errors, and avoidable hospitalizations.

To address these challenges, various organizational models have been developed and tested. Among the most prominent are patient-centered medical homes, integrated care organizations, and accountable care systems. These models differ in structure and context, but they share key principles: coordination, accountability, and person-centeredness.

Patient-centered medical homes, for instance, reorganize primary care practices to provide comprehensive, accessible, and coordinated care. They emphasize continuity, preventive services, and patient engagement. Integrated care organizations seek to unite multiple providers, often across sectors such as health and social care, under a shared governance and financing model. Accountable care systems introduce financial incentives for quality and cost-effectiveness, encouraging providers to collaborate in order to achieve population-level health outcomes (Shortell et al., 2015).

Central to these models is the idea of alignment. Alignment refers to the strategic and operational synchronization of actors, processes, and goals. Without alignment, even the most sophisticated organizational designs can fail. For example, introducing a shared electronic health record may seem like a technical fix, but if clinicians are not trained to use it, if data entry is inconsistent, or if interoperability is lacking, the system may increase complexity instead of reducing it.

Likewise, appointing care navigators to support patients through complex care pathways can improve experience and outcomes, but only if these roles are clearly defined, adequately resourced, and embedded within team workflows.

Organizational trust is a critical enabler of these reforms since it allows for the delegation of responsibility, reduces the need for excessive monitoring, and fosters collaboration across professional and institutional boundaries.

Trust must be cultivated at multiple levels: between managers and clinicians, between different organizations, and between patients and providers.

Professional buy-in is equally essential. Clinicians must see value in new models of care, perceive them as improving their ability to deliver effective care, and believe that leadership is committed to supporting implementation. Without this cultural foundation, organizational change risks being superficial or short-lived.

The role of digital infrastructure cannot be overstated. Technologies such as electronic health records, telemonitoring platforms, and clinical decision support systems can dramatically enhance coordination and continuity. However, technology is not a panacea. Its successful deployment depends on organizational readiness, which includes digital literacy among staff, appropriate governance mechanisms, and a clear alignment between technological tools and clinical workflows. Moreover, equity must be considered.

Digital innovations can exacerbate disparities if they are inaccessible to certain populations or if their use requires skills or devices that not all patients possess.

To move beyond structural reform and into transformative change, healthcare organizations must invest in design thinking and systems approaches. Tools such as process mapping, co-design workshops, and service blueprints provide structured methods for understanding existing care pathways, identifying points of failure, and generating solutions that are grounded in the experiences of users—both patients and professionals.

These approaches promote empathy, creativity, and iterative learning. For instance, co-design workshops bring together patients, clinicians, administrators, and designers to reimagine services, ensuring that reforms are not only clinically effective but also acceptable, usable, and culturally appropriate (Bate & Robert, 2007).

These participatory methods also support cultural change by fostering shared ownership and reducing resistance. When people are involved in shaping solutions, they are more likely to support their implementation. Furthermore, these processes generate valuable insights into the lived experience of chronic illness, insights that are often absent from traditional quality improvement efforts. Understanding what matters most to patients, what barriers they face in navigating the system, and what trade-offs they are willing to make can inform more responsive and humane organizational practices.

Another critical dimension is workforce development. Chronic care requires new skills, roles, and professional relationships. Clinicians must be trained not only in clinical management but also in communication, motivational interviewing, shared decision-making, and cultural competence.

New roles such as care coordinators, health coaches, and peer navigators must be integrated into care teams. These changes challenge existing hierarchies and require thoughtful change management. Leadership development, interprofessional education, and competency-based training programs are key enablers of this transition.

Measurement and evaluation are also vital. Organizations must establish metrics that reflect the goals of chronic care, including patient-reported outcomes, functional status, care continuity, and quality of life. Traditional metrics such as length of stay or readmission rates may capture some aspects of performance but often miss the broader objectives of integrated, person-centered care.

Evaluations should be multidimensional, combining quantitative indicators with qualitative feedback, and should be used not only for accountability but also for learning and adaptation.

Finally, organizations must foster environments that support resilience. Chronic care is complex, unpredictable, and emotionally demanding.

Teams must have the resources, flexibility, and psychological safety to adapt to changing circumstances, learn from failure, and support each other.

Resilient organizations invest in reflective practices, debriefing sessions, and staff well-being programs. They recognize that sustainable chronic care requires not only efficient systems but also engaged and supported professionals.

In sum, the management of chronic conditions is a profound organizational challenge that touches every dimension of healthcare delivery. It requires coherent structures, collaborative cultures, enabling technologies, and responsive leadership.

It demands that organizations shift from reactive, episodic models of care to proactive, integrated, and person-centered systems. While the barriers are considerable, the potential rewards, in terms of health outcomes, patient experience, and system sustainability are equally significant. By embracing complexity and committing to continuous learning, health organizations can rise to the challenge of chronicity and transform it into an opportunity for innovation and improvement.

1.8 Beyond the Pill: Organizational Innovation in Service and Delivery

Pharmaceutical breakthroughs, while essential, are insufficient on their own to transform the outcomes of chronic care. The development of novel therapies and advanced pharmacological treatments may offer clinical potential, but their real-world impact is determined not only by their biochemical efficacy but also by how they are integrated into patient lives and organizational workflows.

The last mile of healthcare delivery, a phrase used to describe the point where health systems meet patients in their everyday contexts, is where the difference between theoretical benefit and lived experience is most acutely felt. At this juncture, organizational variables such as adherence support, health literacy initiatives, and engagement mechanisms become decisive (Berwick et al., 2008).

It is at this crucial interface that service innovation becomes an imperative. Organizations must go beyond product innovation and invest in redesigning the systems, processes, and relationships that shape how care is delivered and received. One of the most promising areas of development is the use of digital adherence platforms.

These include mobile applications that provide reminders, track medication use, offer educational content, and connect patients to care teams. However, their effectiveness hinges on thoughtful integration into clinical workflows and sensitivity to patients' digital access and literacy levels. Technology must support, not complicate, care delivery.

Beyond digital tools, organizations are increasingly turning to community-based outreach programs. These programs, often involving home visits, group education sessions, or partnerships with local organizations, extend the reach of the health system and bridge cultural or linguistic gaps.

They can address social determinants of health, improve patient trust, and reduce barriers to access. When designed and governed appropriately, such programs reinforce the idea that chronic care is not confined to hospitals or clinics, but is woven into the social and familial fabric of daily life.

Effective service innovation in chronic care requires cross-functional collaboration. The complexity of behavioral change and chronic disease management necessitates diverse expertise.

Teams must include not only clinicians but also behavioral scientists, information technology specialists, health communication experts, and community leaders. This multiplicity of perspectives enriches problem-solving, enhances cultural competence, and ensures that innovations are both technically sound and socially grounded.

Hospitals and regional health authorities can foster such collaborative work by establishing innovation labs or transformation units. These organizational spaces are designed to incubate and test new models of care, drawing on design thinking, rapid prototyping, and user feedback.

Innovation labs create a safe environment for experimentation, allowing organizations to pilot new services on a small scale, gather data, and iterate based on results. Importantly, they also signal an institutional commitment to change and can build momentum for broader system transformation (Christensen et al., 2009).

However, innovation must be inclusive if it is to advance equity rather than exacerbate disparities. Evidence shows that without intentional design, new technologies and services often disproportionately benefit already advantaged populations, while leaving behind those who are economically disadvantaged, less digitally literate, or culturally marginalized.

Organizations must therefore embed equity considerations from the outset. This means conducting equity impact assessments, disaggregating outcome data by socioeconomic and demographic variables, and actively involving underrepresented communities in the design and evaluation of new initiatives.

Inclusive innovation models involve a shift in organizational mindset, from doing things "for" communities to doing things "with" them. Participatory design approaches, citizen panels, and co-creation workshops can ensure that patient voices are not tokenized but are central to decision-making. This participatory ethos must extend to governance structures, where community representatives are given real influence in steering committees and advisory boards. Such inclusion enhances legitimacy, increases the likelihood of adoption, and leads to services that better reflect the diversity of patient needs (Greenhalgh et al., 2016).

Organizations also need to build capacity to support continuous learning and adaptation. Innovation is not a one-time event but an ongoing process that requires feedback loops, reflective practices, and resilience in the face of failure.

Evaluation frameworks should incorporate qualitative and quantitative data, including patient-reported outcomes and experiential narratives. Lessons learned from unsuccessful interventions should be shared transparently and used to refine future approaches. This demands an organizational culture that values experimentation and prioritizes learning over blame.

Finally, leadership plays a crucial role in shaping the conditions for successful service innovation. Leaders must articulate a clear vision, align resources, empower frontline staff, and model openness to change. They must also balance the need for agility with the requirements of accountability, ensuring that new initiatives are both innovative and safe. Middle managers, often overlooked, are particularly important in translating strategic goals into operational change. Their support can make the difference between isolated pilot projects and systemic transformation.

To improve chronic care requires more than scientific breakthroughs whereas it calls for organizational creativity, inclusiveness, and commitment to the everyday realities of patients. By investing in service innovation, fostering cross-functional teams, and embedding equity into every stage of the innovation process, health organizations can close the gap between what is medically possible and what is practically achievable. This is the essence of people-centered care: a system that listens, learns, and evolves to meet the needs of all.

1.9 Telemedicine and AI: Organizational Transformation Through Technology

Telemedicine and artificial intelligence, often abbreviated as AI, have emerged as transformative forces in healthcare. They represent both significant opportunities for enhancing access and efficiency and potential disruptions to existing practices and organizational structures.

Their integration into routine care, however, is not merely a matter of acquiring new tools or installing software. It requires comprehensive organizational adaptation across multiple dimensions, including technological infrastructure, clinical processes, management systems, and ethical governance (Baines et al., 2018).

Telemedicine platforms, which enable the remote delivery of health services, compel healthcare organizations to fundamentally rethink how care is delivered. Traditional workflows based on in-person visits must be redesigned to incorporate virtual consultations, asynchronous messaging, and remote monitoring.

This redesign impacts not only clinicians, who must adjust to new modes of communication and clinical judgment, but also administrative staff, who handle scheduling, billing, and patient support. Furthermore, patient onboarding becomes a critical touchpoint. Organizations must ensure that patients understand how to access telemedicine services, navigate digital interfaces, and use home-based diagnostic tools when applicable.

The integration of artificial intelligence tools introduces additional complexities. AI is increasingly used in triage, diagnostics, treatment planning, and risk prediction. While these applications can enhance decision-making and reduce cognitive burden for clinicians, they also raise questions about transparency, accountability, and clinical alignment.

Algorithms must be rigorously validated, regularly audited for bias or error, and updated as new data becomes available. Importantly, their outputs must be interpretable and actionable within clinical workflows. If clinicians do not understand how an AI tool reaches its conclusions, or if the recommendations do not fit the realities of practice, the tool is unlikely to be adopted or trusted.

Organizational governance is essential in managing these dynamics. The ethical implications of AI and telemedicine, including issues of privacy, consent, equity, and liability, require deliberate oversight. Governance structures must include not only technical and legal experts but also frontline staff and patient representatives.

Policies should be developed to guide decision-making around data usage, algorithm selection, error management, and accountability. These policies must be transparent and communicated clearly to all stakeholders.

Implementation science offers valuable insights into how organizations can successfully adopt new technologies. According to the Consolidated Framework for Implementation Research (CFIR), key factors include organizational readiness, leadership engagement, and the adaptability of interventions to local contexts (Damschroder et al., 2009).

Leadership commitment is particularly important in setting priorities, allocating resources, and maintaining momentum. Without visible support from senior leaders, technology projects often stall or remain peripheral to core operations.

Equity remains a pressing concern in digital health innovation. The digital divide refers to the unequal access to and use of digital technologies across populations. Telemedicine can inadvertently deepen existing health disparities if it assumes universal access to high-speed Internet, digital devices, or digital literacy.

Elderly patients, individuals with low income, and residents of rural areas are particularly at risk of being excluded. Organizations must proactively identify these gaps and implement strategies to mitigate them. Solutions include offering digital literacy training, providing loaner devices, establishing telehealth kiosks in community centers, and maintaining alternatives for in-person care.

Hybrid care models are increasingly recognized as a viable and equitable approach. These models combine digital services with traditional face-to-face interactions, allowing care to be tailored to individual needs and preferences. For example, a patient with mobility challenges may conduct routine follow-ups via video but attend in-person visits for diagnostics or procedures. Such models require careful coordination and workflow integration to avoid fragmentation.

Moreover, clinicians must be supported with protocols, training, and decision aids to determine which modality is most appropriate for each patient and scenario.

Training and support are also critical for staff. Telemedicine and AI introduce new skills and responsibilities, including managing virtual interactions, interpreting algorithmic outputs, and troubleshooting technical issues.

Organizations should invest in continuous professional development, peer support networks, and helpdesk services to ensure staff can confidently and competently engage with digital tools. Psychological support may also be needed, as the shift to remote care can alter professional identity and job satisfaction.

From a cultural perspective, the adoption of telemedicine and AI may challenge long-held norms about what constitutes good care. Some clinicians and patients may perceive digital encounters as impersonal or less effective.

Organizations must foster open dialogue about these concerns, collect feedback, and use data to demonstrate the quality and safety of digital modalities. Patient satisfaction surveys, outcome evaluations, and case studies can all help build confidence and refine services.

Finally, sustainability must be considered. Many telemedicine programs expanded rapidly during the COVID-19 pandemic under emergency conditions and temporary reimbursement models. For these services to become a permanent part of healthcare delivery, stable funding, regulatory clarity, and long-term strategic planning are essential. Organizations must collaborate with policymakers, payers, and professional bodies to shape policies that support innovation while protecting standards and equity.

The successful integration of telemedicine and artificial intelligence into healthcare requires much more than technical deployment. It demands holistic organizational change, encompassing governance, workflow design, staff training, patient engagement, and cultural transformation. By approaching these technologies not as isolated solutions but as catalysts for systemic improvement, health organizations can harness their full potential to deliver more accessible, efficient, and equitable care.

1.10 Innovation Systems: Organizational Ecosystems and Adaptive Capacity

Innovation in healthcare rarely emerges in isolation. Instead, it arises from the dynamic and often complex interactions among a wide array of stakeholders including universities, startups, regulatory agencies, healthcare providers, public institutions, and civil society organizations.

These relationships constitute innovation ecosystems that shape how new ideas are generated, tested, and scaled. The capacity of health organizations to innovate is influenced not only by their internal structures and resources but also by their external connections and openness to new knowledge.

As Van de Ven et al. (1999) argue, successful innovation depends on network connectivity, absorptive capacity, and institutional openness, which allow organizations to sense, seize, and adapt to emerging opportunities and challenges.

Frameworks such as the Quadruple Helix model provide a valuable lens to understand and guide health innovation. This model highlights the synergistic potential of collaboration among four key sectors: academia, industry, government, and civil society.

These actors bring different forms of knowledge, capabilities, and legitimacy, and when effectively coordinated, they can co-create solutions that are not only technically robust but also socially responsive. In this context, leadership must evolve from a traditional command and control approach to a more facilitative, distributed, and boundary-spanning style. Leaders need to act as brokers and integrators who can foster mutual understanding, mediate competing interests, and create shared visions across institutional boundaries (Ansell & Gash, 2008).

To support this shift, many health systems and public administrations have established innovation hubs, living labs, and public-private partnerships. Innovation hubs function as organizational platforms that bring together researchers, clinicians, entrepreneurs, and users to collaboratively explore new models of care.

Living labs emphasize user-centered design and real-world testing, allowing for continuous iteration and learning. Public-private partnerships leverage the resources and expertise of different sectors to accelerate the development and dissemination of innovations. These arrangements reflect a growing recognition that no single actor can tackle complex health challenges alone. Instead, innovation must be seen as a collective endeavor that requires ongoing dialogue, joint investment, and shared risk-taking.

However, the expansion of these ecosystems also introduces significant governance challenges. When multiple stakeholders are involved, questions of transparency, accountability, and equitable benefit-sharing become more pressing. Who sets the priorities? Who has access to the data? How are risks and rewards distributed? Without clear and inclusive governance mechanisms, innovation partnerships can reproduce or exacerbate power imbalances, marginalize community voices, or prioritize commercial interests over public good.

Thus, health organizations must invest in participatory governance structures that ensure all relevant stakeholders, including patients and marginalized groups, have a meaningful voice in decision-making processes.

And trust is a cornerstone of such collaborative innovation. It is built through consistent communication, mutual respect, and the demonstration of shared values. Organizations must be transparent about their goals, methods, and outcomes.

They should report both successes and failures and be open to critical feedback. This transparency not only enhances legitimacy but also fosters a learning culture in which innovation is seen not as a heroic act of a few individuals but as the product of collective experimentation and reflection.

Equally important is the development of institutional capacities that support sustained innovation. This includes mechanisms for knowledge management, interdisciplinary collaboration, and evaluation. For instance, organizations can create innovation portfolios that track different initiatives, monitor their progress, and assess their impact using mixed methods.

They can host regular forums or innovation councils that bring together diverse stakeholders to review ongoing projects and identify emerging needs. Capacity-building programs can train staff in innovation methodologies such as design thinking, agile development, and systems thinking, equipping them to contribute actively to transformation efforts.

Moreover, innovation should be aligned with organizational mission and values. It should not be pursued for its own sake or as a response to external pressure, but as a strategic means to improve care quality, equity, and sustainability.

This requires leaders to articulate a clear innovation strategy, allocate adequate resources, and integrate innovation goals into planning, budgeting, and performance management. Innovation should also be grounded in ethical principles and social responsibility. For example, digital innovations should be evaluated not only for their technical performance but also for their impact on privacy, inclusion, and human dignity.

The evaluation of innovation ecosystems must also go beyond conventional metrics. Traditional indicators such as patents or publications, while useful, do not capture the full value of health innovation. More comprehensive evaluation frameworks should include indicators of social impact, user satisfaction, equity, and system-level learning.

Qualitative assessments, including ethnographic studies and participatory evaluations, can reveal insights into how innovations are experienced by different users, how they influence organizational culture, and how they adapt over time.

It can be argued that innovation in healthcare is a deeply organizational phenomenon. It is not merely about discovering new technologies or implementing isolated projects, but about cultivating a culture, structure, and network that supports continuous improvement.

Organizations that thrive in this environment are those that are open to the world, willing to experiment, and committed to collaboration. They recognize that innovation is a journey rather than a destination, and that its success depends as much on governance and relationships as on ideas and inventions. By embracing this perspective, healthcare organizations can play a transformative role in building systems that are more responsive, equitable, and resilient.

1.11 Territorial Health and Organizational Reconfiguration

Territorial health systems offer a promising and increasingly necessary avenue for bringing healthcare services closer to communities. As demographic shifts and patterns of chronic illness continue to evolve, the importance of organizing care at the territorial level becomes more evident.

This approach emphasizes proximity, accessibility, and relevance to the lived realities of populations. It requires a rethinking of traditional models of centralized care delivery, demanding instead the decentralization of authority, strategic investment in community-based providers, and the strengthening of organizational coordination at the local level (Saltman et al., 2006).

In practical terms, territorialization means shifting decision-making closer to where people live and receive care. Local health authorities must be granted the capacity, autonomy, and resources to adapt national strategies to local contexts.

This implies a broader distribution of managerial responsibilities and an enhanced role for frontline professionals in shaping service delivery. However, decentralization must not result in fragmentation or inconsistency. Effective territorial health systems depend on clear governance frameworks, shared goals, and mechanisms that promote coherence across different levels and sectors of care.

Digital innovation can significantly support the development of territorial health systems. Digitally enabled services such as telemonitoring, mobile health units, e-prescriptions, and integrated digital records have the potential to bridge geographic barriers and optimize resource allocation.

Yet, the successful deployment of these tools depends on robust back-office integration, including interoperable platforms, standardized data practices, and coordinated scheduling systems.

Technical solutions must be matched with organizational readiness and investment in human capacity. For example, a mobile clinic equipped with digital diagnostics is only as effective as the systems that interpret results, schedule follow-ups, and communicate with primary care providers.

Moreover, accountability structures must be clearly defined. In territorialized systems, lines of responsibility can blur as multiple actors share roles in care coordination, case management, and community outreach.

Health organizations must adopt governance models that promote transparency, responsiveness, and collaboration. This includes defining performance indicators that reflect territorial priorities, such as continuity of care, population health outcomes, and community satisfaction, rather than simply counting procedures or throughput.

Organizational redesign is central to this transformation whereas efforts must begin with stakeholder mapping to identify all actors involved in the health ecosystem, including formal providers, informal caregivers, local governments, and civil society organizations.

Understanding their respective roles, capacities, and motivations is crucial for effective planning. Workflow redesign is another critical step. Care pathways must be restructured to facilitate seamless navigation across services and settings. This may involve co-locating services, introducing digital triage tools, and empowering community health workers to act as liaisons between patients and the broader system.

Change management strategies are essential to support staff through this transition. Territorial health reform often encounters resistance due to uncertainty, perceived loss of control, or lack of alignment with existing norms. Organizations must therefore communicate a compelling vision, provide training and mentorship, and create feedback loops that enable continuous learning.

Pilot projects can be used to test new models on a small scale, generate data, and refine implementation before broader rollout.

A foundational role in territorial health systems is played by partnerships. Local health authorities should actively create relationships with municipalities, third-sector organizations, schools, housing agencies, and citizen groups. These partnerships are not peripheral but instrumental in co-producing solutions tailored to local needs. For instance, a program to manage diabetes in a rural area might involve collaboration with local food suppliers, fitness instructors, and transportation services to address barriers to nutrition, physical activity, and clinic attendance.

Such intersectoral action acknowledges that health is shaped as much by social conditions as by clinical care.

Finally, territorialization must be guided by a commitment to equity. Bringing care closer to communities must not reinforce existing disparities or create a patchwork of uneven services. Instead, it should be a means to reduce barriers and reach underserved populations. This requires explicit focus on inclusion, cultural competence, and the social determinants of health.

Territorial health systems that succeed are those that listen to communities, adapt to local conditions, and remain accountable to the people they serve. In doing so, they not only improve access and quality, but also strengthen the legitimacy and resilience of health systems as a whole.

1.12 The European Horizon: Organizational Futures for Integrated Care

The European Union has positioned itself as a proactive advocate of integrated and person-centered care. Through its policy frameworks, funding mechanisms, and digital strategies, the EU has sought to encourage member states to reimagine how health services are designed and delivered.

The structural reforms supported by EU instruments such as the Recovery and Resilience Facility and cohesion funds offer a rare opportunity to realign incentives, scale effective practices, and invest in robust digital infrastructure. However, the translation of these high-level ambitions into concrete organizational practices remains highly uneven across member states and regions.

Organizational agility has emerged as a central condition for achieving the impact envisioned by EU strategies. Health systems must not only absorb new funding but also deploy it in ways that reflect local needs, capacities, and cultural contexts. One-size-fits-all models are unlikely to succeed in a union as diverse as Europe.

Adaptive and modular organizational designs, capable of iterative refinement and learning, offer a more viable pathway. These designs must be supported by performance frameworks that are sensitive to territorial diversity, along with real-time feedback mechanisms that allow for continuous adjustment in response to demographic, epidemiological, and technological change (Saltman & Duran, 2016).

EU initiatives such as the European Health Data Space and the Digital Decade Strategy provide a visionary blueprint for the future of healthcare integration and digital transformation. These frameworks promote cross-border data sharing, citizen empowerment, and innovation ecosystems that leverage the full potential of digital tools.

However, their success depends fundamentally on the organizational capacity at national and regional levels. This includes the ability to harmonize data standards, ensure interoperability, safeguard privacy, and operationalize ethical frameworks across institutional boundaries. Technical capacity is necessary, but it is not sufficient. What is equally required is a profound investment in organizational learning, trust-building, and change leadership. Building such capacity entails several interrelated investments.

First, leadership development must be a priority. Health systems need leaders who are not only technically competent but also capable of guiding organizational change in complex and contested environments.

These leaders must navigate the tensions between central direction and local autonomy, between standardization and customization, and between innovation and accountability. Leadership programs supported by EU and national bodies should emphasize distributed and collaborative leadership models, fostering a culture of co-creation and mutual learning across sectors and borders.

Second, systems integration must move beyond technical interoperability to encompass strategic alignment, shared goals, and coordinated action. This requires joint planning processes, multi-stakeholder governance bodies, and integrated performance management systems. Tools such as shared care plans, unified electronic health records, and joint financing mechanisms can support this integration, but their implementation requires sustained political will and institutional alignment.

Third, participatory governance must become a defining feature of organizational renewal in European health systems. Citizens, patients, and community organizations must be actively involved in shaping priorities, evaluating performance, and co-designing services.

This not only enhances legitimacy and responsiveness but also mobilizes new forms of knowledge and capacity that are often overlooked in traditional top-down models. Participatory structures such as deliberative assemblies, patient councils, and citizen panels should be institutionalized and resourced as part of routine governance processes.

Furthermore, attention must be paid to the broader organizational culture within health systems. Cultures that are open to learning, experimentation, and feedback are more likely to succeed in implementing complex reforms.

These cultures value interdisciplinary collaboration, reflective practice, and continuous improvement. EU-level support for communities of practice, cross-border learning exchanges, and knowledge dissemination can help diffuse such cultures across national contexts.

Finally, the future of integrated care in Europe depends on the ability to navigate uncertainty and complexity with resilience and purpose. The dual challenge of population ageing and digital transformation requires not just better tools but also better organizations, that are adaptive, inclusive, and oriented toward the long-term well-being of their communities. The EU can play a catalytic role by fostering policy alignment, funding experimentation, and supporting capacity-building across all levels of the health system. But it is ultimately the work of national and regional organizations, those closest to patients and populations, that will determine whether the European horizon for integrated care becomes a lived reality.

The European commitment to integrated and person-centered care must be understood not only as a policy ambition but also as an organizational transformation.

It calls for leadership, learning, and legitimacy at all levels. By investing in these foundations, European health systems can not only adapt to the demands of the present but also build the capacity to shape a more inclusive, resilient, and sustainable future for health and care.

References

Ahrne, G., & Brunsson, N. (2005). Organizations and meta-organizations. *Scandinavian Journal of Management, 21*(4), 429–449. https://doi.org/10.1016/j.scaman.2005.09.005

Ansell, C., & Gash, A. (2008). Collaborative governance in theory and practice. *Journal of Public Administration Research and Theory, 18*(4), 543–571. https://doi.org/10.1093/jopart/mum032

Bailey, S. R., O'Malley, J. P., Gold, R., Heintzman, J., & Likumahuwa, S. (2017). Receipt of diabetes preventive services differs by insurance status at visit. *American Journal of Preventive Medicine, 52*(6), 735–739. https://doi.org/10.1016/j.amepre.2017.01.013

Baines, D., Cunningham, I., & Shields, J. (2018). Feeling the pinch? Social impact bonds, austerity and the value of co-production. *Social Policy & Administration, 52*(1), 285–301. https://doi.org/10.1111/spol.12324

Bate, P., & Robert, G. (2007). *Bringing user experience to healthcare improvement: The concepts, methods and practices of experience-based design*. Radcliffe Publishing.

Berwick, D. M., Nolan, T. W., & Whittington, J. (2008). The triple aim: Care, health, and cost. *Health Affairs, 27*(3), 759–769. https://doi.org/10.1377/hlthaff.27.3.759

Best, A., Greenhalgh, T., Lewis, S., Saul, J. E., Carroll, S., & Bitz, J. (2012). Large-system transformation in health care: A realist review. *The Milbank Quarterly, 90*(3), 421–456. https://doi.org/10.1111/j.1468-0009.2012.00670.x

Bodenheimer, T., Wagner, E. H., & Grumbach, K. (2002). Improving primary care for patients with chronic illness: The chronic care model, Part 2. *JAMA, 288*(15), 1909–1914. https://doi.org/10.1001/jama.288.15.1909

Briggs, A. M., Valentijn, P. P., Thiyagarajan, J. A., & de Carvalho, I. A. (2018). Elements of integrated care approaches for older people: A review of reviews. *BMJ Open, 8*(4), e021194. https://doi.org/10.1136/bmjopen-2017-021194

Christensen, C. M., Grossman, J. H., & Hwang, J. (2009). *The innovator's prescription*: A disruptive solution for health care. McGraw-Hill.

Cresswell, K., Sheikh, A., & Franklin, B. D. (2022). Organisational governance of artificial intelligence in health and care: A rapid review and conceptual framework. *BMJ Health & Care Informatics, 29*(1), e100536. https://doi.org/10.1136/bmjhci-2021-100536

Damschroder, L. J., Aron, D. C., Keith, R. E., Kirsh, S. R., Alexander, J. A., & Lowery, J. C. (2009). Fostering implementation of health services research findings into practice: A consolidated framework for advancing implementation science. *Implementation Science, 4*(1), 50. https://doi.org/10.1186/1748-5908-4-50

Denis, J. L., Langley, A., & Rouleau, L. (2015). Strategizing in pluralistic contexts: Rethinking theoretical frames. *Human Relations, 68*(1), 33–56. https://doi.org/10.1177/0018726714536932

Ferlie, E. B., & Shortell, S. M. (2001). Improving the quality of health care in the United Kingdom and the United States: A framework for change. *The Milbank Quarterly, 79*(2), 281–315. https://doi.org/10.1111/1468-0009.00206

Friedman, C. P., Rubin, J. C., & Sullivan, K. J. (2017). Toward an information infrastructure for global health improvement. *Yearbook of Medical Informatics, 26*(1), 16–23. https://doi.org/10.15265/IY-2017-014

Gillespie, A., & Reader, T. W. (2018). The healthcare trust imperative: Implications for open data and information sharing. *Journal of Medical Internet Research, 20*(3), e112. https://doi.org/10.2196/jmir.8227

Gittell, J. H. (2009). *High performance healthcare: Using the power of relationships to achieve quality, efficiency and resilience*. McGraw-Hill Education.

Greenhalgh, T., Wherton, J., Papoutsi, C., Lynch, J., & Hughes, G. (2017). Beyond adoption: A new framework for theorizing and evaluating nonadoption, abandonment, and challenges to the scale-up, spread, and sustainability of health and care technologies. *Journal of Medical Internet Research, 19*(11), e367. https://doi.org/10.2196/jmir.8775

Greenhalgh, T., Jackson, C., Shaw, S., & Janamian, T. (2016). Achieving research impact through co-creation in community-based health services: Literature review and case study. *The Milbank Quarterly, 94*(2), 392–429. https://doi.org/10.1111/1468-0009.12197

Greenhalgh, S., Müller, K., Thomas, S., Campbell, M. L., & Harter, T. (2022). Raising the voice of science in complex socio-political contexts: An assessment of contested water decisions. *Journal of Environmental Policy & Planning, 24*(2), 242–260. https://doi.org/10.1080/1523908X.2021.2007762

Ham, C., & Curry, N. (2011). Integrated care: What is it and why is it important? The King's Fund.

Ham, C., Dixon, A., & Brooke, B. (2012). Transforming the delivery of health and social care: The case for fundamental change. The King's Fund. https://www.kingsfund.org.uk/publications/transforming-delivery-health-and-social-care

Heifetz, R. A., & Linsky, M. (2002). *Leadership on the line: Staying alive through the dangers of leading*. Harvard Business Review Press.

Ilmarinen, J. (2006). *Towards a longer worklife: Ageing and the quality of worklife in the European Union*. Finnish Institute of Occupational Health.

Karliner, J., Slotterback, S., Boyd, R., Ashby, B., & Steele, K. (2020). Health care's climate footprint: How the health sector contributes to the global climate crisis and opportunities for action. Health Care Without Harm. https://noharm-global.org/resources/health-care-climate-footprint-repo

Kickbusch, I., Leung, G. M., Bhutta, Z. A., Matsoso, M. P., Ihekweazu, C., & Abbasi, K. (2021). COVID-19: How a virus is turning the world upside down. *BMJ, 372*, n185. https://doi.org/10.1136/bmj.n185

Kodner, D. L., & Kyriacou, C. K. (2000). Fully integrated care for frail elderly: Two American models. *International Journal of Integrated Care, 1*, e08. https://doi.org/10.5334/ijic.10

Llewellyn, S., Procter, R., Harvey, G., & Maniatopoulos, G. (2014). Facilitating technology adoption in the NHS: Negotiating the organisational and policy context – A qualitative study. *Health Services and Delivery Research, 2*(23). https://doi.org/10.3310/hsdr0223

Lupton, D. (2014). The digitally engaged patient: Self-monitoring and self-care in the digital health era. *Social Theory & Health, 11*(3), 256–270. https://doi.org/10.1057/sth.2013.10

Marmot, M., Allen, J., Goldblatt, P., Boyce, T., McNeish, D., Grady, M., & Geddes, I. (2010). Fair society, healthy lives: The Marmot review. The Marmot Review. https://www.instituteofhealthequity.org/resources-reports/fair-society-healthy-lives-the-marmot-review

Martin, G. P., McKee, L., & Dixon-Woods, M. (2015). Beyond metrics? Utilizing 'soft intelligence' for healthcare quality and safety. *Social Science & Medicine, 142*, 19–26. https://doi.org/10.1016/j.socscimed.2015.08.032

Mintzberg, H. (1993). Structure in fives. Designing effective organizations. Prentice-Hall.

Mintzberg, H. (1996). Managing government, governing management. *Harvard Business Review, 74*(3), 75–83.

Nolte, E., & McKee, M. (2008). *Caring for people with chronic conditions: A health system perspective*. McGraw-Hill Education.

Porter, M. E., & Lee, T. H. (2013). The strategy that will fix health care. *Harvard Business Review, 91*(10), 50–70.

Saltman, R. B., & Duran, A. (2016). Governance, government and the search for new provider models. *Health Policy, 120*(2), 135–141. https://doi.org/10.1016/j.healthpol.2016.01.014
Saltman, R. B., Bankauskaite, V., & Vrangbaek, K. (2006). *Decentralization in health care: Strategies and outcomes*. McGraw-Hill Education.
Saltman, R. B., Durán, A., & Dubois, H. F. (2011). *Governing public hospitals: Reform strategies and the movement towards institutional autonomy*. WHO Regional Office for Europe.
Shortell, S. M., Addicott, R., Walsh, N., & Ham, C. (2015). The NHS five year forward view: A critical review of the policy trajectory. *BMJ, 351*, h4719. https://doi.org/10.1136/bmj.h4719
Stone, R. I. (2020). The direct care workforce: Challenges and prospects in an evolving health care system. *Public Policy & Aging Report, 30*(3), 96–101. https://doi.org/10.1093/ppar/praa016
Valentijn, P. P., Schepman, S. M., Opheij, W., & Bruijnzeels, M. A. (2013). Understanding integrated care: A comprehensive conceptual framework based on the integrative functions of primary care. *International Journal of Integrated Care, 13*(1), e010. https://doi.org/10.5334/ijic.886
Van de Ven, A. H., Polley, D. E., Garud, R., & Venkataraman, S. (1999). *The innovation journey*. Oxford University Press.
Van Dijck, J., & Poell, T. (2016). Understanding the promises and premises of platform society. *Social Media + Society, 2*(3), 2056305116662635. https://doi.org/10.1177/2056305116662635
Vayena, E., Blasimme, A., & Cohen, I. G. (2018). Machine learning in medicine: Addressing ethical challenges. *PLoS Medicine, 15*(11), e1002689. https://doi.org/10.1371/journal.pmed.1002689
Wagner, E. H., Austin, B. T., & Von Korff, M. (2001). Organizing care for patients with chronic illness. *The Milbank Quarterly, 74*(4), 511–544. https://doi.org/10.1111/1468-0009.00021
Waring, J., & Currie, G. (2009). Managing expert knowledge: Organizational challenges and managerial futures for the UK medical profession. *Organization Studies, 30*(7), 755–778. https://doi.org/10.1177/0170840609104819
World Health Organization (WHO). 1st ed. World Health Organization; 2013. Global Action Plan For The Prevention and Control of Noncommunicable Diseases 2013–2020. https://apps.who.int/iris/bitstream/handle/10665/94384/?sequence=1
World Health Organization (WHO). (2015). World report on ageing and health. https://apps.who.int/iris/handle/10665/186463.
World Health Organization (WHO). (2017). Global strategy and action plan on ageing and health. https://apps.who.int/iris/handle/10665/345971.

Innovative and Sustainable Accounting Practices for the Management and Prevention of Chronic Diseases

Claudia Salvatore

1 Introduction

The average age of the population in industrialised countries is rising thanks to medical advancements in recent decades. This demographic shift leads to an increase in chronic diseases and multimorbidity with higher healthcare costs, which are expected to rise in the coming years. Chronic diseases are an increasing problem for the economic, financial and social sustainability of health and healthcare systems and for society as a whole, not only from a healthcare perspective, but also because they pose managerial and accountability challenges.

Integrated hospital-community healthcare services and personalised prevention measures can tackle this issue by improving patients' quality of life, health outcomes and also reduce costs. This work identifies innovative and sustainable management approaches, planning and control systems, and accounting practices for chronic disease management and cost-effective operational models for high-quality care. Furthermore, remote healthcare and artificial intelligence (AI) tools have the potential to reduce hospitalisation costs while improving care for patients with chronic conditions, providing a positive impact on patients, their caregivers, and society as a whole.

Healthcare systems are actually patient-centred in the sense that patients and citizens should actively participate in the management of health systems in view of co-creating public value (Cavacece, 2023). Thus, the framework of this study is the *value-based health system perspective* (Smith et al., 2023) which is a management model based on value in health systems that emphasised the integration and

C. Salvatore (✉)
Department of Public Health, University of Naples Federico II,
Naples, Italy
e-mail: claudia.salvatore@unina.it

A. Ricciardelli, L. Mercurio (eds.), *Building Innovation in Ageing and Health Policy*, Springer Series in Healthcare Management and Innovation,
https://doi.org/10.1007/978-3-032-09163-5_2

partnership of the patient/citizen with the territory and communities in which they operate in order to reach a societal well-being. This framework moves from a *Value-Based Health Care* (VBHC) model to a very recent *value-based health system perspective* which includes also health promotion and prevention activities.

Demographic decline and increasing life expectancy due to the progress of medical sciences has caused an increased mean age of the population, thereby jeopardising the management of healthcare systems in the last few years. Indeed, population aging is one factor strictly connected with an increasing level of chronic illnesses that occur particularly in people over 65 years of age (Sosto, 2020).

The increasing incidence of chronic diseases among the older population in Italy, in Europe and worldwide, needs to be managed under economic, social and environmental conditions in order to achieve the sustainability of the health system.

In this context, the present work conducts a narrative review of the literature to explore the current state of the art on this topic, taking into account recent policy frameworks such as the Next Generation EU and the EU4Health Program, both introduced in response to the Covid-19 pandemic to strengthen health systems and foster innovation in healthcare delivery. In fact, the Covid pandemic has changed the organisation and management of healthcare. Thus, this chapter discusses the problems which have emerged during and in the aftermath of the Covid pandemic and highlights strategies to be implemented in the near future. The Italian case is explored in this work in order to identify how is possible to lessen the burden of chronic diseases.

With this purpose, the aim of this work is to analyse the literature on the topic and discuss innovative and sustainable practices for the management of chronic diseases, considering also the chronic patient management processes, in order to reduce costs and, consequently, the burden of chronic illnesses for patients and society as a whole. This will improve sustainability of national health systems, together with regional healthcare systems. Another challenge of chronicity is to create value for patients and their caregivers, co-creating and collaborating in the delivery of health services to meet patient specific needs.

The findings of the narrative review highlight the urgent need to redesign the management of chronic diseases, the essential role of interprofessional collaborations through integrated care networks, hospital-territory, and the growing necessity to leverage digital technologies in a more consistent, efficient and effective manner.

In this context, in order to ensure an active and healthy life course it is necessary to implement health prevention activities through a planning strategy and a budgeting phase in order to allocate financial resources, as well as other assets, to these activities accordingly. In addition, health promotion activities will facilitate and support the urgent transformation of public health systems.

It is crucial that the implementation of integrated care (between patient, hospital and territory) for chronic disease management is undertaken with the cooperation of new healthcare professionals, the community and with the use of smart technologies, such as digital tools, remote monitoring and AI.

Thus, new health professionals could have a positive impact on the development of territorial assistance in addition to hospital care. In fact, the recent Italian

Ministerial Decree (the DM 77/2022) on new scenarios of territory-hospital integration, identifies not only new infrastructures of great utility for the development of territorial assistance (health centres, community hospitals, territorial operations centres, as previously underlined), but also new professional figures to be involved in the management of these pathologies, such as the family and community nurse—IFoC (De Lorenzo et al., 2020; Noto et al., 2022) in order to monitor the state of health, promote healthy lifestyles, plan interventions to be provided to communities.

Another important finding that emerges from this study is the creation of "*continuum of care*" for chronicity which refers to maintaining continuous care for patients as they move across multiple and different caregivers, procedures, facilities and treatments. This will facilitate the shift from "disease management" in hospital settings towards a "person-centred integrated care" with stronger community services and facilities.

2 A Picture on Chronic Disease Data Offered by National and International Organisations

The percentage of older adults increases yearly in Italy, in Europe and worldwide. Elderly population is steadily growing and there is a shortage of caregivers (Sosto, 2020).

In Italy around 39.9% of the entire population lives with at least one chronic disease (ISTAT, 2022a).

The issue of chronic diseases is inextricably linked to population ageing. In Italy, people living with a chronic disease account for 60% of those aged 60–64, 75% of those aged 65–74 and 85% of those over 75 (ISTAT, 2022b). The age-related gradient of chronicity varies depending on the specific disease considered, in some cases leading to markedly different estimates across age groups. This is evident, for example, in the case of hypertension: fewer than 10% of people under the age of 40 are affected, whereas approximately 65% of those around 80 years of age suffer from it (Tozzi & Longo, 2023).

Beyond this necessary premise regarding population ageing, exploring the realm of chronicity means uncovering some recurring characteristics, such as multichronicity (or multimorbidity) and the presence of comorbidities. In Italy, 21% of the population lives with more than one chronic disease. The presence of multiple coexisting diseases makes the management and care of individuals more complex.

Each year, 74% of deaths worldwide are caused by chronic diseases (WHO, 2022). Moreover, it should be noted that, prior to death, people affected by chronic illnesses often experience several years with a lower quality of life, due to the limitations imposed by complications, disabilities, frailty and comorbidities. This reality explains the World Health Organisation's (WHO) ongoing calls to increase attention to this issue, identifying five non-communicable diseases (NCDs) as particularly significant: cardiovascular diseases, cancer, diabetes, chronic respiratory diseases and mental health disorders.

The Global Burden of Disease (GBD) collects recent epidemiological data of around 195 countries in order to evaluate which is the burden on health of different chronic diseases and risk factors. Just to give a few examples: cardiovascular diseases remain the leading cause of death and disability worldwide, accounting for over 17 million deaths annually. Diabetes prevalence has also sharply increased, affecting more than 400 million people globally. Chronic respiratory diseases, such as chronic obstructive pulmonary disease (COPD), contribute significantly to morbidity, especially in regions with high levels of air pollution and smoking rates (Pacileo et al., 2019). Additionally, risk factors like high blood pressure, smoking and poor diet are among the main contributors to the global burden, causing millions of premature deaths every year.

3 Methodology

The research methodology of this work is *a narrative literature review* (Pautasso, 2019), through an overview of the literature on the topic, which has been taken as reference in order to analyse the problem.

This narrative descriptive literature review adopts a *value-based health system perspective* to provide an overview of the existing models for chronic disease management, particularly those accelerated by pandemic-driven changes, and their economic impact on health systems. The study reveals innovative approaches and models to patient-centred care for individuals with chronic conditions and multimorbidity, as well as measures to promote chronic disease prevention across the individual's life course.

The narrative review consists of a qualitative summary of the relevant literature on the field.

4 The State of the Art on Chronic Disease Management: The Results of the Narrative Literature Review

It is important to underline the urgent need for better chronic disease management strategies that include also an analysis of chronic patient management processes, as well as the implementation of appropriate technology innovations.

The incidence and prevalence of chronic diseases are critical issues in many countries around the world, especially in industrialised countries where multiple chronic diseases are rapidly increasing, as are the related costs of healthcare, especially those linked to hospital care (Ramli & Taher, 2008; García-Goñi et al., 2012; Milani & Lavie, 2015; Lavergne, 2017; Trankle et al., 2020; Karimi et al., 2021).

Therefore, as highlighted in literature from different scholars worldwide, it appears necessary to remodel the traditional hospital-based care system for chronic diseases, implementing a decentralised management system in order to exploit the various available management models. The final objective is to involve different professionals to promote an increasing level of primary and territorial care systems to combat chronicity (Hwang et al., 2019; Sayani et al., 2019).

The traditional healthcare system designed on a model of sudden, episodic care is no longer able to satisfy the needs of chronic patients; chronicity no longer fits this model. This is why it was decided to develop new models of chronicity management, such as the *Chronic Care Model* (CCM) and the *Kaiser's permanent pyramid*.

To achieve this goal, it is first necessary to identify which elements belonging to the architecture of the health system best responding to the challenge of chronic diseases, in particular which are the key elements that allow to obtain health systems based on high-performance chronic care and try to apply them (García-Goñi et al., 2012).

Population Health Management (PHM) is a strategy designed to stratify the population into homogeneous subgroups based on healthcare needs. This segmentation enables the design of operational activities and policy measures that are tailored to the specific subgroup to which individuals belong. The logic of personalisation thus replaces that of standardisation, allowing interventions to be adapted to the clinical, social and personal characteristics of each individual. Individualisation becomes instrumental in upholding both the principle of patient-centred care and individual choice, as well as the requirements of effectiveness and efficiency by reducing inappropriate interventions (Ministry of Health, 2016).

Through PHM, stratification should be understood as both an approach and a practical tool that various healthcare stakeholders can leverage—both in the different stages of patient care and in proactive healthcare initiatives (Tozzi & Longo, 2023).

Most of the health services in the world continue to be organised mainly according to a traditional acute, episodic and limited-duration care model that no longer meets the needs and preferences of individuals who have or are at risk of developing chronic conditions and multiple pathologies. To this end, it is important to implement new models for the management of high-performance chronic care, such as the *Chronic Care Model* (CCM), a model present in Italy in the Tuscany Region (Barsanti & Guarneri, 2019), the *Kaiser's permanent pyramid* (as an evolution of the CCM) and the *Chronic Disease Self-Management Model*, a programme which aims to increase patient empowerment, identifying the elements of the architecture of a health system that contribute to a better response to the challenge of chronic diseases (García-Goñi et al., 2012; Beretta & Demartini, 2020).

The reallocation of resources towards urgent care for Covid-19 patients caused inadequate ongoing care for chronic conditions. Chronic diseases require, as underlined several times, continuous assistance in order to avoid negative health outcomes. Covid-19 prevented this continuity and interaction as healthcare for non-Covid-19 cases was affected by the reallocation of resources towards urgent care for Covid-19 patients. To this have been added many other barriers, hindering the ability of people with chronic conditions to receive timely and effective access to primary and specialist care. The solution was found in telemedicine. Primary care centres around the world have switched to remote consultations with ad hoc in person medical visits. Potential benefits of virtual care include more effective daily disease monitoring, better patient satisfaction and better treatment compliance and higher follow-up rates (Kendzerska et al., 2021).

Embuldeniya et al. (2020) observed that in order to correlate clinical and economic efficiency, the Canadian province of Ontario has launched an integrated care programme (Integrated Funding model) that requires coordination of services between different sectors of acute and post-acute healthcare. Therefore, acute care, primary care, social and community services have been linked in order to significantly reduce the length of hospital stays and obtain more harmonised and cost-effective therapies. In fact, territorial assistance results in a perfect care of patients before and after hospitalisation.

Other scholars underline that, in order to simultaneously improve population health, patient experience and treatment costs, some countries, especially in Northern Europe (e.g. Sweden, Finland), have decided to adopt the logic of healthcare based on patient value (value-based approach). This logic is implemented mainly in developing hospitals in order to reduce fragmentation and ensure *continuity of care*, trying to facilitate both the vertical integration of services in primary and secondary care, as well as the horizontal integration of health and social services for the development of health policies which emphasise patient needs and align performance based on individual demands. It is necessary to listen to the requirements and goals of each patient, which may not be the same as those of healthcare professionals. Health systems that choose to adopt this type of approach must also increasingly clarify the patient's pathways. The outcome measures to be used must emerge from a shared decision-making process between professionals, the patient and any caregiver, leading to better collaboration, integration and communication across multiple sectors and organisations, and a greater capacity to manage chronic diseases in primary care (Elf et al., 2017; Embuldeniya et al., 2020; Kokko & Kork, 2020; Trankle et al., 2020).

Another strategy is represented by the use of technology: it is important to support healthcare through digital factors such as technologies and especially digital platforms, expanding the responsibility and availability of the actors involved in sharing their resources to co-create continuous and mutual value, which is essential for the sustainability of healthcare systems. Technologies help to enhance interactions between individuals by offering more effective management of information and allowing the co-production of personalised healthcare services. To do this, healthcare, both public and private, should promote a more intelligent use of these factors to encourage a language that is understandable to the different actors with the aim of combining the need for effectiveness, efficiency and healthcare sustainability (Faggini et al., 2019). Thanks to technology innovations, such as telemedicine, it is also possible to help disadvantaged areas, low and middle-income countries, where it is increasingly difficult to gain access to primary and specialist care (Paul & McDaniel, 2016). This is an attempt to reduce the poverty barrier that represents a risk factor for the development of chronic diseases and the same, in turn, increase poverty in those affected (Sayani et al., 2019).

The same concept is reiterated by Seixas et al. (2021) whose study examined the digital solutions for health and telemedicine which emerged during the pandemic.

There are numerous advantages that can be enjoyed without compromising the quality of healthcare which also becomes faster and more convenient for the patient. This represents the fastest way to change a fragmented healthcare system.

The Covid pandemic has highlighted the difficulties that the population has to face, together with unmet health needs. The reduced access to healthcare among Italian citizens was linked to various causes such as: delay of a medical service scheduled by decision of the professional/provider, mainly associated with socio-demographic variables; fear of being infected; level of trust towards politicians; non-Italian citizenship. Chronically ill and elderly patients are those who most need healthcare services on a scheduled basis, and yet they are the most affected by the postponement of non-urgent services (Gualano et al., 2021). Covid-19 has prevented what is fundamental for a chronically ill patient, namely, *continuity of care*, which can be realised thanks to telemedicine. Primary care centres around the world have switched to remote consultations with ad hoc medical visits per person. Virtual care allows for more effective daily monitoring of the disease, improved patient satisfaction, greater compliance with treatment and higher follow-up rates (Kendzerska et al., 2021). Among the possible strategies to be implemented, prevention is an absolutely priority, which allows for the analysis of risk factors, but above all to address them to avoid the onset or worsening of the disease, focusing more on the weakest individuals (such as women, the elderly, and people living in rural/remote areas) (Sahle et al., 2016). The solutions to chronicity are evident; what we need to understand is how to implement them based on the characteristics of each territory, with the hope of collaboration and sharing between different countries.

In Italy, for example, all the critical issues of the National Health Service (NHS) are addressed in a synergic way through a series of institutional projects, such as the *National Recovery and Resilience Plan* (PNRR), which (in its Mission 6: "Health") intends to consolidate the services provided in the territory, thanks to the creation of territorial structures and facilities (such as Community Houses and Community Hospitals, etc.), the strengthening of home care, the development of telemedicine and a more effective integration with all social and health services. Furthermore, the PNRR finances investments aimed at renewing existing technological and digital structures, such as completing and disseminating the *Electronic Health Record* (Fascicolo Sanitario Elettronico—FSE), improving the provision and monitoring of the *Levels of Essential Assistance* (Livelli Essenziali di Assistenza—LEA) through more effective information systems. The PNRR should also consolidate the skills of human capital of the NHS by strengthening staff training.

It is necessary to plan prevention strategies that protect the social and environmental, as well as economic and financial sustainability of the systems and healthcare entities that must manage the elderly population and chronically ill patients, often affected by multiple pathologies. Thus, a new role is given to the general practitioners (GPs), and to IFOC (family and community nurses) which assume a primary role in the patient journey and in the development of territorial assistance (Schiavone et al., 2023).

Another strategy could be the implementation of the living lab approach; a new paradigm in which end-users, technological developers, and stakeholders live together in a real or virtual environment to test the use of new technologies for digital health to care chronicity. Living lab is an open innovation environment. Some living labs struggle to transition from pilot phases to fully operational healthcare solutions. This is due to the absence of a long-term funding policy that hinders financial sustainability (Almeida et al., 2022; Cuomo et al., 2021).

A possible solution in terms of a new care formula, in a context in which healthcare can be understood as a service ecosystem, concerns home hospitalisation practices (Hospitalisation at Home—HaH), which allow new types of hospitalisation, much more in line with the real needs of patients and caregivers. HaH can be considered an alternative approach to consolidated healthcare, offering a care environment equivalent to the hospital one, but at the patient's home, useful for improving the quality of life of patients and reducing the costs of healthcare processes. Home hospitalisation is thus identified as a method through which healthcare services ecosystems (HSES) can be managed in the light of economic and social sustainability (Polese et al., 2018).

To achieve what has been stated above, great attention must be given towards a vision based on collaboration (no longer competition), so as to conceive healthcare as an "ecosystem of services" guided by the principles of sustainability. This new vision is based on home hospitalisation practices that are much closer to the patient and the caregiver, with a reduction in hospital admissions and treatment costs and a reduction in clinical risks (Polese et al., 2018).

Consequently, management and accounting practices for chronic diseases need to be implemented in order to avoid the high costs of healthcare services, in particular the cost of hospitalisations, which is increasing worldwide. These costs are of different types, including managerial, social and medical costs.

Furthermore, another issue concerns management practices that rely on conventional financial accounting that do not consider social and sustainability impacts, because social resources are not represented in the entities' balance sheets. This leads to incomplete accountability because social costs are not included in the organisations' decision-making processes because they are not visible in reporting documents. Non-financial and sustainability reporting, that is voluntary in private and public entities and thus in healthcare organisations, could help to communicate non-financial information to the public, to the territories and communities, only if it involves external stakeholders and is used as an accountability tool. This is why a management accounting process is strategic in healthcare entities in order to control the high costs of chronicity.

Population ageing observed in recent decades has led to an increase in the prevalence of chronic diseases, which often coexist within the same individual (multimorbidity). The disease burden experienced by people suffering from these conditions frequently results in years lived with disability, inevitably compromising quality of life and increasing the risk of premature mortality. In fact, chronic conditions require more frequent medical consultations and hospital admissions, and the expenditure for chronic patients accounts for more than 50% of total healthcare costs.

It is necessary to improve not only patient health, but also patient literacy, and costs (Gualano et al., 2021). For example, elderly patients have a lower digital literacy. If patients with low education enjoyed the same benefits as patients with high education (no inequity), there would be many more financial resources to redistribute or request for higher-value services. Therefore, the improvement of equity leads to obtaining positive results on sustainability in financial terms (Cafagna et al., 2018).

It is, in fact, well documented in the literature that higher levels of education are traditionally associated with better health outcomes, including a lower prevalence and incidence of chronic diseases (Choi et al., 2008; Oude Hengel et al., 2019; Raghupathi & Raghupathi, 2020; CERGAS–SDA Bocconi, 2024). In this case, the breakdown by specific type of chronic condition is reported: osteoarthritis/arthritis, chronic bronchitis, diabetes, nervous disorders, hypertension, allergies, heart diseases, osteoporosis, and gastric or duodenal ulcer. Furthermore, fewer chronic conditions are observed among those holding a university or postgraduate degree compared to those with a high school diploma; fewer chronic conditions among those with a high school diploma compared to those with only a middle school certificate, and so on.

5 Discussion, Conclusion and Future Research Lines

From the analysis of the literature review it clearly emerges that the challenges posed by population ageing require a systematic and multidisciplinary approach for the management of chronic diseases that encompasses:

1. The reorganisation of health and healthcare systems towards a decentralised model leveraging the expertise of different healthcare professionals.
2. An expanded approach towards preventive and personalised care and increased coordination among primary care and specialists (with a greater involvement of general practitioners).
3. The optimisation of the offer of digital health solutions (e.g. remote monitoring, AI-driven tools and smart wearables) to improve healthcare delivery. Such an approach requires coordinated human and financial resources.

Moreover, the implementation of community care models needs the reorganisation of the healthcare delivery system towards a greater integration between patient, hospital and territory. Experiences show how these models can ultimately improve healthcare financial and social sustainability (Salvatore, 2023).

Among the experiences identified, living lab is a novel model of open innovation ecosystem that could be applied to digital health. It is a collaborative physical or virtual environment for continuum of care. The living lab consists of a network of various actors (universities, businesses, public and private institutions, patients, end-users) that collaborate to drive digital health innovations and improve health outcomes, prevention, and patient support in real life contexts. Such a model could be especially beneficial for patients with chronic conditions.

Living labs are increasingly prevalent in primary care, as evidenced by numerous studies (Samuelson et al., 2023; Demiris et al., 2013). Living labs often focus on addressing various chronic diseases, a significant area of concern in health. Research highlights their application in managing diabetes, cardiovascular diseases, and other long-term health challenges (Benvenuto et al., 2017; Kanstrup, 2014; Swinkels et al., 2018).

The health-related innovations emerging from living labs primarily focus on developing new technological solutions. These innovations include mobile applications (Kim & Choi, 2023; Lobo et al., 2022) software platforms (Haux et al., 2014; Santa et al., 2023), wearable devices and sensors (Noublanche et al., 2019; Montalva Colomer et al., 2014; Rahman et al., 2022), as well as robotics and chatbots (Leminen et al., 2017; Luengo-Polo et al., 2021; Kwon & Ju, 2023; Phanareth et al., 2017).

Further synergies resulting from collaboration can be observed in the management and control of non-communicable chronic diseases (NCDs), which incorporate broader population-based perspectives into clinical practice, including vaccination and screening programmes. This integration is supported by the implementation of evidence-based, patient-centred "*Preventive Diagnostic Therapeutic Care Pathways*" (PPDTA) (CERGAS–SDA Bocconi, 2024). In the Veneto region, in particular, this involves a wide range of coordinated interventions at different levels aimed at preventing the onset of diseases such as diabetes and obesity, avoiding clinical complications, ensuring early care for individuals at risk or in the initial stages of disease, and slowing disease progression. In the case of obesity-related conditions, for example, integrated care pathways are designed for the entire family unit.

Furthermore, the *Cardio50 project* represents another successful example of integration, involving multiple levels and actors within the healthcare system. Its objective is to identify cardiovascular risk factors early in a strategically significant age group, in order to make preventive interventions more effective.

Similar experiences of coordination in chronic disease management have also emerged in other regional contexts. In healthcare organisations in the Italian city of Milan, hospital specialists and community-based physicians collaborate with public health departments to provide personalised vaccination programmes for the most vulnerable patients (e.g. dialysis patients). In the Emilia-Romagna region, in Italy, hospital specialists and general practitioners, together with public health services, coordinate care for patients with chronic diseases. For instance, the diabetes care pathway includes the administration of vaccines (such as the influenza vaccine) and the monitoring of patient health through specialist visits. Screening activities are also incorporated into the care pathways of chronic patients.

Management of chronic diseases can be optimised thanks to a greater use of in-home care (hospitalisation at home) and "illness management in the community" in order to reduce hospitalisations and their costs.

This review highlights the importance of strengthening local healthcare services, community care, primary care, and home services in order to reduce the burden of chronic diseases and create value for the patients.

The implementation of innovative digital health solutions, such as telemedicine and smart health applications, plays a significant role in promoting the economic, social, and environmental sustainability of health systems and also for the continuum of care.

This study aims at advancing knowledge of innovative and sustainable approaches and practices, which may support decision-making processes for policymakers and practitioners in order to implement innovative health policies. The overview and analysis conducted may be useful in the post-pandemic period and as well as in other context of emergencies.

The limits of this work are explained herein. This narrative review focuses on industrialised countries. A broader scope and a more systematic approach would identify other practices proposed for different healthcare systems.

References

Almeida, M., Taveira, A., Macedo, A., & Crispim, J. (2022). Co-design of a routine that implements an equity and quality checklist to vulnerable elders on primary care: A living lab approach. *Procedia Computer Science, 196*, 517–524. https://doi.org/10.1016/j.procs.2021.12.044

Barsanti, S., & Guarneri, F. (2019). Chronic disease management: discussing the perspectives of general practitioners in Italy. *Health Services Management Research, 33*(1), 13–23. https://doi.org/10.1177/0951484819871011

Benvenuto, M., Viola, C., & Sambati, F. (2017). A new social and technological paradigm to assess chronic patient management process: preliminary results. *Management, 5*(6), 525–540. https://doi.org/10.17265/2328-2185/2017.06.005

Beretta, V., & Demartini, M. C. (2020). La gestione della cronicità nelle aziende sanitarie: una rassegna della letteratura. *Mecosan, 116*(4), 7–30. https://doi.org/10.3280/MESA2020-116002

Cafagna, G., Seghieri, C., Vainieri, M., & Nuti, S. (2018). A turnaround strategy: improving equity in order to achieve quality of care and financial sustainability in Italy. *International Journal for Equity in Health, 17*(1), 1–12. https://doi.org/10.1186/s12939-018-0878-x

Cavacece, Y. (2023). *Management sanitario tra innovazione digitale e partecipazione del cittadino: prospettive teoriche ed evidenze empiriche*. Franco Angeli.

CERGAS–SDA Bocconi. (2024). *Rapporto OASI 2024: Osservatorio sulle aziende e sul sistema sanitario italiano*. Egea.

Choi, H.-J., Lee, S. Y., Arozullah, A. M., & Crittenden, K. S. (2008). Effects of health literacy on health status and health service utilisation among the elderly. *Social Science & Medicine, 66*(8), 1809–1816. https://doi.org/10.1016/j.socscimed.2007.11.034

Cuomo, F., Lambiase, N., & Castagna, A. (2021). Living lab on sharing and circular economy: The case of Turin. *Health Informatics Journal, 27*(1). https://doi.org/10.1177/1460458220987278

De Lorenzo, A., Esposito, E., Maffei, C. M., & Zuccatelli, G. (2020). Coronavirus e cronicità, due battaglie da vincere sullo stesso campo (il territorio) e anche con una "nuova" figura (l'infermiere di famiglia e di comunità). *Mecosan, 113*, 201–208. https://doi.org/10.3280/MESA2020-113025

Demiris, G., Thompson, H. J., Reeder, B., Wilamowska, K., & Zaslavsky, O. (2013). Using informatics to capture older adults' wellness. *International Journal Medical Informatics, 82*(11), e232–e241. https://doi.org/10.1016/j.ijmedinf.2011.03.004

Elf, M., Flink, M., Nilsson, M., Tistad, M., von Koch, L., & Ytterberg, C. (2017). The case of value-based healthcare for people living with complex long-term conditions. *BMC Health Services Research, 17*(1), 1–6. https://doi.org/10.1186/s12913-016-1957-6

Embuldeniya, G., Gutberg, J., & Wodchis, W. P. (2020). The reimagination of sustainable integrated care in Ontario, Canada. *Health Policy, 125*(1), 83–89. https://doi.org/10.1016/j.healthpol.2020.11.001

Faggini, M., Cosimato, S., Nota, F. D., & Nota, G. (2019). Pursuing sustainability for healthcare through digital platforms. *Sustainability, 11*(1), 165. https://doi.org/10.3390/su11010165

García-Goñi, M., Hernández-Quevedo, C., Nuño-Solinís, R., & Paolucci, F. (2012). Pathways towards chronic care-focused healthcare systems: evidence from Spain. *Health Policy, 108*(2–3), 236–245. https://doi.org/10.1016/j.healthpol.2012.09.014

Gualano, M. R., Corradi, A., Voglino, G., Bert, F., & Siliquini, R. (2021). Beyond Covid-19: a cross-sectional study in Italy exploring the Covid collateral impacts on healthcare services. *Health Policy, 125*(7), 869–876. https://doi.org/10.1016/j.healthpol.2021.03.005

Haux, R., Hein, A., Kolb, G., Künemund, H., Eichelberg, M., Appell, J. E., et al. (2014). Information and communication technologies for promoting and sustaining quality of life, health and self-sufficiency in ageing societies–outcomes of the Lower Saxony research network design of environments for aging (GAL). *Informatics for Health and Social Care, 39*(3–4), 166–187. https://doi.org/10.3109/17538157.2014.931849

Hwang, R., Morris, N. R., Mandrusiak, A., Bruning, J., Peters, R., Korczyk, D., & Russell, T. (2019). Cost-utility analysis of home-based telerehabilitation compared with centre-based rehabilitation in patients with heart failure. *Heart, Lung and Circulation, 28*(12), 1795–1803. https://doi.org/10.1016/j.hlc.2018.12.013

ISTAT. (2022a). Indagine MULTISCOPO sulle famiglie, aspetti della vita quotidiana.

ISTAT. (2022b). Rapporto annuale 2022.

Kanstrup, A. M. (2014). Design concepts for digital diabetes practice: Design to explore, share, and camouflage chronic illness. *International Journal of Design, 8*(3), 49–60. www.ijdesign.org/ojs/index.php/IJDesign/article/view/1568/652

Karimi, L., Leggat, S. G., Bartram, T., et al. (2021). Emotional intelligence: predictor of employees' wellbeing, quality of patient care, and psychological empowerment. *BMC Psychology, 9*, 93. https://doi.org/10.1186/s40359-021-00593-

Kendzerska, T., Zhu, D. T., Gershon, A. S., Edwards, J. D., Peixoto, C., Robillard, R., & Kendall, C. E. (2021). The effects of the health system response to the Covid-19 pandemic on chronic disease management: a narrative review. *Risk Management and Healthcare Policy, 14*, 575–584. https://doi.org/10.2147/RMHP.S293471

Kim, H., & Choi, Y. (2023). A practical development protocol for evidence-based digital integrative arts therapy content in public mental health services: digital transformation of mandala art therapy. *Frontiers in Public Health, 11*, 1175093. https://doi.org/10.3389/fpubh.2023.1175093

Kokko, P., & Kork, A. A. (2020). Value-based healthcare logics and their implications for Nordic health policies. *Health Services Management Research, 34*(1), 3–12. https://doi.org/10.1177/0951484820971457

Kwon, J., & Ju, D. (2023). Living lab-based service interaction design for a companion robot for seniors in South Korea. *Biomimetics, 8*(8), 609. https://doi.org/10.3390/biomimetics8080609

Lavergne, M. R. (2017). Financial incentives for physicians to improve health-care. *Canadian Medical Association Journal, 189*(49), E1505–E1506. https://doi.org/10.1503/cmaj.171126

Leminen, S., Westerlund, M., & Rajahonka, M. (2017). Innovating with service robots in health and welfare living labs. *International Journal of Innovation Management, 21*(8), 1740013. https://doi.org/10.1142/S1363919617400138

Lobo, E. H., Kensing, F., Frølich, A., Rasmussen, L. J., Livingston, P. M., Islam, S. M. S., et al. (2022). mHealth intervention for carers of individuals with a history of stroke: Heuristic evaluation and user perspectives. *Digital Health, 8*, 20552076221089070. https://doi.org/10.1177/20552076221089070

Luengo-Polo, J., Conde-Caballero, D., Rivero-Jiménez, B., Ballesteros-Yáñez, I., Castillo-Sarmiento, C. A., & Mariano-Juárez, L. (2021). Rationale and methods of evaluation for

ACHO, a new virtual assistant to improve therapeutic adherence in rural elderly populations: A user-driven living lab. *International Journal of Environmental Research and Public Health, 18*(15), 7904. https://doi.org/10.3390/ijerph18157904
Milani, R. V., & Lavie, C. J. (2015). Health care 2020: Reengineering health-care delivery to combat chronic disease. *The American Journal of Medicine, 128*(4), 337–343. https://doi.org/10.1016/j.amjmed.2014.10.047
Ministry of Health. (2016). Piano Nazionale della Cronicità, disponibile online: https://www.salute.gov.it/imgs/C_17_pubblicazioni_2584_allegato.pdf
Montalva Colomer, J. B., Salvi, D., Cabrera-Umpierrez, M. F., Arredondo, M. T., Abril, P., Kimenez-Mixco, V., et al. (2014). Experience in evaluating AAL solutions in living labs. *Sensors, 14*(4), 7277–7311. https://doi.org/10.3390/s140407277
Noto, G., Noto, A., & Borgonovi, E. (2022). Le basi dell'approccio sistemico al DM 77 e all'integrazione territorio-ospedale: dalla pianificazione strategica all'attuazione operativa. *Mecosan, 124*, 113–136.
Noublanche, F., Jaglin-Grimonprez, C., Sacco, G., Lerolle, N., Allain, P., & Annweiler, C. (2019). The development of gerontechnology for hospitalized frail elderly people: The ALLEGRO hospital-based geriatric living lab. *Maturitas, 125*, 17–19. https://doi.org/10.1016/j.maturitas.2019.04.002
Oude Hengel, K., Groothoff, J. W., Geuskens, G. A., & Brouwer, S. (2019). Socioeconomic inequalities in reach, compliance and effectiveness of workplace health promotion programs: a systematic review. *BMC Public Health, 19*, 1234. https://doi.org/10.1186/s12889-019-7545-0
Pacileo, G., Tozzi, V. D., Sotgiu, G., Aliberti, S., Morando, V., & Blasi, F. (2019). Administrative databases and clinical governance: the case of COPD. *International Journal of Health Planning and Management, 34*(1), 177–186. https://doi.org/10.1002/hpm.2609
Paul, D. L., & McDaniel, R. R. (2016). Facilitating telemedicine project sustainability in medically underserved areas: a healthcare provider participant perspective. *BMC Health Services Research, 16*(1), 1–14. https://doi.org/10.1186/s12913-016-1401-y
Pautasso, M. (2019). The structure and conduct of a narrative literature review. In M. Shoja, A. Arynchyna, M. Loukas, A. V. D'Antoni, S. M. Buerger, M. Karl, & R. S. Tubbs (Eds.), *A guide to the scientific career: Virtues, communication, research and academic writing* (pp. 299–310). https://doi.org/10.1002/9781118907283.ch31
Phanareth, K., Vingtoft, S., Christensen, A. S., Nielsen, J. S., Svenstrup, J., Berntsen, G. K. R., et al. (2017). The Epital care model: a new person-centered model of technology-enabled integrated care for people with long-term conditions. *JMIR Research Protocols, 6*(1), e6506. https://doi.org/10.2196/resprot.6506
Polese, F., Carrubbo, L., Caputo, F., & Sarno, D. (2018). Managing healthcare service ecosystems: abstracting a sustainability-based view from hospitalization at home (HaH) practices. *Sustainability, 10*(11), 3951. https://doi.org/10.3390/su10113951
Raghupathi, V., & Raghupathi, W. (2020). The influence of education on health: an empirical assessment of OECD countries for the period 1995–2015. *Archives of Public Health, 78*, 20. https://doi.org/10.1186/s13690-020-00402-5
Rahman, M. J., Morshed, B. I., Harmon, B., & Rahman, M. (2022). A pilot study towards a smart-health framework to collect and analyze biomarkers with low-cost and flexible wearables. *Smart Health, 23*, 100249. https://doi.org/10.1016/j.smhl.2021.100249
Ramli, A. S., & Taher, S. W. (2008). Managing chronic diseases in the Malaysian primary health-care: A need for change. *Malaysian Family Physician, 3*(1), 7–13.
Sahle, B. W., Owen, A. J., Mutowo, M. P., Krum, H., & Reid, C. M. (2016). Prevalence of heart failure in Australia: A systematic review. *BMC Cardiovascular Disorders, 16*(1), 1–6. https://doi.org/10.1186/s12872-016-0208-4
Salvatore C. (a cura di). (2023). Il management delle malattie croniche. Profili economico-aziendali. Milano: Franco Angeli.
Samuelson, S., Svensson, A., Svenningsson, I., & Pennbrant, S. (2023). Learning in living lab collaboration in primary care–a qualitative study. *Journal of Workplace Learning, 35*(9), 218–234. https://doi.org/10.1108/JWL-01-2023-0012

Santa, K., Dixon, C., Ganga, R. N., Trainor, G., Smith, G., Furfie, V., et al. (2023). Facilitating the access of the broader community into child and adolescent mental health services in Liverpool and Sefton (UK): The co-customisation of the CYP as one platform with young people; parents and health service providers. *Research Square*. Preprint. https://doi.org/10.21203/rs.3.rs-2521427/v1

Sayani, S., Muzammil, M., Saleh, K., Muqeet, A., Zaidi, F., & Shaikh, T. (2019). Addressing cost and time barriers in chronic disease management through telemedicine: An exploratory research in select low-and middle-income countries. *Therapeutic Advances in Chronic Disease, 10*, 1–10. https://doi.org/10.1177/2040622319891587

Schiavone, F., Russo, S., & Montanino, F. (2023). Monitoraggio e Referral dei pazienti cronici: i risultati di uno studio empirico. *Mecosan, 127*(3), 29–42. https://doi.org/10.3280/mesa2023-127oa17873

Seixas, A. A., Olaye, I. M., Wall, S. P., & Dunn, P. (2021). Optimizing healthcare through digital health and wellness solutions to meet the needs of patients with chronic disease during the Covid-19 era. *Frontiers in Public Health, 9*, 667654. https://doi.org/10.3389/fpsyg.2021.667654

Smith, P. C., Sagan, A., Siciliani, L., & Figueras, J. (2023). Building on value-based health-care: Towards a health system perspective. *Health Policy, 138*, 104918. https://doi.org/10.1016/j.healthpol.2023.104918

Sosto, G. (2020). Una popolazione a strati. *Modelli previsionali, population health management, stratificazione e targeting della popolazione.* Strumenti integrati per la governance in sanità, Rubbettino, Soveria Mannelli (CZ).

Swinkels, I. C. S., Huygens, M. W. J., Schoenmakers, T. M., Oude Nijeweme-D'Hollosy, W., van Velsen, L., Vermeulen, J., et al. (2018). Lessons learned from a living lab on the broad adoption of eHealth in primary health care. *Journal of Medical Internet Research, 20*(3), e83. https://doi.org/10.2196/jmir.9110

Tozzi, V., & Longo, F. (a cura di). (2023). Management della cronicità. Logiche aziendali per gestire i nuovi setting sanitari finanziati dal PNNR. Egea, .

Trankle, S. A., Usherwood, T., Abbott, P., Roberts, M., Crampton, M., Girgis, C. M., & Reath, J. (2020). Key stakeholder experiences of an integrated healthcare pilot in Australia: a thematic analysis. *BMC Health Services Research, 20*(1), 1–12. https://doi.org/10.1186/s12913-020-05794-2

WHO. (2022). Primary health-care: making our commitments happen: realizing the potential of primary health-care: lessons learned from the Covid-19 pandemic and implications for future directions in the WHO European Region, World Health Organisation, Regional Office for Europe.

A Multimodal Data Collection Approach in a Health Promotion Event: "The Futuro Remoto" Living Lab Experience

Arianna Scala, Michele Virgolesi, Angela Palomba, Antonio Picone, Antonio Bianco, Alessandra Cuomo, Erminia Attaianese, Mariangela Perillo, Vincenzo De Luca, Sara Aprano, Enrica Mastantuoni, Tiziana Russo Spena, Francesco Garifalos, Davide Menafra, Daniela Lemmo, Fabrizio Mezza, Lorenzo Mercurio, and Maddalena Illario

1 Introduction

Health promotion is widely recognized as a fundamental pillar of public health, aiming to empower individuals and communities to take greater control over their health and its determinants (World Health Organization [WHO], 1986). As populations age and chronic diseases become more prevalent, there is growing consensus

A. Scala (✉) · M. Virgolesi · A. Palomba · A. Picone · A. Bianco · V. De Luca · L. Mercurio · M. Illario
Department of Public Health, University of Naples Federico II, Naples, Italy
e-mail: arianna.scala@unina.it; michele.virgolesi@unina.it; angela.palomba@unina.it; antonio.picone@unina.it; antonio.bianco@unina.it; lorenzo.mercurio@unina.it; maddalena.illario@unina.it

A. Cuomo · S. Aprano · F. Garifalos · D. Menafra
Department of Clinical and Surgical Medicine, University of Naples "Federico II", Naples, Italy
e-mail: alessandra.cuomo@unina.it; sara.aprano@unina.it; davide.menafra@unina.it

E. Attaianese · M. Perillo
Department of Architecture, University of Naples Federico II, Naples, Italy
e-mail: erminia.attaianese@unina.it; mariangela.perillo@unina.it

E. Mastantuoni
Department of Neuroscience, Reproductive Science and Dentistry, University of Naples "Federico II", Naples, Italy
e-mail: enrica.mastrantuoni@unina.it

A. Ricciardelli, L. Mercurio (eds.), *Building Innovation in Ageing and Health Policy*, Springer Series in Healthcare Management and Innovation,
https://doi.org/10.1007/978-3-032-09163-5_3

on the need for proactive, preventive approaches that address behavioral and environmental risk factors (Nutbeam, 2000; Kickbusch, 2012).

Public engagement events offer unique opportunities to translate health promotion principles into practice, particularly by combining education, interaction, and self-assessment in real-life settings (Rowe & Frewer, 2005). Such initiatives are increasingly aligned with the concept of the Living Lab, a user-centered, open-innovation ecosystem that integrates research and innovation processes in real-life communities and settings (European Network of Living Labs, 2020; Schuurman et al., 2016). Within the field of health promotion, Living Labs have demonstrated the capacity to foster co-creation, raise awareness, and collect data in a context that is both experiential and participatory (Pallot et al., 2011; Leminen et al., 2012).

The event Futuro Remoto—a long-standing science communication festival in Naples—was chosen as a platform for implementing an interactive public health intervention based on the Living Lab model. The primary goal was to increase awareness of modifiable health factors such as physical activity, nutrition, cognitive function, and social engagement, while also collecting integrated, multimodal health-related data through guided self-assessment pathways.

The methodological approach combined structured questionnaires, educational tools, and the support of trained nurse navigators, facilitating not only data collection but also meaningful participant involvement. This type of setting provides fertile ground for the application of mixed-methods research, which is increasingly used in health sciences to capture both behavioral complexity and individual perspectives (Creswell & Plano Clark, 2017; Johnson et al., 2007).

The aim of this article is to present the design, implementation, and methodological implications of the *Futuro Remoto* intervention, highlighting its relevance as a model for participatory public health strategies and interdisciplinary health promotion.

2 Methods

The methodology adopted in this study was based on a multimodal, mixed-methods approach, designed to offer participants an integrated and engaging health assessment experience. The setting was the public engagement event Futuro Remoto, where a Living Lab format was implemented to simultaneously promote health literacy and collect valuable population health data.

The intervention was structured into eight thematic stations, each addressing specific dimensions of health and well-being. Upon enrollment, participants

T. R. Spena
Department of Economics, Management, Institutions, University of Naples "Federico II", Naples, Italy
e-mail: tiziana.russospena@unina.it

D. Lemmo · F. Mezza
Department of Humanities, University of Naples Federico II, Naples, Italy
e-mail: daniela.lemmo@unina.it; fabrizio.mezza@unina.it

provided informed consent ($n = 99$) and were assigned a unique anonymized code to ensure confidentiality and enable traceability of responses across stations.

Self-assessment tools—both qualitative and quantitative—were administered with the assistance of trained nurse navigators, enhancing data reliability and participant adherence. Each station was equipped with validated instruments suitable for field-based health screenings, and participants received immediate feedback on their results, including recommendations for further assessment where necessary.

Below is a summary of the eight health screening stations:

Healthy Nutrition and Chronobiology: This station addressed the importance of balanced nutrition in relation to physical activity, sleep quality, and sedentary behavior. Key self-assessment tools included:

KIDMED Index for evaluating adherence to the Mediterranean diet (López-Gajardo et al., 2022).

Pittsburgh Sleep Quality Index (PSQI) for assessing sleep patterns (Curcio et al., 2013).

IPAQ (International Physical Activity Questionnaire) for measuring physical activity levels (Mannocci et al., 2010).

IAT (Internet Addiction Test) for evaluating digital device dependence (Young, 1998).

Anthropometric measurements such as weight and BMI were recorded. Participants received an anonymized report summarizing their results. Based on these assessments, participants could be referred to a second-level evaluation for more in-depth functional assessments.

Skeletal Disease Screening in Children: This station focused on early detection of kyphosis and other spinal conditions in children aged 6–14. Clinical assessments were conducted by a team led by Prof. Carlo Ruosi. Emphasis was placed on postural education related to backpack use and digital device exposure. Screening outcomes helped identify candidates for postural reeducation, physical therapy, or orthotic interventions.

Physical Strength Assessment: Standardized physical fitness tests were used to assess muscular strength and endurance. These included:

Handgrip Strength Test for upper limb function.

Chair Stand Test for lower limb strength and endurance.

These tests were particularly relevant for identifying early signs of frailty, especially in older adults.

Psychophysical Well-Being and the Built Environment: Two structured questionnaires evaluated the relationship between the participant's environment and perceived walking quality:

One focused on neighborhood walkability and mobility challenges.

The second assessed indoor environmental risks such as poor lighting, flooring, and architectural barriers that may increase fall risk.

Maternal and Neonatal Health: This station targeted women of reproductive age, pregnant women, and new mothers. Participants completed questionnaires (quantitative and qualitative) focused on:

Preconception health awareness

Physical and psychological well-being during pregnancy and postpartum

Early signs of anxiety and mood disorders

Participants received tailored information and access to specialist referrals for further assessments.

Male Sexual Health: This station addressed male sexual health using validated instruments:

IIEF-15 (International Index of Erectile Function): A score < 26 suggested erectile dysfunction (Rosen et al., 1997).

PEDT (Premature Ejaculation Diagnostic Tool): A score ≥ 11 indicated potential premature ejaculation (Symonds et al., 2007).

Information materials on sexual health, contraception, and STI prevention were distributed, especially targeting younger male participants.

Lifestyle, Motivation, and Subjective Well-Being: Participants completed structured questionnaires examining lifestyle choices, self-care behaviors, readiness to change, and perceptions of health and well-being. A brief interpretative report was provided to stimulate self-reflection and promote behavioral changes.

Frailty in the Elderly Older adults were assessed for frailty using the Handgrip Strength Test and Chair Stand Test. These tools are validated measures for identifying physical decline and sarcopenia. Participants received information on physical activity recommendations from the WHO, encouraging at least 150 minutes of moderate aerobic activity weekly.

All data were recorded in a digital spreadsheet using standardized scores and metrics, allowing for cross-sectional analysis and comparability. The mixed-methods framework enhanced both data reliability and contextual interpretation (Creswell & Plano Clark, 2017; Johnson et al., 2007). Instruments used were validated in prior research and selected for their feasibility in public engagement contexts.

This structured, participatory approach allowed not only for comprehensive health screening but also served as a powerful educational and behavioral intervention tool, consistent with health promotion principles outlined by the WHO (1986) and expanded in later frameworks (Kickbusch, 2012).

3 Results

A total of 395 questionnaires were administered during the event, following the collection of 99 informed consents. On average, each participant completed approximately 3.5 questionnaires, with a range from 1 to 9. The highest number of responses was collected at Station 1 (Healthy Nutrition and Chronobiology), accounting for 165 questionnaires. This was followed by 55 questionnaires at Station 3 (Physical Strength Assessment), 48 at Station 4 (Psychophysical Well-Being and the Built Environment), 34 at Station 6 (Male Sexual Health), and 41 at Station 7 (Lifestyle, Motivation, and Subjective Well-Being). Additionally, 52 questionnaires were dedicated to evaluating participants' perceptions of the quality of the overall process and organizational experience.

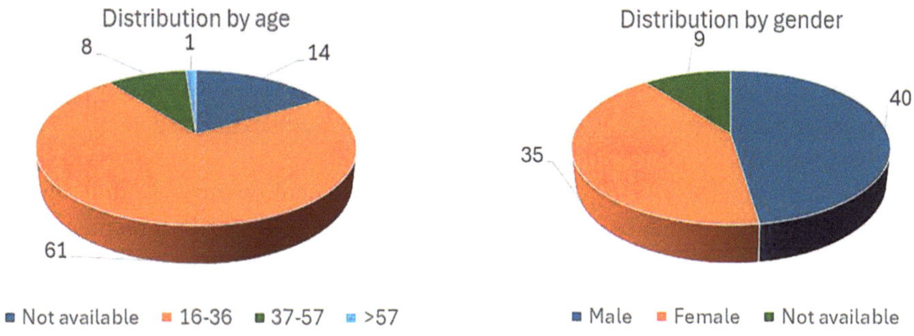

Fig. 1 Age and gender distribution of participants

All questionnaires were linked through a unified, anonymized coding system and entered into a centralized digital database designed to integrate data from multiple sources in real time. This methodological infrastructure enabled consistent tracking of participant responses across stations, facilitated the detection of patterns in health behaviors and needs, and allowed for a cross-sectional view of the population reached during the event. The integration of qualitative and quantitative measures within a unified dataset ensured data comparability and supported a deeper contextual analysis of health determinants and outcomes. This approach exemplifies a living lab methodology applied to public health screening and education, with the database acting as a core tool for both operational coordination and subsequent research exploitation.

From a demographic standpoint, participation skewed toward younger age groups, with 61 individuals aged 16–36, 8 aged 37–57, and just 1 participant over 57 years old. Age was not reported for 14 individuals. In terms of gender, 40 participants identified as male, 35 as female, and 24 did not report gender information. These distributions are visually represented in Fig. 1. These data highlight both the potential and limitations of voluntary public engagement models and underscore the value of tailored outreach strategies for underrepresented demographic groups in future health promotion initiatives.

4 Discussion and Conclusions

This study demonstrates how a Living Lab approach, implemented within a science communication festival, can serve as both a public engagement strategy and a rigorous model for integrated health data collection. Central to the success of the intervention was the methodological framework, which enabled simultaneous delivery of health promotion content and real-time acquisition of multimodal health data.

The use of a unified, anonymized coding system and a centralized digital database represented a methodological innovation in the context of field-based public health interventions. This infrastructure allowed for consistent linkage of data across different thematic stations, making it possible to analyze participant profiles from a multidimensional perspective. The integration of both qualitative and quantitative self-assessment tools, each validated in previous research, ensured that the data collected were not only robust but also highly contextualized to individual health behaviors and perceptions.

The centralization of data also facilitated operational coordination during the event and laid the groundwork for future longitudinal analyses. By creating a unified dataset with standardized metrics, the intervention overcame one of the main challenges in public engagement initiatives: the fragmentation of data collected through heterogeneous, nonintegrated tools. Moreover, the involvement of trained nurse navigators not only supported the quality of data entry but also enhanced participant engagement and trust—an essential aspect in voluntary, nonclinical health screening contexts.

From a practical standpoint, the results highlight a strong interest among participants in lifestyle-related domains such as nutrition, sleep, and physical activity. However, lower participation rates in stations focusing on male sexual health or environmental risk factors suggest the persistence of cultural stigmas or lower perceived relevance. These findings point to the importance of designing inclusive and targeted communication strategies that consider age, gender, and cultural sensitivities.

Despite its strengths, the intervention had several limitations. First, the sample was not representative of the general population. Participation was voluntary and skewed toward younger individuals (predominantly aged 16–36), with limited engagement from older adults—an important target group for preventive interventions. Gender data were also incomplete, with 24 participants not reporting their sex, limiting disaggregated analysis. Second, while the integration of questionnaires into a centralized database was a methodological asset, it also required significant manual data entry and real-time coordination. This introduces potential risks of data inconsistency or input errors, despite the efforts of trained personnel. Third, the self-administered nature of many of the instruments, even when guided, may have introduced response bias, particularly in domains such as sexual health or mental well-being. Moreover, the cross-sectional design does not allow for evaluation of behavioral change or long-term health impact.

This pilot intervention demonstrates the feasibility and potential of combining participatory health promotion with integrated data collection in real-life settings. The methodological core—centered on interoperability, data standardization, and user engagement—offers a replicable model for future public health interventions in nonclinical environments.

Going forward, efforts should focus on improving demographic inclusivity, enhancing digital data collection tools to reduce manual processing, and developing follow-up mechanisms to assess the longitudinal impact of such interventions. The Living Lab approach, if scaled and adapted to diverse contexts, has the potential to bridge the gap between public engagement, education, and actionable health data generation.

References

Creswell, J. W., & Plano Clark, V. L. (2017). *Designing and conducting mixed methods research* (3rd ed.). SAGE Publications.

Curcio, G., Tempesta, D., Scarlata, S., Marzano, C., Moroni, F., Rossini, P. M., Ferrara, M., & De Gennaro, L. (2013). Validity of the Italian version of the Pittsburgh sleep quality index (PSQI) in a clinical sample. *International Journal of Environmental Research and Public Health, 10*(10), 4339–4349. https://doi.org/10.3390/ijerph10104339

European Network of Living Labs. (2020). What is a Living Lab? Retrieved from https://enoll.org.

Johnson, R. B., Onwuegbuzie, A. J., & Turner, L. A. (2007). Toward a definition of mixed methods research. *Journal of Mixed Methods Research, 1*(2), 112–133. https://doi.org/10.1177/1558689806298224

Kickbusch, I. (2012). Twenty-first century determinants of health and wellbeing: A new challenge for health promotion. *Global Health Promotion, 19*(3), 5–7. https://doi.org/10.1177/1757975912454783

Leminen, S., Westerlund, M., & Nyström, A.-G. (2012). Living labs as open-innovation networks. *Technology Innovation. Management Review, 2*(9), 6–11. https://doi.org/10.22215/timreview/602

López-Gajardo, M. A., García-Marín, L., & García-Marín, J. A. (2022). KIDMED 2.0: An update of the KIDMED questionnaire. *Frontiers in Nutrition, 9*, 945721. https://doi.org/10.3389/fnut.2022.945721

Mannocci, A., Di Thiene, D., Del Cimmuto, A., Masala, D., Boccia, A., De Vito, E., & La Torre, G. (2010). International physical activity questionnaire: validation and assessment in an Italian sample. *Italian Journal of Public Health, 7*(4), 369–376. https://doi.org/10.2427/5672

Nutbeam, D. (2000). Health literacy as a public health goal: A challenge for contemporary health education and communication strategies into the 21st century. *Health Promotion International, 15*(3), 259–267. https://doi.org/10.1093/heapro/15.3.259

Pallot, M., Trousse, B., Senach, B., & Scapin, D. (2011). Living lab research landscape: From user centred design and user experience towards user cocreation. In *Technologies and innovation* (pp. 287–298). Springer. https://doi.org/10.1007/978-3-642-22094-7_31

Rosen, R. C., Riley, A., Wagner, G., Osterloh, I. H., Kirkpatrick, J., & Mishra, A. (1997). The international index of erectile function (IIEF): A multidimensional scale for assessment of erectile dysfunction. *Urology, 49*(6), 822–830. https://doi.org/10.1016/S0090-4295(97)00238-0

Rowe, G., & Frewer, L. J. (2005). A typology of public engagement mechanisms. *Science, Technology, & Human Values, 30*(2), 251–290. https://doi.org/10.1177/0162243904271724

Schuurman, D., De Marez, L., & Ballon, P. (2016). The impact of living lab methodology on open innovation contributions and outcomes. *Technology Innovation Management Review, 6*(1), 7–16. https://doi.org/10.22215/timreview/956

Symonds, T., Perelman, M. A., Althof, S., Giuliano, F., Martin, M., & May, K. (2007). Development and validation of a premature ejaculation diagnostic tool. *European Urology, 52*(2), 565–573. https://doi.org/10.1016/j.eururo.2007.01.028

World Health Organization. (1986). *Ottawa charter for health promotion*. Retrieved from https://www.who.int/publications/i/item/ottawa-charter-for-health-promotion.

Young, K. S. (1998). Internet addiction: The emergence of a new clinical disorder. *Cyberpsychology & Behavior, 1*(3), 237–244. https://doi.org/10.1089/cpb.1998.1.237

References

Creswell, J. W., & Plano Clark, V. L. (2018). *Designing and conducting mixed methods research* ... SAGE Publications.

Interprofessional Health Workforce Development in the Context of an Ageing Population

Sonja Lindner-Rabl and Regina Roller-Wirnsberger

1 Introduction: Demographic and Policy Context – Ageing as a Global Health Challenge

The demographic landscape of the European Union (EU) is undergoing significant transformations characterized by declining fertility rates, increasing life expectancy, and resultant population ageing. These changes have profound implications across social, health, and related economic sectors (SAPEA, 2019). Life expectation at birth has risen significantly with an average of 81.5 years for the EU in 2023, with variations among member states (OECD/European Commission, 2024). The global population aged 60 years and older amounted to 1 billion people in 2020 and is expected to rise up to nearly 2.1 billion by 2050 (World Health Organization, 2020). This increase is due to advancements in healthcare, improved living conditions, and public health initiatives. While lifespan has increased, the challenge remains to extend the health span (the period of life spent in good health), which has not kept pace with the increase in life expectancy (SAPEA, 2019).

In parallel to these demographic transformations, health systems are increasingly challenged by a growth in chronic diseases, multimorbidity and geriatric syndromes, leading to an intensification in complexity of care needs among older adults (World Health Organization, 2020; Polidori et al., 2018). These highly individual clinical patterns emphasize the inadequacy of fragmented, disease-centred models of care and call for a paradigm shift towards integrated, person-centred approaches that holistically address the physical, psychological, and social dimensions of ageing (Kaehne & Nies, 2021; Duque et al., 2021). The accumulation of vulnerabilities

S. Lindner-Rabl · R. Roller-Wirnsberger (✉)
Research Unit Services for Old Age and Lifelong Health, Department of Internal Medicine, Medical University of Graz, Graz, Austria
e-mail: sonja.lindner@medunigraz.at; regina.roller-wirnsberger@medunigraz.at; aging-ukim@medunigraz.at

A. Ricciardelli, L. Mercurio (eds.), *Building Innovation in Ageing and Health Policy*, Springer Series in Healthcare Management and Innovation,
https://doi.org/10.1007/978-3-032-09163-5_4

over the lifespan, commonly manifesting as frailty, further necessitates comprehensive and coordinated health and social care responses (Hendry et al., 2019).

Substantial differences in the development and availability of geriatric care infrastructure across EU member states lead to highly unequal opportunities for older adults to access specialized and coordinated healthcare services (World Health Organization, 2020; Mateos-Nozal & Beard, 2011; Grund et al., 2020; Fisher et al., 2017). This fragmentation is mirrored in the education and training systems for health and social care professionals, which differ markedly in structure, content, and emphasis on "geriatric competencies" needed for the complex care of the ageing population. This heterogeneity of health workforce professional capacity across Europe, in turn, reflects a persistent underestimation of the strategic importance of geriatric care and interprofessional collaboration in workforce development (Fisher et al., 2017; Michel et al., 2008; Lindner-Rabl et al., 2023; Roller-Wirnsberger et al., 2025). Consequently, professionals often lack adequate preparation to address the complex and multidimensional needs of ageing populations, including multimorbidity, functional decline, social vulnerability and the capacity for interprofessional collaborative practice (IPC) (SAPEA, 2019).

Strategic workforce planning therefore needs to prioritize the development of interprofessional education (IPE) initiatives and training programmes that foster a collaborative practice culture across disciplines. IPE is a key enabler in equipping health professionals with the transversal competencies necessary to manage complexity, promote resilience among older adults, and deliver integrated care (SAPEA, 2019; Interprofessional Education Collaborative, 2016). Embedding these competencies systematically into educational curricula is imperative to support a sustainable transformation towards health systems that are responsive to the needs of ageing societies. Consequently, the urgency to strengthen interprofessional health workforce capacity represents not only an educational imperative but a critical systemic response to safeguard the quality, accessibility, and equity of needs-oriented healthcare in the decades to come (World Health Organization, 2016).

Recognizing the pressing demand for a resilient, future-ready health workforce necessitates a critical exploration of the theoretical underpinnings and empirical evidence supporting IPE. To lay the foundation for strategic workforce development, it is essential to understand, how IPE concepts have evolved, how they address the complexities inherent in geriatric care, and what evidence exists regarding their effectiveness. The following section systematically examines the theoretical frameworks, pedagogical principles, and outcome data that underpin IPE, thereby informing the design and implementation of targeted strategies to meet the health and social care needs of ageing populations.

2 Theoretical and Empirical Foundations of IPE

The concept of IPE is anchored in the recognition that effective collaboration among health and social care professionals is essential to manage the growing complexity of care—particularly in the context of ageing populations (Hean et al., 2012). IPE is defined as an educational approach in which

> *learners from two or more professional backgrounds learn about, from, and with each other to enable effective collaboration and improve health outcomes* (World Health Organization, 2010).

As such, it serves as a cornerstone of integrated care models that seek to respond to the multidimensional needs of older adults through coordinated and person-centred service delivery (Bookey-Bassett et al., 2022).

IPE is informed by theoretical foundations, such as the Social Learning Theory by Bandura (Bandura, 1977) or the concept of Social Capital (Gillies, 1997), that highlight the importance of interaction, reciprocity and shared learning, especially in complex systems. The concept emphasizes experiential learning, reflective practice, and social interaction as critical mechanisms for fostering shared understanding and interprofessional competence. Central to these frameworks is the development of transversal skills such as communication, role clarification, conflict resolution, and collaborative decision-making—all of which are indispensable in geriatric care settings characterized by high levels of medical, functional, and psychosocial complexity (Doornebosch et al., 2022; Nancarrow et al., 2013; Bunn et al., 2018).

Empirical evidence increasingly underscores the value of IPE in enhancing both learner outcomes and health system performance. Systematic reviews and evaluation studies have demonstrated that IPE interventions can improve learners' knowledge, skills, and attitudes toward collaborative practice (Lindner-Rabl et al., 2023; Guraya & Barr, 2018; Oudbier et al., 2024; Al-Qallaf et al., 2024; Knebl et al., 2019; Montano et al., 2022; Joosten-Hagye et al., 2024). Evidence for better care coordination and improved patient satisfaction in clinical contexts involving older adults is growing as well (Cadet et al., 2024; Reeves et al., 2016). Importantly, these effects are most pronounced when IPE is embedded in authentic, practice-oriented environments that reflect the realities of interprofessional teamwork (Patel et al., 2025; Krystallidou et al., 2018).

However, the effectiveness and efficacy of IPE is mediated by a range of contextual factors, including institutional support, curricular integration, faculty readiness, and the presence of clearly defined interprofessional learning outcomes (Oudbier et al., 2024; Bogossian et al., 2023). Moreover, the evidence base remains heterogeneous, with considerable variation in intervention design, target populations, assessment methods, and reported outcomes (Jiang et al., 2024; Mattiazzi et al., 2024; Babin et al., 2023). This underscores the need for further research employing robust, longitudinal designs and standardized evaluation frameworks to assess the sustained impact of IPE on workforce preparedness and health outcomes in geriatric care.

In the following sections, key competency frameworks will be examined to provide a more in-depth analysis of major principles underpinning IPE and to offer guidance for the strategic planning and development, implementation and evaluation of interprofessional collaborative practices in geriatric health workforce education and training.

3 IPE and Competency Frameworks for Interprofessional Care in General

Competency frameworks offer structured and evidence-informed guidance for cultivating the essential knowledge, skills, and attitudes required for effective interprofessional collaboration in geriatric contexts. An exemplary selection of frameworks guiding IPE and competency development as well as consolidation in geriatric care will be presented in this section. These frameworks serve as foundational tools to align educational strategies with the realities of integrated, person-centred care, ensuring that health professionals are equipped to respond to the multidimensional and complex needs of older adults.

3.1 Integrated Care for Older People (ICOPE) Implementation Framework: Guidance for Systems and Services (World Health Organization, 2019)

The ICOPE Implementation Framework was developed by WHO to address the complex health and social care needs of older populations (World Health Organization, 2019). It aims to support the integration of health and social care services to maintain and improve intrinsic capacity and functional ability among older adults.

The framework outlines 19 macro- and meso-level actions designed to facilitate integrated care, as outlined in the Fig. 1 below. As a special feature, actions needed to realize strategy implementation are structurally presented according to health-systems' maturity level. In this way, the importance of local, regional, and national context is recognized and considered throughout framework adoption. Maturity level is defined based on three indicators of the implementation level: no to minimal implementation, initiating implementation, and sustaining implementation and assessment will logically result in different actions needed for a successful framework adoption (World Health Organization, 2019).

In this context, focus is put on System Action 14, which specifically addresses workforce capacity development as a critical component for ensuring that health-care systems are equipped to deliver integrated, person-centred care efficiently and sustainably (World Health Organization, 2019).

The primary aim of System Action 14 is to develop capacity within the current and emerging workforce (both paid and unpaid) to deliver integrated care effectively. This involves:

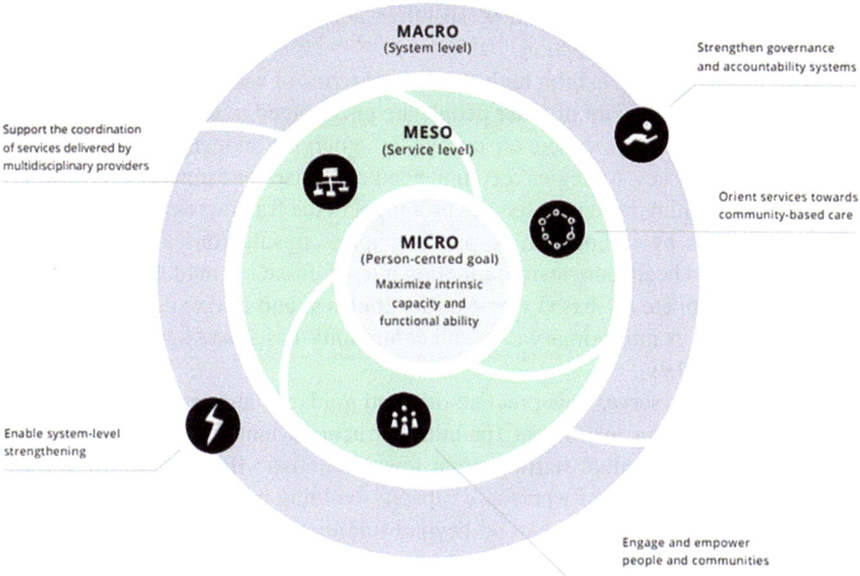

Fig. 1 Depicts a holistic approach across three levels of care to realize integrated care for older adults (World Health Organization, 2019)

- Building workforce competencies to ensure professionals can conduct person-centred assessments, develop personalized care plans, and deliver services that enhance functional ability.
- Promoting interdisciplinary collaboration, recognizing that effective integrated care requires coordinated efforts from a diverse set of healthcare and social care professionals.
- Fostering ongoing education to adapt to evolving healthcare demands, including emerging roles in the healthcare workforce (e.g. community health workers).
- Supporting both paid and unpaid caregivers, acknowledging the vital role of family members and community volunteers in delivering care.

If there are no or only minimal processes in place to develop knowledge and skills of the health workforce, the framework demonstrates a range of foundational competencies current and future health professionals need to develop and advocates for an evaluation of the current capacity of the workforce. Moreover, suggested capacity-building initiatives, such as progression towards competency-based curricula; the adoption of IPE modules and training expansions towards primary care and community-based settings, are identified (World Health Organization, 2019).

In case of limited existing initiatives for health workforce knowledge and skill development or capacity-building—mainly without the interdisciplinary component, systems are advised to also strive for fostering foundational competencies as mentioned above and moreover to expand existing capacity building processes by including all workforce roles and perspectives, also reflecting on interdisciplinary care (World Health Organization, 2019).

Systems that already exhibit high maturity in terms of workforce capacity development for integrated care of older people are encouraged to continue, update, and monitor their initiatives based on current or emerging evidence and resources. Moreover, further key strategies recommended comprise for example the provision of in-service training for competencies promoted in the framework; enabling supervision processes by senior staff; supporting joint consultations and meetings of interprofessional healthcare teams; adopting interprofessional models and progressing towards competency-based curricula for trainees; and also expanding capacity building initiatives into primary care and community-based settings (World Health Organization, 2019).

The framework serves as a practice-oriented guidance and implementation tool also incorporating an instrument for initial structured maturity assessments, that allow to set the individual starting point towards holistic IPE in geriatric care. It encourages the adoption of workforce capacity-building processes and interprofessional education models that extend beyond traditional roles, integrating community-based health workers and non-medical caregivers into the learning ecosystem.

3.2 European Collaborative and Interprofessional Capability Framework for Prevention and Management of Frailty (Roller-Wirnsberger et al., 2020)

The European Collaborative and Interprofessional Capability Framework for the Prevention and Management of Frailty was developed as part of the Joint Action on Frailty Prevention (ADVANTAGE) initiative, supported by the European Geriatric Medicine Society (EuGMS) (Roller-Wirnsberger et al., 2020). The consensus-based framework was designed to address the increasing complexity and prevalence of frailty among older adults in Europe.

Frailty, characterized by reduced resilience and increased vulnerability, presents unique challenges requiring coordinated, interprofessional care. This framework aims to provide a structured approach to developing skills and knowledge among healthcare professionals to support integrated, person-centred care for frail older adults.

Against this background, this concept strives for a standardization of IPE and collaborative practice to enhance the care and management of frailty. The specific goals include:

- Improving competences of the healthcare workforce involved in care of older adults by promoting evidence-based approaches.
- Enabling multiprofessional collaboration through standardized training that aligns with the needs and pre-conditions of various healthcare settings.
- Enhancing the quality of integrated care by embedding interprofessional collaborative practice as a fundamental element in frailty management.

- Promoting prevention and early detection of frailty, thus reducing the risk of adverse outcomes and maintaining independence and quality of life among older adults.

The framework is grounded in interprofessional collaborative practice (ICP), which is characterized by 1) flat hierarchy in teams with clear role definitions; 2) relationship-focused care that prioritizes communication and collaboration among healthcare professionals; and 3) team-based decision-making that incorporates perspectives from different disciplines.

While not providing particular strategies for IPE itself, the framework (Roller-Wirnsberger et al., 2020) rather focusses on four core domains where development of competencies are crucial for efficient care of older adults:

1. *Understanding frailty*: This domain deals with competencies necessary to fully grasp the condition of frailty.
2. *Identification of frailty*: This domain covers necessary capabilities to correctly screen, diagnose, and assess frailty based on prevailing evidence base.
3. *Person-centred collaborative working:* Within this domain, capabilities around the subjects of effective communication, shared decision-making and holistic care planning are presented.
4. *Managing frailty and its prevention*: The last domain integrates required competencies for the implementation of preventative strategies, the promotion of independence of older adults and the integration of community resources.

3.3 Knowledge and Skills Framework for Healthcare Professionals Working with the Older Persons (Brennan et al., 2023)

The Knowledge and Skills Framework developed by the National Clinical Programme for Older People (NCPOP), in collaboration with the Royal College of Physicians of Ireland (RCPI) (Brennan et al., 2023), provides a comprehensive and context-specific guide to professional development for interdisciplinary teams involved in the care of older adults. It defines both shared and discipline-specific competencies within an interprofessional model across various healthcare settings.

The framework was designed with three core objectives:

- Support of high-quality, integrated care provision across healthcare settings by clarifying competencies needed by healthcare professionals (HCPs).
- Facilitation of interdisciplinary team-working by means of clearly defined shared knowledge and skill domains.
- Guidance for continuous professional development (CPD) and workforce planning for individual professionals and system-level leadership.

Against this background, the framework presents five shared competency domains that are applicable across all professions engaged in geriatric care;

discipline-specific competencies according to professional roles such as nursing, physiotherapy, or dietetics, amongst others; as well as core and enhanced competence levels offering flexibility to different career stages and practice contexts (Brennan et al., 2023).

To enable alignment with policy and practice, the instrument was jointly designed with other strategic tools and is intended to be used with curricula and other organizational planning tools. Educators and health system managers can use it for role development and recruitment, team training plans, or maturity evaluation of interdisciplinary practice (Brennan et al., 2023).

By providing a unified language and competency set for the entire health and social care workforce, this framework represents a critical and valuable tool for operationalizing interprofessional collaboration in the care of older people.

4 Implications for Practice

4.1 How to Recognize and Analyse Needs for Interprofessional Geriatric Education

Before implementing IPE interventions and programmes to enhance geriatric health workforce capabilities, it is important to recognize and understand current and emerging learning needs amongst the health and social care staff. In this regard, especially local social and cultural contexts as well as the degree of health system maturity will determine implementation interventions and outcomes (World Health Organization, 2019).

Within this chapter, two methodologies to recognize and analyse needs for IPE in geriatrics are suggested:

Competence Gap Mapping is defined as a systematic process to identify what competencies are required for effective interprofessional geriatric care versus what is currently present in the respective workforce or learning programme. Educators and managers will then be able to prioritize development and operationalize implementation. A simple and practical tool in this regard are competency checklists that allow a structured assessment of staff or learner proficiency. Several established frameworks provide specific learning outcomes or competencies with performance indicators that can be assessed and mapped against existing competencies in the workforce or learning cohort (Brennan et al., 2023; Aerts & De Weerdt, 2023; Dijkman et al., 2018).

Contextual Maturity Assessments represent another methodology to comprehensively assess the individual maturity for supporting and implementing IPE in a particular system by reflecting how well a health system, educational institution or care team is prepared and exhibits basic requirements to support and implement IPE and collaborative practice. The ICOPE Framework (World Health Organization, 2019) (see Sect. 3.1) offers a comprehensive self-assessment template to elaborate different dimensions and facilitates institutional or system-level benchmarking as well as linking maturity levels to resulting interventions or educational milestones.

4.2 Key Elements to Consider for IPE in Geriatric Care

When designing and implementing geriatric IPE, there are several key elements to be considered and integrated during the educational process. These elements are also recognized in major competency frameworks (Brennan et al., 2023; Aerts & De Weerdt, 2023; Dijkman et al., 2018; Wang & Zorek, 2016) and ensure educational effectiveness in geriatric contexts as well as ethical fidelity.

Shared Values and Ethical Foundations: Values serve as foundation for collaboration and ensure alignment around a shared moral commitment (Rider et al., 2021). Exemplary core values in this regard are compassion, empathy, sensitivity, respect for diversity, dignity, human rights, self-determination, flexibility, and ethical competence (Brennan et al., 2023; Aerts & De Weerdt, 2023; Dijkman et al., 2018; Wang & Zorek, 2016).

To cultivate these values effectively, educational programmes should *embed reflective practice on values* throughout the curriculum, enabling a critical examination of learners' believes and behaviours. *Ethical dilemmas and collaborative moral reasoning* should be explored through case-based learning to deepen ethical sensitivity. Additionally, *training in cultural competence and anti-ageism* is vital to prepare learners for equitable and inclusive care for diverse ageing populations.

Role Clarity and Interprofessional Identity Formation: Understanding one's own professional role and identity as well as the complementary role of colleagues within a team is essential in collaborative practice and therefore prevents interprofessional friction. Major frameworks recognize this aspect as critical key competency for effective geriatric care by identifying aspects such as interprofessional practice (IP) and interprofessionalism (IPM) (Aerts & De Weerdt, 2023), and "roles and responsibilities" as well as "interprofessional collaboration" (Brennan et al., 2023), as key domains of the respective framework or integrating and defining core competencies for the canMED role (Frank et al., 2015) of the "collaborator" (Dijkman et al., 2018).

To foster this clarity, educational programmes should *include role-shadowing or interprofessional placements* to allow learners to directly observe how different professionals contribute to care. Additionally, structured *team-based simulations with post-activity debriefs focussing on role performance* enable learners to practice and refine their contributions within a team context. Finally, the development of *shared learning objectives across professions* ensures alignment in educational goals and reinforces mutual understanding.

Effective Communication: Especially in complex geriatric cases involving multiple providers, communication is a vital aspect to ensure a relationship-based care. Selected frameworks integrate this feature by ensuring that healthcare professionals are able to communicate with patients, families and the interprofessional team effectively (Aerts & De Weerdt, 2023), integrating and defining core competencies for the canMED role (Frank et al., 2015) of the "communicator" (Dijkman et al., 2018), or identifying communication as key domain of the respective framework (Brennan et al., 2023).

To build these skills in practice, educators should incorporate *interprofessional case conferences and structured feedback sessions* that emphasize collaborative dialogue. In addition, learners should receive *training in working with interpreters and addressing sensory impairments in older adults*. The use of *structured communication tools*—such as the Situation, Background, Assessment, Recommendation—(SBAR) tool (Shahid & Thomas, 2018)—can further enhance clarity and consistency in both clinical and educational interactions.

Person-Centredness and Family Involvement: Geriatric care is defined by complexity and social vulnerability (World Health Organization, 2020; Polidori et al., 2018). Person- and family-centred care ensures that healthcare professionals avoid fragmented care processes. Guidance in this regard can be retrieved from competency frameworks, as they emphasize partnerships with the older adult and their families (Aerts & De Weerdt, 2023), put focus on personalized care planning (World Health Organization, 2019) or identify advocacy and person-centredness as key principles of gerontological care (Brennan et al., 2023).

To translate these principles into practice, educators should integrate *training in narrative-based care and shared decision-making*. *Exposure to patient voices*—via interviews, panels, or lived experience narratives—can further reinforce empathy. In addition, promoting *family systems understanding* in training helps professionals to understand broader relational and caregiving contexts.

Competency-Based and Context-Sensitive Curriculum Design: Geriatric care occurs across healthcare settings and in diverse contexts. Educators need to be aware about shifts in competency needs according to learner levels and care settings. As presented in Sect. 4.1 (How to Recognize and Analyse Needs for Interprofessional Geriatric Education), there are several methodologies to define contextual learning and competency needs.

To operationalize this, curricula should follow *staged learning models* that guide learners progressively from initial exposure through immersion to mastery (Charles et al., 2010). Furthermore, *learning goals should be adapted to different care environments*, such as acute care, primary care, and long-term care. To maximize relevance and authenticity and ensure contextual realism, *practitioners should be involved in curriculum design* and integrate their first-hand insights.

4.3 Suitable Learning Methods According to Competence Level

To ensure effective development of interprofessional competencies in geriatric care, learning methods need to correspond with the learners' stage of professional development (e.g. undergraduate, early-career, experienced professionals), the complexity of the care context (e.g. academic, clinical, hospital, community) and targeted collaboration outcomes (e.g. communication, shared decision-making, team leadership). Several frameworks offer tiered models for aligning teaching and learning approaches to learners' progression in interprofessional competency (Brennan et al., 2023; Wang & Zorek, 2016; Aldriwesh et al., 2022), placing IPE along a continuum from mere functional awareness to experiential mastery.

In this section, pedagogical strategies to support progressive skill acquisition are explored based on three levels of learner proficiency.

Foundational Level (Awareness and Formation of Professional Identity)

- *Target audience*: Early-stage undergraduates or professionals with no prior IPE exposure
- *Learning goals*:
  - Understand one's own professional role
  - Gain conceptual awareness of other disciplines and team collaboration
- *Suggested methods*:
  - Didactic input: Lectures, readings on gerontology, team dynamics, and health systems
  - Case-based learning: Profession-specific analysis of geriatric cases
  - Self-directed exploration: Reflective assignments on professional identity and values

This level corresponds with Stage 1 of the Undergraduate interprofessional teaching and learning framework (Aldriwesh et al., 2022), where team-based activities occur mainly within single disciplines. It also aligns with the Level 0 and Level 1 of the "Learning and Development" domain of the INPRO Competency framework (Aerts & De Weerdt, 2023), which emphasizes continuous interprofessional growth. Similarly, the NCPOP Knowledge and Skills framework (Brennan et al.,

2023) identifies this level as part of the "core" knowledge base required for all health professionals engaged in care of older adults.

Intermediate Level (Role Clarification and Interprofessional Exposure)

- *Target audience*: Advanced undergraduates, postgraduates, or early-career professionals transitioning into interdisciplinary roles
- *Learning goals*:
  - Understand others' roles and develop interprofessional communication skills
  - Practice collaborative problem-solving in structured settings
- *Suggested methods*:
  - Simulation-based learning: Realistic team-based geriatric scenarios (e.g. falls, frailty, polypharmacy)
  - E-Learning/blended learning: Modules on team decision-making and ethics in geriatric care
  - Interprofessional team placements: Short rotations with joint supervision

This phase is consistent with Stage 2 of the Undergraduate interprofessional teaching and learning framework (Aldriwesh et al., 2022), which highlights the importance of simulation, blended learning and virtual or in-person case-based interaction. It also reflects the application of an Interprofessional Experience Education (IEE) model (Wang & Zorek, 2016), which advocates for implementation of IPE within an experiential education setting, as students can fully dive into their future professional environment and discover realistic aspects of their profession while also making early experiences with interprofessional teamwork. Furthermore, competencies in relation to effective communication and collaborative relationships (Brennan et al., 2023; Aerts & De Weerdt, 2023) are becoming active learning targets.

Advanced Level (Interprofessional Mastery and Leadership)

- *Target audience*: Senior professionals, team leads, or educators in geriatric settings
- *Learning goals*:
  - Integrate interprofessional collaboration into complex decision-making
  - Mentor and support team performance and influence system-level change
- *Suggested methods*:
  - Deliberate practice: Repeated, goal-directed practice of interprofessional tasks (e.g. joint Comprehensive Geriatric Assessments (CGAs), family meetings)
  - Interprofessional peer coaching: Facilitated feedback from colleagues across disciplines
  - In-service continuous professional development (CPD) programmes: Custom training on team leadership, integrated care pathways, and digital tools
  - Communities of practice: Learning collaboratives for sustained interprofessional exchange

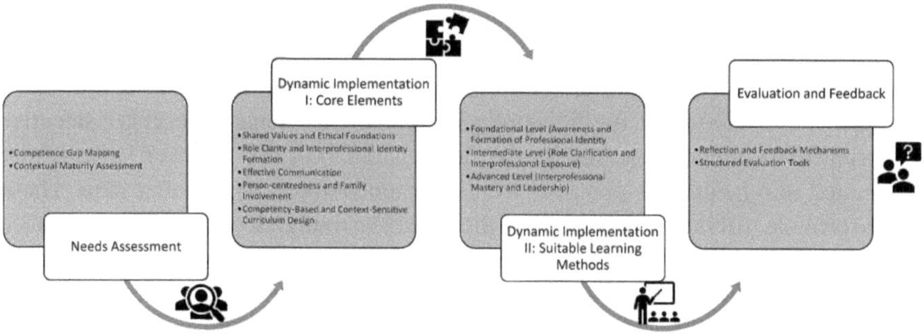

Fig. 2 Presents a schematic model on how to design, implement, and evaluate practice-oriented IPE in geriatric care based on evidence-based guidance from established frameworks presented

This level draws directly on capabilities of Management and Leadership and Research (Aerts & De Weerdt, 2023), where professionals are expected to enhance team and service performance and apply evidence in interprofessional practice contexts. It is also consistent with the NCPOP Knowledge and skills framework's (Brennan et al., 2023) "enhanced" levels of capabilities, where HCPs are not only recognized for their technical expertise but also for their contribution to system innovation and collaborative practice culture. The IEE model (Wang & Zorek, 2016) supports this level through deliberate, repeated experiential learning embedded in real-world settings with active feedback cycles.

Considerations for Implementation

Application of a staged approach is essential and learning methods should build progressively. Directly engaging into full interprofessional simulations without preceding role understanding may lead to frustration and ineffective or superficial outcomes. Moreover, practice-based learning environments (e.g. joint ward rounds) are regarded most effective and sustainable when coupled with reflection and feedback (Oudbier et al., 2024; Maqsood et al., 2025). Effectiveness of IPE events should be evaluated by means of structured tools, such as the Interprofessional Collaborator Assessment Rubric—ICAR (Curran et al., 2011) to assess learning outcomes at each level. Figure. 2 below illustrates a dynamic model outlining key components for the design of IPE in geriatric care across progressive learning stages.

5 Case Studies: Implementation of IPE in Practice

In this chapter, the necessity of IPE implementation as critical component for fostering collaborative practice has been emphasized so far, especially as healthcare systems evolve to meet the growing complexity of care in ageing populations. Translating IPE principles from theoretical frameworks into real-world practice, however, remains a complex endeavour. As analysed in the previous section, a successful implementation requires innovative educational models, institutional commitment, and continuous evaluation to ensure that health professionals are prepared to work effectively within multidisciplinary teams. This chapter presents a selective overview of exemplary case studies that demonstrate how IPE has been successfully integrated into healthcare practice, with a particular focus on geriatric care. These cases provide valuable insights into the diverse strategies employed to enhance interprofessional collaboration and underscore the tangible benefits of IPE in improving healthcare outcomes. By additionally examining these real-world applications, readers will gain a deeper understanding of the practical challenges and opportunities inherent in fostering interprofessional competence in diverse healthcare settings.

5.1 Interprofessional Education in Geriatric Medicine: Towards Best Practice – A Controlled Before–After Study of Medical and Nursing Students (Thompson et al., 2020)

This initiative (Thompson et al., 2020) involved a controlled before–after study assessing the readiness for interprofessional learning of nursing and medical students from a tertiary care university hospital setting.

Implementation of IPE was realized by utilizing problem-based learning (PBL) case scenarios centred on geriatric patients, reflecting real-world clinical challenges that require multidisciplinary collaboration. Central methodology were workshop sessions designed and facilitated by experienced geriatricians. Sessions began with a structured introduction, followed by self-directed group work and facilitated discussions. Each subgroup consisted of no more than 10 students and emphasis was put on a balanced representation of medical and nursing perspectives to foster an environment enabling meaningful interaction and collaborative problem-solving.

Evaluation was facilitated by the Readiness for Interprofessional Learning Scale (RIPLS) (Parsell & Bligh, 1999) both before and after the intervention. The results demonstrated statistically significant improvements in students' understanding of team roles, confidence in collaborative clinical decision-making, and positive professional identity, especially among nursing students. The structured, case-based IPE approach was shown to reduce apprehension regarding joint learning and foster a deeper appreciation of interprofessional roles within geriatric care.

Integration of problem-based learning (PBL) with real-world case scenarios
Experiential learning through direct interaction, reflective discussions and role clarification
Incorporating and alleviating potential hierarchical challenges between professions

5.2 Geriatric Interprofessional Education: In-Person Simulation (Brown, 2021)

The educational intervention described in this case study represents a structured, multi-layered approach aimed at enhancing collaborative competencies among healthcare students. This programme uniquely combines theoretical foundations with hands-on simulation-based learning to bridge the gap between knowledge acquisition and practical application (Brown, 2021).

The programme was designed by using an active learning approach, integrating multiple educational stages to build competencies progressively. The implementation involved the following key steps: 1) knowledge acquisition with online didactic content; 2) skills reinforcement through interactive in-person sessions to bridge theoretical understanding and practical application; 3) profession-specific huddles to communicate patient assessment findings; 4) interprofessional team meeting simulation centred around a complex geriatric case; 5) supervised patient assessment; and 6) reflective debrief where students critically analysed their collaborative outcomes.

This comprehensive approach effectively bridged theoretical knowledge and practical skills, enhancing students' readiness for interprofessional teamwork in geriatric settings.

Integration of theoretical instruction and hands-on simulation
Gradual and progressive approach starting from theory over intra-professional towards interprofessional collaborative practice
Use of diverse educational methods

5.3 Interprofessional Trainees Using the Geriatric 5Ms Framework in a Workshop (Schwartz et al., 2020)

This case study represents an innovative approach to IPE designed to enhance collaborative competencies among healthcare trainees (Schwartz et al., 2020).

IPE implementation was facilitated by a workshop, conducted at the New England Geriatric Research, Education, and Clinical Center, involving 66 trainees from 10 different healthcare professions. The training aimed to improve interprofessional collaboration through the structured application of the Geriatrics 5Ms framework—Mobility, Mind, Medications, Multicomplexity, and What Matters Most (Tinetti et al., 2017). The workshop began with sessions focused on motivating trainees to pursue careers in ageing and understanding the relevance of interprofessional collaboration in geriatric care. Next, trainees engaged in interactive discussions through "Speed Circles", where they shared insights with peers from other professions. In the next phase, trainees gathered in professional subgroups to discuss their unique training paths, common misconceptions, and key competencies. The core of the workshop was applying the Geriatrics 5Ms in small interprofessional groups. Each group addressed one of the 5Ms, using case scenarios involving frail older adults with complex healthcare needs. The final session involved reflective debriefing, where trainees discussed their experiences, challenges, and insights gained from collaborative practice.

The programme was evaluated through pre- and post-workshop surveys using a 5-point Likert scale. Trainees reported significant improvements in understanding other professions, familiarity with the Geriatrics 5Ms framework, and comfort in identifying patient problems related to mobility, medications, and multicomplexity.

Integration of a theoretically grounded framework (Geriatrics 5Ms) with experiential learning and practical application
Combination of structured didactic content with interactive case discussions and reflective practice
Learning enhancement by requiring learners to teach and learn from each other in dynamic, team-based settings

6 Conclusion

The evolving demographic realities and rising complexity of geriatric care demand a health workforce that is not only clinically competent but also proficient at interdisciplinary collaboration. IPE emerges as a pivotal strategy to address these needs, aligning educational innovation with the goals of integrated, person-centred care for ageing populations. This chapter has underscored the theoretical and empirical foundations of IPE and highlighted how competency frameworks, contextual assessments, and tailored pedagogical methods can operationalize its potential in geriatric contexts.

The integration of IPE into geriatric workforce development requires more than curricular adjustments; it necessitates a systemic transformation. Educational initiatives need to be grounded in shared values, foster interprofessional identity formation, and be sensitive to learner level and care settings. Furthermore, maturity assessments and competency mapping can guide context-sensitive implementation, ensuring that training aligns with local health system needs and readiness.

Empirical evidence and case studies illustrate that when implemented with strategic foresight—through staged, practice-based, and reflective methodologies—IPE enhances collaborative skills, professional confidence, and ultimately care quality for older adults. Moving forward, a unified effort by educators, policymakers, and healthcare institutions is essential to embed IPE as a structural element of geriatric education and practice.

References

Aerts, I., De Weerdt, C. (2023). INPRO competency framework. Competency Book: INPRO Consortium.

Aldriwesh, M. G., Alyousif, S. M., & Alharbi, N. S. (2022). Undergraduate-level teaching and learning approaches for interprofessional education in the health professions: A systematic review. *BMC Medical Education, 22*(1), 13. https://doi.org/10.1186/s12909-021-03073-0

Al-Qallaf, A., Akhtar, M., Fouda, M., Alyas, O., Akram, J., Mashal, R., et al. (2024). Understanding pathways for effective interprofessional education: A thematic analysis of medical and nursing students' insights. *Bmc Medical Education, 24*. https://doi.org/10.1186/s12909-024-06489-6

Babin, C., Salem, Y., Quiben, M., & Davis, B. (2023). Interprofessional education (IPE) faculty development—a scoping review. *Health Interprofessional Practice, 5*(2), 1–26. https://doi.org/10.61406/hipe.269

Bandura, A. (1977). *Social learning theory*. Prentice-Hall.

Bogossian, F., New, K., George, K., Barr, N., Dodd, N., Hamilton, A. L., et al. (2023). The implementation of interprofessional education: A scoping review. *Advances in Health Sciences Education, 28*(1), 243–277. https://doi.org/10.1007/s10459-022-10128-4

Bookey-Bassett, S., Espin, S., & Lawrence, K. (2022). The role of interprofessional education in training healthcare providers for integrated healthcare: A scoping review. *Health Interprofessional Pract., 4*(3), eP2191. https://doi.org/10.7710/2641-1148.2191

Brennan, J., Claffey, A., Coleman, S., Cosgrave, S., Devaney, C., Donnelly, S., et al. (2023). *Knowledge and skills framework for healthcare professionals working with the older persons*. Health Service Executive.

Brown, D. (2021). Geriatric interprofessional education: In-person simulation. *Innovation in Aging, 5*(Suppl 1), 1. https://doi.org/10.1093/geroni/igab046.002

Bunn, F., Goodman, C., Russell, B., Wilson, P., Manthorpe, J., Rait, G., et al. (2018). Supporting shared decision making for older people with multiple health and social care needs: a realist synthesis. *BMC Geriatrics, 18*(1), 165. https://doi.org/10.1186/s12877-018-0853-9

Cadet, T., Joseph, C., Shelley, M., Julie, H., Cynthia, O. N., Reza, T., et al. (2024). Describing the evidence linking interprofessional education interventions to improving the delivery of safe and effective patient care: a scoping review. *Journal of Interprofessional Care, 38*(3), 476–485. https://doi.org/10.1080/13561820.2023.2283119

Charles, G., Bainbridge, L., & Gilbert, J. (2010). The University of British Columbia model of interprofessional education. *Journal of Interprofessional Care, 24*(1), 9–18. https://doi.org/10.3109/13561820903294549

Curran, V., Hollett, A., Casimiro, L. M., McCarthy, P., Banfield, V., Hall, P., et al. (2011). Development and validation of the interprofessional collaborator assessment rubric (ICAR). *Journal of Interprofessional Care, 25*(5), 339–344. https://doi.org/10.3109/13561820.2011.589542

Dijkman, B., Roodbol, P., Achtschin-Stieger, S., Aho, J., Andruszkiewicz, A., Coffey, A., et al. (2018). *European core competences framework for health and social care professionals working with older people*. University of Limerick.

Doornebosch, A. J., Smaling, H. J. A., & Achterberg, W. P. (2022). Interprofessional collaboration in long-term care and rehabilitation: A systematic review. *Journal of the American Medical Directors Association, 23*(5), 764–77.e2. https://doi.org/10.1016/j.jamda.2021.12.028

Duque, S., Inzitari, M., Albayrak, A., & van der Cammen, T. (2021). Integrated care for older patients: Geriatrics. In V. Amelung, V. Stein, E. Suter, N. Goodwin, E. Nolte, & R. Balicer (Eds.), *Handbook integrated care*. Springer.

Fisher, J. M., Masud, T., Holm, E. A., Roller-Wirnsberger, R. E., Stuck, A. E., Gordon, A., et al. (2017). New horizons in geriatric medicine education and training: The need for pan-European education and training standards. *European Geriatric Medicine, 8*(5), 467–473. https://doi.org/10.1016/j.eurger.2017.07.022

Frank, J., Snell, L., & Sherbino, J. (2015). *CanMEDS 2015 physician competency framework*. Royal College of Physicians and Surgeons of Canada.

Gillies, P. (1997). Social capital: Recognising the value of society. *Healthiness, 45*, 15–17.

Grund, S., van Wijngaarden, J. P., Gordon, A. L., Schols, J., & Bauer, J. M. (2020). EuGMS survey on structures of geriatric rehabilitation across Europe. *Eur Geriatr Med., 11*(2), 217–232. https://doi.org/10.1007/s41999-019-00273-2

Guraya, S. Y., & Barr, H. (2018). The effectiveness of interprofessional education in healthcare: A systematic review and meta-analysis. *The Kaohsiung Journal of Medical Sciences, 34*(3), 160–165. https://doi.org/10.1016/j.kjms.2017.12.009

Hean, S., Deborah, C., Marilyn, H., & Hammick, M. (2012). Theoretical insights into interprofessional education: AMEE guide no. 62. *Medical Teacher, 34*(2), e78–e101. https://doi.org/10.3109/0142159X.2012.650740

Hendry, A., Vanhecke, E., Carriazo, A. M., López-Samaniego, L., Espinosa, J. M., Sezgin, D., et al. (2019). Integrated care models for managing and preventing frailty: A systematic review for the European joint action on frailty prevention (ADVANTAGE JA). *Translational Medicine UniSa, 19*, 5–10.

Interprofessional Education Collaborative. (2016). *Core competencies for interprofessional collaborative practice: 2016 update*. Interprofessional Education Collaborative. https://ipec.memberclicks.net/assets/2016-Update.pdf. Accessed May 8, 2025

Jiang, Y., Yan, C., Xue, Z., & Wang, C. (2024). Interprofessional education interventions for healthcare professionals to improve patient safety: A scoping review. *Medical Education Online, 29*(1), 2391631. https://doi.org/10.1080/10872981.2024.2391631

Joosten-Hagye, D., Tatyana, G., Cheryl, R., Freddi, S.-G., Marie, R. J., Thayer, E. K., et al. (2024). A community-based geriatric interprofessional education experience and its impact on postgraduate collaborative practice. *Journal of Interprofessional Care, 38*(5), 855–863. https://doi.org/10.1080/13561820.2024.2371337

Kaehne, A., & Nies, H. (2021). Integrated care—an introduction. In A. Kaehne & H. Nies (Eds.), *How to deliver integrated care: A guidebook for managers* (pp. 1–14). Emerald Publishing Limited.

Knebl, J., Severance, J., & Hartos, J. (2019). Interprofessional education and training to expand the geriatrics workforce. *Journal of Gerontology & Geriatric Medicine, 5*, 030. https://doi.org/10.24966/GGM-8662/100030

Krystallidou, D., Van De Walle, C., Deveugele, M., Dougali, E., Mertens, F., Truwant, A., et al. (2018). Training "doctor-minded" interpreters and "interpreter-minded" doctors the benefits of collaborative practice in interpreter training. *Interpreting, 20*(1), 126–144. https://doi.org/10.1075/intp.00005.kry

Lindner-Rabl, S., Singler, K., Polidori, M. C., Herzog, C., Antoniadou, E., Seinost, G., et al. (2023). Effectiveness of multi-professional educational interventions to train comprehensive geriatric assessment (CGA)—a systematic review. *International Journal of Integrated Care, 23*(3), 9. https://doi.org/10.5334/ijic.7549

Maqsood, Z., Sajjad, M., & Yasmin, R. (2025). Effect of feedback-integrated reflection, on deep learning of undergraduate medical students in a clinical setting. *BMC Medical Education, 25*(1), 66. https://doi.org/10.1186/s12909-025-06648-3

Mateos-Nozal, J., & Beard, J. R. (2011). Global approaches to geriatrics in medical education. *European Geriatric Medicine, 2*(2), 87–92. https://doi.org/10.1016/j.eurger.2011.01.001

Mattiazzi, S., Neil, C., Norman, N., & Beckman, E. (2024). Behavioural outcomes of interprofessional education within clinical settings for health professional students: A systematic literature review. *Journal of Interprofessional Care, 38*(2), 294–307. https://doi.org/10.1080/13561820.2023.2170994

Michel, J. P., Huber, P., & Cruz-Jentoft, A. J. (2008). Europe-wide survey of teaching in geriatric medicine. *Journal of the American Geriatrics Society, 56*(8), 1536–1542. https://doi.org/10.1111/j.1532-5415.2008.01788.x

Montano, A. R., Shellman, J., & Malcolm, M. (2022). Outcomes from an interprofessional geriatric outreach and training program. *Innovation in Aging, 6*(6), igac044. https://doi.org/10.1093/geroni/igac044

Nancarrow, S. A., Booth, A., Ariss, S., Smith, T., Enderby, P., & Roots, A. (2013). Ten principles of good interdisciplinary team work. *Human Resources for Health, 11*(1), 19. https://doi.org/10.1186/1478-4491-11-19

OECD/European Commission. (2024). *Health at a glance: Europe 2024: State of health in the EU cycle*. OECD Publishing. https://www.oecd.org/en/publications/health-at-a-glance-europe-2024_b3704e14-en.html. Accessed May 14, 2025

Oudbier, J., Verheijck, E., van Diermen, D., Tams, J., Bramer, J., & Spaai, G. (2024). Enhancing the effectiveness of interprofessional education in health science education: A state-of-the-art review. *BMC Medical Education, 24*(1), 1492. https://doi.org/10.1186/s12909-024-06466-z

Parsell, G., & Bligh, J. (1999). The development of a questionnaire to assess the readiness of health care students for interprofessional learning (RIPLS). *Medical Education, 33*(2), 95–100. https://doi.org/10.1046/j.1365-2923.1999.00298.x

Patel, H., Perry, S., Badu, E., Mwangi, F., Onifade, O., Mazurskyy, A., et al. (2025). A scoping review of interprofessional education in healthcare: Evaluating competency development, educational outcomes and challenges. *BMC Medical Education, 25*(1), 409. https://doi.org/10.1186/s12909-025-06969-3

Polidori, M. C., Singler, K., & Roller-Wirnsberger, R. (2018). Introduction: Age-attuning medical education, fostering geriatric thinking. In R. Roller-Wirnsberger, K. Singler, & M. C. Polidori (Eds.), *Learning geriatric medicine—a study guide for medical students* (pp. 3–6). Springer.

Reeves, S., Simon, F., Hugh, B., Ivan, B., Sylvain, B., Nigel, D., et al. (2016). A BEME systematic review of the effects of interprofessional education: BEME guide no. 39. *Medical Teacher, 38*(7), 656–668. https://doi.org/10.3109/0142159X.2016.1173663

Rider, E. A., Frost, J. S., & Longmaid, H. E. (2021). Embedding shared interprofessional values in healthcare organizational culture: The National Academies of practice experience. *Journal of Interprofessional Education & Practice, 23*, 100348. https://doi.org/10.1016/j.xjep.2020.100348

Roller-Wirnsberger, R., Herzog, C., Lindner-Rabl, S., Schlögl, M., Illario, M., Polidori, M. C., et al. (2025). Teaching comprehensive geriatric assessment (CGA) in medical education: a scoping review. *European Geriatric Medicine, 16*(2), 425–433. https://doi.org/10.1007/s41999-025-01157-4

Roller-Wirnsberger, R., Lindner, S., Liew, A., O'Caoimh, R., Koula, M.-L., Moody, D., et al. (2020). European collaborative and interprofessional capability framework for prevention and Management of Frailty—a consensus process supported by the joint action for frailty prevention (ADVANTAGE) and the European geriatric medicine society (EuGMS). *Aging Clinical and Experimental Research, 32*(4), 561–570. https://doi.org/10.1007/s40520-019-01455-5

SAPEA. (2019). *Transforming the future of ageing: Evidence review report (1.2)*. SAPEA. https://scientificadvice.eu/advice/transforming-the-future-of-ageing/. Accessed May 8, 2025

Schwartz, A. W., Hawley, C. E., Strong, J. V., Phillips, S. C., Amir, O., Ludwin, B. M., et al. (2020). A workshop for interprofessional trainees using the geriatrics 5Ms framework. *Journal of the American Geriatrics Society, 68*(8), 1857–1863. https://doi.org/10.1111/jgs.16574

Shahid, S., & Thomas, S. (2018). Situation, background, assessment, recommendation (SBAR) communication tool for handoff in health care—a narrative review. *Safety in Health, 4*(1), 7. https://doi.org/10.1186/s40886-018-0073-1

Thompson, S., Metcalfe, K., Boncey, K., Merriman, C., Flynn, L. C., Alg, G. S., et al. (2020). Interprofessional education in geriatric medicine: Towards best practice. A controlled before–after study of medical and nursing students. *BMJ Open, 10*(1), e018041. https://doi.org/10.1136/bmjopen-2017-018041

Tinetti, M., Huang, A., & Molnar, F. (2017). The geriatrics 5M's: A New way of communicating what we do. *Journal of the American Geriatrics Society, 65*(9), 2115. https://doi.org/10.1111/jgs.14979

Wang, J. M., & Zorek, J. A. (2016). Deliberate practice as a theoretical framework for interprofessional experiential education. *Frontiers in Pharmacology, 7*, 188. https://doi.org/10.3389/fphar.2016.00188

World Health Organization. (2010). *Framework for action on Interprofessional Education & Collaborative Practice*. World Health Organization. https://www.who.int/publications/i/item/framework-for-action-on-interprofessional-education-collaborative-practice. Accessed May 6, 2025

World Health Organization. (2016). *Global strategy on human resources for health: workforce 2030*. World Health Organization. https://iris.who.int/bitstream/handle/10665/250368/9789241511131-eng.pdf. Accessed May 6, 2025

World Health Organization. (2019). *Integrated care for older people (ICOPE) implementation framework: Guidance for systems and services*. World Health Organization. https://www.who.int/publications/i/item/9789241515993. Accessed May 6, 2025. License: CC BY-NC-SA 3.0 IGO

World Health Organization. (2020). Decade of healthy ageing: baseline report Geneva World Health Organization. https://www.who.int/publications/i/item/9789240017900. Accessed May 6, 2025.

Use Cases of Active and Healthy Aging

Managing Vaccine Hesitancy Among Adults and Elderly People

Pier Luigi Lopalco, Fabiana Nuccetelli, and Valeria Gabellone

1 Vaccine Hesitancy as a Major Threat for Public Health

Vaccine hesitancy (VH) has been defined by the WHO as "delay in acceptance or refusal of vaccines despite availability of vaccination services" (SAGE Working Group on Vaccine Hesitancy, 2015). Delay or refusal of any medical intervention is always an issue for people's health, but in the case of vaccination programs it becomes also a public health problem, as it undermines the collective efforts to control and eradicate infectious diseases. Benefits of vaccination do not only concern individuals but the whole society. Vaccines directly protect individuals against infection or disease and indirectly do benefit the community limiting the spread of pathogen agents, protecting the health care services from overload, producing resource savings or even economic gain. Through herd immunity, even those who cannot be vaccinated, such as immunocompromised individuals or newborns, receive indirect protection, highlighting the broader societal impact of immunization programs. The reduction in morbidity and mortality associated with vaccine-preventable diseases has historically represented one of the greatest achievements of public health, and any decline in vaccination coverage threatens to reverse these hard-won gains.

In 2019 WHO named top 10 threats to global health including VH among them, at the same level as antimicrobial resistance or noncommunicable diseases (World Health Organization, 2019). This inclusion reflects the growing concern over how behavioral, cultural, and informational factors are influencing public health policies and outcomes worldwide. Definitively, it is evident that VH has become

P. L. Lopalco (✉) · F. Nuccetelli · V. Gabellone
Department of Experimental Medicine, University of Salento, Lecce, Italy
e-mail: pierluigi.lopalco@unisalento.it; fabiana.nuccetelli@unisalento.it; valeria.gabellone@unisalento.it

A. Ricciardelli, L. Mercurio (eds.), *Building Innovation in Ageing and Health Policy*, Springer Series in Healthcare Management and Innovation,
https://doi.org/10.1007/978-3-032-09163-5_5

increasingly worrying over the last decades. This phenomenon is multifactorial, driven by complex and often intersecting determinants, including mistrust in health authorities, misinformation, religious or philosophical beliefs, and concerns about vaccine safety or side effects. Nevertheless, opposition to vaccination programs is a well-known phenomenon, born with vaccination itself. Following widespread smallpox vaccination in the early 1800s, organized anti-vaccination movements began their activity in England and rapidly grew fueled by the Vaccination Act, ordering mandatory vaccination for children (Porter & Porter, 1988). This historical resistance was often rooted in fears of state control, infringement of personal liberties, and lack of understanding of the science behind immunization. Towards the end of nineteenth century similar movements become established also in Northern America, such as Anti Vaccination Society of America (1879), the New England Anti Compulsory Vaccination League (1882), and the Anti-vaccination League of New York City (1885) (Williamson, 1984).

More recently, vaccine controversies were raised around diphtheria, tetanus, and pertussis (DTP) immunization in 1970s starting from a signal at the Great Ormond Street Hospital for Sick Children in London regarding 36 children allegedly suffering some neurological conditions after DTP vaccination (Kulenkampff et al., 1974). These reports, although later challenged or disproven, triggered widespread fear and skepticism among parents, showing how even isolated events can significantly erode public confidence in vaccination. In the 1990s the famous Wakefield's article on the alleged link between measles, mumps, and rubella (MMR) vaccination and autism (firstly published and then retracted from *The Lancet*) started a never-ending controversy which is still the pet subject of the contemporary anti-vaccination movements (Hackett, 2008). The damage caused by this fraudulent study continues to influence public perception and vaccination rates, particularly in certain countries and communities. Safety signals have been continuously raised and amplified by vaccine opponents and contributed to make VH stronger. In many cases, these concerns persist even in the face of overwhelming scientific evidence supporting vaccine safety and efficacy, showing the powerful role of emotional reasoning and confirmation bias in shaping public opinion. On the other hand, public health response to anti-vaccination sentiment has not been strong enough. Communication campaigns have often failed to effectively counter misinformation, and the lack of coordinated global strategies has left room for disinformation to thrive.

Nowadays, VH has grown stronger and spread across the continents. The wide availability of new communication tool like web publishing and social media have been effectively used by anti-vaccination activists. These platforms have enabled the rapid and unfiltered spread of unverified or false information, often reaching large audiences before accurate data from institutional sources can be disseminated. Their propaganda pervades all socio-economical layers and, unfortunately, involves also health care professionals, thus becoming a very serious threat to global public health. The involvement of medical personnel in antivaccine rhetoric adds a dangerous layer of credibility to unfounded claims, undermining trust in scientific institutions and jeopardizing the health of entire populations. Addressing VH today requires not only scientific evidence but also culturally competent communication, proactive policy measures, and sustained public engagement to rebuild confidence in vaccines as vital tools of prevention.

2 Importance of a Lifelong Vaccination Calendar Including Adult and Elderly People

The World Health Assembly (WHA), following the dramatic experience of the COVID-19 pandemic, has endorsed a new strategy aiming at saving over 50 million lives during the third decade of the twenty-first century, called Immunization Agenda 2030 (IA2030) (MacDonald & Dubé, 2022). In the IA2030 seven strategic priorities are identified, among which strategic priority 4 "Life-course and integration." The goal related to such strategy is that "all people benefit from recommended immunizations throughout the life-course, effectively integrated with other essential health services." The evidence bases for including adult vaccination among the top priority of IA2030 are solid.

Vaccine-preventable diseases cause a significant burden throughout the entire life course. Thanks to pediatric immunization programs, infant mortality has been dramatically reduced globally together with disease burden during the first years of life. Since 1974, when the Expanded Program of Immunization (World Health Organization, 2021) started, is estimated that vaccination has prevented 146 million deaths among children younger than 5 years and has accounted for the 40% of the observed decline of global infant mortality (Keja et al., 1988).

Proportion of DALYs (disability-adjusted life years) associated with 85 infectious pathogens in 2019 globally represented the 27.7% of the total burden of disease considering all ages and the 19.1% considering the age group >5 years (Shattock et al., 2024). In 2021, excluding COVID-19, globally 344 million cases of lower respiratory infections were estimated with 1.68 million deaths in people >5 years of age. In the European Union a total burden of 1.38 million DALYs was estimated to be caused by infectious agents between 2009 and 2013. Adults 65 years of age and over had 24% of the total. Influenza alone represented the 30% of the burden (Naghavi et al., 2024). In addition, infectious disease burden in fragile subjects is not only linked to the direct effect of the pathogen but is also represented by long-term consequences of the infection. Increased risk for cardiovascular events and exacerbation of underlying chronic conditions have been reported after influenza (Cassini et al., 2018). Reduced functional independence in activities of daily living—like eating, dressing, or bathing—is reported among elderly persons after acute respiratory events caused by vaccine preventable agents like influenza or respiratory syncytial virus (RSV) (Macias et al., 2021; Branche et al., 2022).

Infectious disease burden is therefore disproportionately represented at both ends of people lifespan, with both infants and the elderly experiencing higher rates of disease incidence and mortality. Observing the history of vaccination programs, adult vaccination has been often implemented to protect military personnel. The first inactivated influenza vaccine was developed with the help of the US Army and was tested on US military for efficacy and safety, before its wider use in 1945

(Gupta & Mohan, 2023). Tetanus toxoid vaccine, that becomes commercially available in 1938, was widely used among soldiers during the World War II (Liang et al., 2018). Otherwise, over the decades, vaccination programs have been targeting primarily children and led to develop an articulated pediatric immunization schedule. The first global initiative led by the WHO was the Expanded Programme on Immunization (EPI) launched in 1974 to warrant protection to all children against six life-threatening diseases: tuberculosis, diphtheria, pertussis, tetanus, polio, and measles. The EPI program is nowadays known as Essential Programme on Immunization and covers 13 diseases adding *Haemophilus influenzae* type B, hepatitis B, rubella, pneumococcal disease, rotavirus, human papillomavirus, and COVID-19 to the original EPI program. All EPI vaccines, excluding COVID-19, address infants and children. In fact, the concept of a lifelong vaccination calendar is relatively recent and is not considered top priority at global level.

Influenza vaccine has been the one traditionally associated to adult and elderly immunization. In 1983 a 23-valent pneumococcal polysaccharide vaccine was introduced to protect adults and high-risk individuals. More recently, effective vaccines against herpes zoster, COVID-19, and respiratory syncytial virus (RSV) become available for adult and elderly immunization.

Such wide availability of immunization opportunities makes today a lifelong vaccination calendar a reality but poses several challenges to public health. A thorough analysis of the obstacles may identify the correct strategy to fully implement a lifelong vaccination calendar. As an example, the IA2030 suggests an integration between immunization services and delivery points of other public health interventions (MacDonald & Dubé, 2022). In any case, awareness of disease burden among adults with risk conditions and elderly persons is the starting point for any preventive intervention in such population group.

3 Challenges for Implementing Lifelong Vaccination Calendar and Role of Vaccine Hesitancy

Despite clear evidence supporting vaccine efficacy and safety, the introduction and adherence to a lifelong vaccination calendar face significant challenge worldwide. These difficulties are especially pronounced among adults and older adults, where coverage for vaccines such as influenza, pneumococcal, herpes zoster, respiratory syncytial virus (RSV), and COVID-19 remains well below recommended targets (Doherty et al., 2018; Bonanni et al., 2020; European Centre for Disease Prevention and Control (ECDC), n.d.).

A key obstacle is the limited awareness at both individual and societal levels regarding the importance of vaccination beyond childhood. Many adults do not realize that vaccines often require periodic boosters or that new immunizations may be recommended later in life. This misunderstanding is rooted in the widespread perception of vaccination as primarily a pediatric issue, a belief reinforced by decades of health policies and communication efforts focused on childhood immunization (Dube et al., 2015). Consequently, the risks posed by infectious diseases in adulthood and older age, as well as the benefits of vaccination in preventing severe illness, hospitalizations, and death, tend to be underestimated.

Data on vaccine coverage highlight these issues. Influenza vaccine uptake among Italians aged 65 and over falls short of the 75% goal established by national and international authorities, with notable regional disparities (Italian Ministry of Health, 2021). Vaccination rates for pneumococcal and herpes zoster vaccines are even lower. These gaps partly result from low awareness among healthcare professionals and the public, alongside insufficient proactive vaccination offers (Gianfredi et al., 2022; Gabutti et al., 2019). Similar trends have been observed in other high-income countries. In the United States, coverage for influenza among adults aged ≥65 years reached only 68% during the 2022–2023 season, with even lower rates for pneumococcal (59%) and zoster (48%) vaccines (McLaughlin et al., 2024). A recent review by the European Centre for Disease Prevention and Control (ECDC) also confirms substantial variability in vaccine coverage across EU/EEA countries, with suboptimal uptake in most adult immunization programs (ECDC, 2017). The recent rollout of the RSV vaccine and ongoing COVID-19 booster campaigns further complicate an already fragmented adult immunization landscape, characterized by inconsistent messaging and unclear guidance (Bertin et al., 2020).

To overcome these challenges, a cultural shift is needed to frame vaccination as a lifelong, shared responsibility. Strengthening vaccine literacy at all ages is crucial to encourage informed decision-making and build confidence. The COVID-19 pandemic underscored the vital role of vaccines in protecting public health and mitigating infectious threats (Wilson & Wiysonge, 2020). Yet, emergency-driven communication, widespread misinformation, and political polarization during the pandemic may have inadvertently fueled mistrust toward vaccines and institutions, especially among adults and older adults (Report of the SAGE Working Group on Vaccine Hesitancy, 2014; Razai et al., 2021).

VH plays a central role in this context (Caserotti et al., 2021). VH is complex and influenced by confidence, complacency, and convenience, and it varies by time, place, and vaccine type. Among adults, VH often manifests as skepticism toward newer vaccines (such as COVID-19 or RSV vaccines), low perceived vulnerability to disease, or fear of side effects, especially when faced with contradictory or incomplete information (Betsch et al., 2018; Schmid et al., 2017). On top of this, perceived low priority by health authorities and practical organizational issues are important component of VH.

Addressing these barriers requires targeted, transparent, and inclusive communication strategies, supported by evidence-based policies. Healthcare professionals, who remain the most trusted sources of vaccine information, must be actively engaged in these efforts (Gualano et al., 2021). Moreover, interventions should be tailored to the needs of specific groups, including older adults, people with chronic conditions, caregivers, and those in vulnerable socioeconomic circumstances, to ensure equitable vaccine access and uptake throughout the life course (MacDonald & Dubé, 2022).

In summary, although vaccines are a cornerstone of public health, implementing a lifelong vaccination calendar faces persistent challenges linked to awareness, perception, and hesitancy. Enhancing vaccine literacy, fostering trust, and promoting equitable delivery are essential steps toward improving adult immunization coverage and protecting population health.

4 Understanding the Determinants of Vaccine Hesitancy in Adults and Elderly

VH among adults and elderly populations remains a significant obstacle to achieving optimal vaccine coverage and controlling vaccine-preventable diseases. VH is a multifaceted phenomenon shaped by psychological, sociocultural, and logistical-organizational determinants that interact in complex ways. These determinants acquire specific characteristics in adults and elderly people due to factors related to aging, social context, health status, and healthcare access. A thorough understanding of these factors is crucial for public health stakeholders to design targeted and effective interventions to enhance vaccine acceptance and uptake.

4.1 Psychological and Cognitive Determinants

Psychological and cognitive factors strongly influence vaccine attitudes among adults, particularly the elderly. One of the most critical psychological determinants is risk perception. The assessment of risks related to both vaccine-preventable diseases and potential adverse effects of vaccines affects vaccination decisions (Gualano et al., 2021). Older adults frequently underestimate their susceptibility to infections and the potential severity of these diseases. This underestimation partly results from an optimism bias and the decreased prevalence of vaccine-preventable diseases today, thanks to widespread vaccination programs (Kharroubi et al., 2022). Consequently, perceived vulnerability is often low, reducing motivation to vaccinate.

Concerns about vaccine safety and side effects tend to be heightened in older populations. The presence of chronic illnesses and polypharmacy, common in the elderly, often amplifies fears about possible adverse interactions or worsening of existing conditions (Betsch et al., 2015). Additionally, cognitive decline or mild impairments in memory and executive function, more frequent with advancing age, may hinder effective processing of health information, thereby increasing misunderstanding and hesitancy (Berkman et al., 2011).

Trust is a central psychological factor influencing vaccine acceptance: trust in healthcare providers, government agencies, and pharmaceutical companies correlates positively with vaccine uptake. Elderly individuals who express higher trust in their physicians and health systems are more inclined to get vaccinated (Yaqub et al., 2014). Conversely, past negative experiences, misinformation, or perceived conflicts of interest can erode trust and reduce confidence in vaccines.

Health literacy and cognitive abilities play an equally important role. Lower health literacy is linked with difficulties in understanding vaccine benefits and risks, navigating health systems, and distinguishing credible information from misinformation (Larson et al., 2016). Older adults often face challenges related to digital literacy, making them vulnerable to misinformation spread via social media and other online platforms (Santini et al., 2020).

4.2 Sociocultural Determinants

Sociocultural factors affect vaccine hesitancy through beliefs, social norms, and community influences. Religious beliefs, for example, can be a powerful determinant of vaccine refusal or delay. Certain religious groups oppose vaccination due to doctrinal objections, ethical concerns regarding vaccine ingredients, or faith-based healing preferences (Wilson & Wiysonge, 2020). Although less prevalent among elderly populations in Western countries, such influences persist in specific communities worldwide.

Cultural values and traditions shape attitudes toward vaccination as well. Skepticism towards Western medicine or preference for traditional healing practices may reduce vaccine acceptance in some cultural contexts (Quinn et al., 2017). Cultural norms also influence perceptions of illness, vaccination, and preventive health behaviors, thereby affecting hesitancy.

Social isolation and limited social support are especially relevant among older adults. Many elderly people live alone or have restricted social networks, reducing opportunities to receive encouragement or accurate vaccine information from family and peers (Zimmerman et al., 2017). Social connectedness has been shown to promote vaccine uptake, as trusted relationships often reinforce positive health behaviors.

The pervasive role of misinformation cannot be overstated: in fact, social media and other communication channels have accelerated the spread of vaccine misinformation and conspiracy theories. Older adults, who may have less facility in critically appraising digital content, are disproportionately affected by such misinformation (Shapiro et al., 2018). False claims about vaccine safety, efficacy, or conspiracies linking vaccines to political or social agendas are significant contributors to hesitancy.

Levels of community and societal trust also impact VH. Societies characterized by high institutional trust tend to show higher vaccination rates. In contrast, historical events that have caused distrust, such as unethical medical experiments or systemic neglect, have fostered entrenched skepticism, particularly among marginalized groups (Brewer et al., 2017).

4.3 Logistical and Organizational Determinants

Logistical and organizational barriers heavily influence vaccine uptake in adult and elderly populations. Accessibility is a fundamental factor. Physical limitations like reduced mobility, chronic pain, or disability can make travel to vaccination sites difficult (Opel et al., 2013). In rural or underserved urban areas, inadequate transportation further exacerbates these challenges.

Healthcare system factors such as the availability, convenience, and user-friendliness of vaccination services also shape uptake. Clinics with limited hours, complex appointment procedures, or long waiting times discourage vaccination, particularly among elderly individuals who may depend on caregivers for support (Glanz et al., 2013). The absence of proactive outreach, reminder systems, or follow-ups further limits vaccine acceptance.

Communication and information dissemination strategies often fail to address the specific needs of adults and elderly. Information is frequently overly technical, not culturally adapted, or unavailable in accessible formats for individuals with sensory impairments such as vision or hearing loss (Lu et al., 2015). Healthcare providers may lack training in effectively discussing vaccines with hesitant adults or may not prioritize vaccination counseling amid busy clinical workloads (Larson et al., 2015).

Fragmented healthcare services contribute to missed opportunities for vaccination. Many adults, especially the elderly, consult multiple specialists and providers, and responsibility for vaccination may be unclear or poorly communicated (Kaur & Gupta, 2020). Integration of vaccination records and reminder systems across providers remains insufficient.

Economic factors, while less prominent in many high-income countries due to free or subsidized vaccines, can still affect uptake. Costs related to transportation or lost income due to time off work may pose barriers for some individuals (Habersaat et al., 2020).

4.4 Interaction of Determinants and Implications

The determinants of vaccine hesitancy rarely act independently but rather interact in multifaceted ways to influence individual vaccine decisions. For instance, low health literacy (psychological) combined with social isolation (sociocultural) and poor access to vaccination services (logistical) can synergistically increase hesitancy and lower vaccine uptake (Gualano et al., 2021). Conversely, strong trust in healthcare providers may mitigate concerns about vaccine safety or logistical inconveniences.

Recognizing these interacting layers is essential for designing effective interventions. Psychological interventions might include tailored educational materials addressing specific fears and misinformation, delivered through trusted sources. Sociocultural approaches could involve engaging community leaders and faith-based organizations to build vaccine confidence and counteract misinformation. Logistical strategies should focus on improving accessibility by implementing mobile clinics, home visits, extended service hours, and integrated care pathways (SAGE Working Group on Vaccine Hesitancy, 2015).

Health communication must be adapted to the preferences and needs of adult and elderly populations, employing clear, simple language, diverse formats (print, audio, visual), and culturally sensitive messaging. Training healthcare providers to engage empathetically and effectively with hesitant individuals is paramount.

In conclusion, vaccine hesitancy among adults and elderly is driven by an intricate network of psychological, sociocultural, and logistical factors. Addressing these determinants requires comprehensive, evidence-based strategies incorporating education, community engagement, improved service delivery, and supportive policies to increase vaccine acceptance and coverage in these vulnerable populations.

5 Lessons Learned from the COVID-19 Pandemic and Lasting Effects on Vaccine Hesitancy

The COVID-19 pandemic has profoundly reshaped the global landscape of vaccine hesitancy (VH), presenting both significant challenges and novel opportunities for public health systems worldwide. The unprecedented speed of vaccine development, combined with the global scale of the crisis, revealed deep societal vulnerabilities, altered public perceptions of vaccines, and transformed the dynamics of vaccine acceptance. This section reviews key lessons learned from the COVID-19 pandemic concerning VH, focusing on its drivers, the responses implemented, and the potential lasting effects on vaccination attitudes and behaviors.

5.1 Rapid Vaccine Development and Trust Challenges

A hallmark of the COVID-19 response was the rapid development and emergency authorization of multiple vaccines within a year of identifying SARS-CoV-2. This scientific achievement marked a milestone in biomedical innovation; however, it also contributed to public skepticism regarding vaccine safety and efficacy (Van Bavel et al., 2020). Many individuals questioned whether the vaccines had undergone sufficient testing due to the accelerated timelines and the emergency use authorization framework (Jamison et al., 2019).

Public confidence was further undermined by inconsistent messaging from health authorities, especially in the early phases of the pandemic. Changing guidelines on mask usage, social distancing, and vaccine eligibility created confusion and doubt (Lazarus et al., 2021). Meanwhile, misinformation and conspiracy theories proliferated across social media platforms, amplifying fear and distrust (Keja et al., 1988).

The critical lesson is that rapid vaccine development must be accompanied by transparent, consistent communication that acknowledges uncertainties and clearly explains the scientific process to build and sustain public trust (Jamison et al., 2019).

5.2 Impact of Politicization and Polarization

COVID-19 vaccination attitudes became highly politicized in many countries, with acceptance often aligning with political identity and ideology (Khubchandani et al., 2021). Political leaders' rhetoric and policies sometimes intensified public distrust and contributed to vaccine resistance, complicating public health messaging (Quinn et al., 2017).

This politicization heightened societal polarization, making it difficult to convey unified health messages. Vaccine promotion efforts were often interpreted through partisan lenses, reducing their effectiveness regardless of scientific evidence (Quinn et al., 2017). These developments emphasize the necessity of shielding public health strategies from political interference and engaging trusted community leaders across the political spectrum to foster broader acceptance (Kulenkampff et al., 1974).

5.3 Disparities and Equity Issues

The pandemic exposed and often exacerbated existing social and health inequities influencing VH and vaccine access. Marginalized populations, including racial and ethnic minorities, socioeconomically disadvantaged groups, and those with limited healthcare access, consistently showed lower vaccination rates and higher hesitancy (Freimuth et al., 2017).

Such disparities stem from historical medical mistrust, rooted in unethical research and systemic discrimination, alongside practical barriers including transportation difficulties, limited digital access, and language obstacles (Zarocostas, 2020). Addressing these inequities requires culturally tailored interventions and equitable resource allocation (Kulenkampff et al., 1974).

Importantly, community engagement proved crucial to overcoming hesitancy in underserved populations. Collaborations with local organizations, faith leaders, and community health workers were instrumental in building trust and improving vaccine uptake (Roozenbeek et al., 2020).

5.4 Role of Misinformation and the Infodemic

The COVID-19 crisis was accompanied by an unprecedented "infodemic", the rapid spread of misinformation and disinformation about the virus and vaccines (Michie & West, 2020). False claims ranged from questioning vaccine safety to conspiracy theories involving government control or microchips.

Social media platforms became primary vectors for misinformation, influencing public attitudes and behaviors worldwide. This phenomenon exposed vulnerabilities in public health communication systems and underscored the urgent need for proactive measures (Williams et al., 2020).

Effective management of misinformation requires real-time monitoring of emerging narratives and rapid, targeted communication responses. Partnerships between health authorities and media companies are essential to flag and limit false information while amplifying credible sources (Williams et al., 2020). Equally important is promoting media literacy and critical thinking among the public to empower individuals to independently identify misinformation (Williams et al., 2020).

5.5 Psychological Impacts and Pandemic Fatigue

The prolonged duration of the pandemic induced significant psychological strain, including anxiety, fear, and pandemic fatigue, which influenced vaccine attitudes. Over time, some individuals became increasingly skeptical or complacent about vaccination, weary of ongoing public health restrictions and messaging (Dada et al., 2022).

Mental health and emotional factors are thus key determinants of VH. Effective communication must be empathy-driven, and vaccination campaigns should integrate mental health support to address these issues. Recognizing and mitigating pandemic fatigue is vital to sustaining vaccine uptake, especially as booster doses and new vaccinations become necessary (Schwarzinger et al., 2021).

5.6 Innovations in Vaccine Delivery and Communication

COVID-19 accelerated innovation in vaccine delivery and communication strategies. The establishment of mass vaccination sites, mobile clinics, pop-up centers, and workplace vaccination programs significantly enhanced accessibility (Schwarzinger et al., 2021). Digital tools for appointment scheduling and vaccine passports became widespread, though they highlighted digital divide challenges.

Communication evolved to include social media influencers, targeted advertising, and multilingual campaigns designed for diverse populations (Larson et al., 2018). These approaches demonstrated the value of adaptive, multichannel communication strategies tailored to meet people where they are.

5.7 Lasting Effects on Vaccine Hesitancy

The pandemic's impact on VH will likely extend beyond the immediate crisis. Increased public attention to vaccines has raised awareness and may improve acceptance of other adult immunizations. The successful deployment of novel vaccine platforms such as mRNA technology holds promise for enhancing future vaccine development and acceptance, provided communication remains effective (Community Preventive Services Task Force (CPSTF), 2015).

Conversely, persistent distrust, misinformation, and politicization may continue to sustain VH in certain populations. The erosion of trust in public institutions observed during the pandemic represents a significant barrier for future vaccination efforts (Community Preventive Services Task Force (CPSTF), 2014).

5.8 Implications for Future Vaccination Strategies

Moving forward, public health authorities must apply these lessons to strengthen vaccine confidence and coverage. Transparent, consistent, and empathetic communication should be institutionalized. Strategies must prioritize equity, community engagement, and culturally appropriate messaging that addresses specific concerns.

Investment in infrastructure to improve vaccine access and the integration of vaccination into routine healthcare for adults and elderly populations are essential. Continuous monitoring of vaccine attitudes and rapid responses to emerging concerns can prevent the spread of hesitancy.

Finally, fostering resilience against misinformation through education and partnerships with trusted community leaders will be crucial to sustaining public trust and ensuring vaccination success.

6 Role of Healthcare Workers in VH in Adults and Elderly

Healthcare workers occupy a pivotal role in shaping vaccine acceptance among adults and elderly individuals, as they are often regarded as the most trustworthy source of immunization information (MacDonald & Dubé, 2022). Their attitudes, knowledge, and communication strategies can decisively influence whether a patient chooses to receive (or postpone) a recommended vaccine. In older cohorts, where routine childhood immunization campaigns no longer apply and chronic comorbidities elevate both perceived vulnerability and concerns about adverse events, the impact of a healthcare professional's recommendation becomes even more pronounced (Dube et al., 2015; Gualano et al., 2021).

Physicians, nurses, and pharmacists serve as primary interpreters of vaccine risks and benefits. During consultations, adult and senior patients frequently raise questions regarding vaccine effectiveness, safety profiles, and potential interactions with existing medications. When healthcare workers provide clear, evidence-based explanations, they dispel myths and correct misinformation that patients may have encountered online or through social networks (Razai et al., 2021). Conversely, if a provider harbors doubts, whether due to gaps in continuing education, personal beliefs or exposure to misleading content, their uncertainty may be communicated unintentionally, reinforcing patient hesitancy instead of alleviating it (SAGE Working Group on Vaccine Hesitancy, 2015).

The way healthcare workers frame their recommendations strongly affects patient confidence and motivation. A presumptive recommendation ("Today you will receive your influenza and pneumococcal vaccines" has been shown to increase uptake more effectively than an open-ended suggestion "What do you think about getting your flu shot today?") especially among older adults (Lu et al., 2015).

Nevertheless, participatory techniques that invite patients to express their concerns and address those concerns with empathy foster lasting trust. Training in motivational interviewing and empathetic communication enables professionals to balance authority with responsiveness, ensuring that high-risk patients feel informed and respected in their decision-making (Glanz et al., 2013).

Healthcare workers also contribute significantly to improving access and convenience, factors that are often decisive for elderly patients facing mobility or transportation challenges. Proactive systems such as in-clinic reminders, coordination with community pharmacies and home-visit vaccination programs help overcome logistical barriers (Brewer et al., 2017). Integrating vaccine counseling into routine chronic-care visits, such as follow-ups for diabetes, cardiovascular disease or COPD, allows clinicians to build on existing patient relationships and minimizes the burden of additional appointments (Kaur & Gupta, 2020). Including vaccination in the routine therapeutic pathways of adult and elderly patients (e.g., in the management of chronic conditions) can strengthen the perception of vaccination as an integral part of basic care, rather than as an optional intervention. Telemedicine platforms and digital health tools can be employed to send automated reminders, schedule virtual pre-vaccination assessments and share tailored educational materials, further reducing friction in the vaccination process.

At the organizational and policy levels, healthcare workers act as advocates for adult immunization. By leading institution-wide vaccination campaigns, organizing educational workshops and contributing to the development of local immunization guidelines, they help embed vaccine practices into the culture of primary care (Larson et al., 2018). Their frontline experience, insights into prevalent patient concerns, common misconceptions and systemic bottlenecks, can inform targeted interventions such as extending clinic hours, deploying mobile vaccination units in underserved neighborhoods or creating culturally tailored communication materials for diverse patient populations (Habersaat et al., 2020).

A patient-centered approach is crucial. Beyond conveying facts, healthcare workers must appreciate the values, preferences and lived experiences of adult and elderly patients. Shared decision-making models that involve patients in weighing the pros and cons of vaccination, while addressing individual health goals and quality of life considerations, ensure that immunization strategies align with what matters most to each person. For example, understanding an elderly patient's fear of potential side effects or logistical hurdles can prompt the provider to offer alternative scheduling options or additional follow-up support.

Continuous professional development is essential to maintain healthcare workers' ability to counter vaccine hesitancy effectively. Rapid innovations in vaccine mean that providers must stay up to date on safety data, emerging contraindications and evolving efficacy evidence (Van Bavel et al., 2020). Structured training programs, peer-to-peer learning networks and easy access to authoritative resources such as WHO reports and regulatory guidance empower healthcare professionals to deliver confident, accurate recommendations for both established and novel immunizations (Jamison et al., 2019).

In conclusion, healthcare workers are linchpins in addressing vaccine hesitancy among adults and the elderly. Their influence encompasses direct patient communication, facilitation of access, organizational advocacy and policy development. By investing in targeted training on empathetic, evidence-based dialogue, integrating vaccination into routine adult care pathways and leveraging digital health tools to streamline access, we can enhance vaccine confidence and uptake in these vulnerable populations.

7 Organizational Strategies to Counteract VH in Adults and Elderly

Vaccine hesitancy (VH) among adults and elderly persons can be effectively addressed by intervening on each of its distinct components, confidence, complacency, and convenience, through targeted and evidence-based strategies. Organizational issues play an important role, since comprehensive and multifaceted approaches must be developed to enhance vaccine confidence, raise awareness about the risks associated with vaccine-preventable diseases, and facilitate equitable and timely access to vaccination services. Each of these pillars requires careful consideration in the context of specific population needs and systemic healthcare dynamics.

At the foundation of vaccine acceptance lies an accurate and individualized risk-benefit assessment. Vaccine refusal among adults is frequently driven by a cognitive bias that leads to overestimation of vaccine-associated risks while simultaneously underestimating the potential severity and likelihood of contracting the disease. This misperception is particularly significant in older adults, who may experience reduced perception of vulnerability or rely on outdated information. Education and well-structured communication campaigns represent essential tools to promote correct understanding of risks and benefits, contributing to informed decision-making. However, it is important to note that informational interventions alone may be insufficient to significantly raise vaccination coverage. A systematic review conducted by the US Community Preventive Services Task Force (CPSTF) found that community-wide education programs, when implemented in isolation, show limited effectiveness. Conversely, robust evidence supports the efficacy of community-based communication interventions when integrated with broader strategies aimed at improving immunization uptake (Community Preventive Services Task Force (CPSTF), 2016). At this purpose, it is important that communication interventions are integrated in a consistent manner into different healthcare services. As an example, if a poster inviting to the flu vaccination is displayed in the waiting room of a hospital ward, the same message should be promoted over the counter of the pharmacies and the general practitioners should be trained to consistently convey the same message to their patients. Therefore, organizational efforts are needed to implement effective training, integrate efficient logistics, and finally evaluate the effectiveness of the integrated program.

Moreover, the implementation of multicomponent interventions requires coordinated action and partnership across various levels of society. Collaboration between community organizations, local authorities, healthcare providers, and public health institutions is crucial. Among the operational strategies that have demonstrated success are reminder and recall systems, direct client incentives, expanded availability of healthcare access points, and policies designed to reduce or eliminate out-of-pocket expenses related to vaccination (Galanakis et al., 2013). Furthermore, there is consistent and strong evidence supporting the role of home visits in improving vaccine adherence. These visits may be conducted by trained healthcare personnel capable of administering vaccines on site, or by community health workers and social care providers who can counsel and refer individuals to vaccination clinics (Savulescu, 2021). Home-based interventions can be particularly valuable for frail elderly individuals or those with limited mobility, reducing structural barriers to access. Unfortunately, home care is severely affected by budget availability. In healthcare systems that are under pressure because of financial constraints home care is often considered low priority in comparison with hospital care. In such situation it is important to demonstrate cost-effectiveness of home-based interventions. Adding vaccination to home care provisions may improve the economic balance of the intervention and make it more palatable to decision makers.

A longstanding and controversial debate surrounds the role and ethical implications of vaccine mandates. The imposition of mandatory vaccination policies raises fundamental questions about individual autonomy, public good, and the proportionality of public health interventions. In adult populations, the ethical acceptability of mandates has been explored both in the context of healthcare professionals and the general public (Mello et al., 2022; Okpani et al., 2024). Generally speaking, mandatory vaccination may be ethically justified when three conditions are met: there exists a serious threat to public health; no less coercive alternatives are available that achieve comparable outcomes; and there is strong scientific evidence regarding vaccine efficacy and safety. In the case of healthcare workers, these justifications are reinforced by professional and ethical duties to "do no harm" and protect vulnerable patients. In this sense, vaccine mandates for healthcare personnel have proven particularly effective in increasing coverage rates, as seen during the COVID-19 pandemic, when employer-imposed mandates led to high uptake among staff in hospitals and long-term care facilities (Lynch, 2024; Goodson & Rota, 2022; Chang Blanc et al., 2024). Outside emergency contexts or sectors of public interest such as healthcare or defense, however, mandatory vaccination policies are rarely adopted for the general adult population due to ethical, legal, and practical concerns. On the other hand, it is important to underline that vaccine mandates often represent a shortcut for public health being less resource-intensive in comparison to other interventions that require managerial changes, training activities, need for innovation.

Addressing the "convenience" dimension of VH presents substantial challenges. It requires not only policy will and political commitment but also the availability of sufficient financial resources and the presence of a robust, resilient, and well-coordinated health system. One of the key reasons for the historical success of childhood immunization programs lies in the clear societal awareness of the threats posed by infectious diseases in early life and the logistical feasibility of targeting a relatively small number of annual birth cohorts. In contrast, the adult population is demographically much larger, more heterogeneous, and subject to a wider range of risk factors. Moreover, many adult-targeted vaccines require regular or seasonal administration, such as the influenza vaccine, which introduces additional complexities in sustaining high coverage over time.

To ensure the feasibility and long-term sustainability of adult immunization programs, it is essential to enhance the overall efficiency of service delivery. This can be achieved through better integration of vaccination with other preventive and curative healthcare services. A cross-sectoral and interdisciplinary approach is key: collaboration among general practitioners, specialists, pharmacists, public health authorities, and social services can create a supportive ecosystem for vaccine uptake. Missed opportunities for vaccination during any healthcare contact should be minimized by ensuring that immunization services are available at multiple points of entry, including hospitals, nursing homes, outpatient clinics, and community pharmacies. Furthermore, all healthcare professionals should be equipped with up-to-date knowledge on vaccination benefits and trained to provide consistent, empathetic, and scientifically accurate information. Their role as trusted sources of information cannot be overstated. Innovation both in organizational pathways and immunization delivery systems is therefore key for increasing and sustaining vaccine coverage [74]. Make vaccination easy should be the password for a healthy ageing and an overall sustainable universal healthcare system [75].

Ultimately, promoting a life-course approach to vaccination is fundamental. Immunization should be perceived as an essential component of healthy ageing, equivalent in importance to other widely accepted health promotion measures such as smoking cessation, balanced nutrition, and regular physical activity. Embedding vaccination into the broader framework of preventive medicine and active ageing not only supports individual well-being but also contributes to the sustainability of healthcare systems in ageing societies. This perspective, accompanied by the necessary organization and management changes, must be at the core of future vaccination policies if we aim to effectively reduce VH and ensure equitable protection for all age groups.

References

Berkman, N. D., Sheridan, S. L., Donahue, K. E., Halpern, D. J., & Crotty, K. (2011). Low health literacy and health outcomes: An updated systematic review. *Annals of Internal Medicine, 155*(2), 97–107.

Bertin, P., Nera, K., & Delouvée, S. (2020). Conspiracy beliefs, rejection of vaccination, and support for hydroxychloroquine: A conceptual replication and extension. *Psychological Medicine, 52*(6), 1230–1234.

Betsch, C., Böhm, R., & Chapman, G. B. (2015). Using behavioral insights to increase vaccination policy effectiveness. *Policy Insights From the Behavioral and Brain Sciences, 2*(1), 61–73.

Betsch, C., Schmid, P., Heinemeier, D., et al. (2018). Beyond confidence: Development of a measure assessing the 5C psychological antecedents of vaccination. *PLoS One, 13*(12), e0208601.

Bonanni, P., Boccalini, S., & Bechini, A. (2020). Vaccination in the elderly: the challenge of coverage. *BMC Public Health, 20*, 1164.

Branche, A. R., Saiman, L., Walsh, E. E., Falsey, A. R., Jia, H., Barrett, A., Alba, L., Phillips, M., & Finelli, L. (2022). Change in functional status associated with respiratory syncytial virus infection in hospitalized older adults. *Influenza and Other Respiratory Viruses, 16*(6), 1151–1160.

Brewer, N. T., Chapman, G. B., Rothman, A. J., Leask, J., & Kempe, A. (2017). Increasing vaccination: Putting psychological science into action. *Psychological Science in the Public Interest, 18*(3), 149–207.

Caserotti, M., Girardi, P., Rubaltelli, E., et al. (2021). Associations of COVID-19 risk perception with vaccine hesitancy over time for Italian residents. *Social Science & Medicine, 272*, 113688.

Cassini, A., Colzani, E., Pini, A., Mangen, M. J., Plass, D., McDonald, S. A., et al. (2018). Impact of infectious diseases on population health using incidence-based disability-adjusted life years (DALYs): Results from the burden of communicable diseases in Europe study, European Union and European Economic Area countries, 2009 to 2013. *Eurosurveillance, 23*(16) 17-00454.

Chang Blanc, D., Grundy, J., Sodha, S. V., O'Connell, T. S., Montenegro, H. J., von Mühlenbrock, J., Grevendonk, T. R., Patel, M., Olayinka, F., Brooks, A., Wahl, B., Bar-Zeev, N., Nandy, R., & Lindstrand, A. (2024). Immunization programs to support primary health care and achieve universal health coverage. *Vaccine, 42*(Suppl 1), S38–S42.

Community Preventive Services Task Force (CPSTF). (2014). Increasing Appropriate Vaccination: Community-Based Interventions Implemented in Combination. https://www.thecommunityguide.org/media/pdf/Vaccination-Community-Based-in-Combination.pdf.

Community Preventive Services Task Force (CPSTF). (2015). Increasing appropriate vaccination: Community-wide education when used alone. https://doi.org/10.15620/cdc/168614.

Community Preventive Services Task Force (CPSTF). (2016). Increasing appropriate vaccination: Home visits to increase vaccination rates. https://doi.org/10.15620/cdc/168616.

Dada, D., Djiometio, J. N., McFadden, S. M., et al. (2022). Strategies to counter vaccine hesitancy: A systematic review. *Vaccine, 10*(1), 1–18.

Doherty, T. M., Connolly, M. P., Del Giudice, G., et al. (2018). Vaccination programs for older adults in an era of demographic change. *European Geriatric Medicine, 9*(3), 289–300.

Dube, E., Vivion, M., & MacDonald, N. E. (2015). Vaccine hesitancy, an overview. *Human Vaccines & Immunotherapeutics, 9*(8), 1763–1773.

European Centre for Disease Prevention and Control. (2017). Catalogue of interventions addressing vaccine hesitancy. Stockholm: ECDC.

European Centre for Disease Prevention and Control (ECDC). (n.d.) Vaccine Schedule. https://vaccine-schedule.ecdc.europa.eu/.

Freimuth, V. S., Jamison, A., An, J., Hancock, G. R., & Quinn, S. C. (2017). Determinants of trust in the flu vaccine for African Americans and Whites. *Social Science & Medicine, 193*, 70–79.

Gabutti, G., Stefanati, A., & Kuhdari, P. (2019). Herpes zoster vaccination in Italy: current status and perspectives. *Journal of Preventive Medicine and Hygiene, 60*(1), E1–E8.

Galanakis, E., Jansen, A., Lopalco, P. L., & Giesecke, J. (2013). Ethics of mandatory vaccination for healthcare workers. *Eurosurveillance, 18*(45), pii=20627.

Gianfredi, V., Santangelo, O. E., Provenzano, S., et al. (2022). Adult vaccination coverage in Italy: The regional divide. *Human Vaccines & Immunotherapeutics, 18*(1), 2029182.

Glanz, J. M., Newcomer, S. R., Narwaney, K. J., et al. (2013). A population-based cohort study of undervaccination in 8 managed care organizations across the United States. *JAMA Pediatrics, 167*(3), 274–281.

Goodson, J. L., & Rota, P. A. (2022). Innovations in vaccine delivery: Increasing access, coverage, and equity and lessons learnt from measles and rubella elimination. *Drug Delivery and Translational Research, 12*(5), 959–967.

Gualano, M. R., Bert, F., Passi, S., et al. (2021). Attitudes towards vaccination and intention to vaccinate against COVID-19: Results from a representative survey in Italy. *Vaccine, 9*(4), 366.

Gupta, D., & Mohan, S. (2023). Influenza vaccine: A review on current scenario and future prospects. *Journal, Genetic Engineering & Biotechnology, 21*(1), 154.

Habersaat, K. B., Betsch, C., Danchin, M., et al. (2020). Ten considerations for effectively managing the COVID-19 transition. *Nature Human Behaviour, 4*(7), 677–687.
Hackett, A. J. (2008). Risk, its perception and the media: The MMR controversy. *Community Practitioner, 81*, 22–25.
Italian Ministry of Health. (2021). *Coperture vaccinali in Italia.* https://www.salute.gov.it/new/it/tema/vaccinazioni/. Accessed on 9/11/2025
Jamison, A. M., Broniatowski, D. A., & Quinn, S. C. (2019). Malicious actors on Twitter: A guide for public health researchers. *American Journal of Public Health, 109*(S3), S329–S330.
Kaur, S. P., & Gupta, V. (2020). COVID-19 vaccine: A comprehensive status report. *Virus Research, 288*, 198114.
Keja, K., Chan, C., Hayden, G., & Henderson, R. H. (1988). Expanded programme on immunization. *World Health Statistics Quarterly, 41*(2), 59–63.
Kharroubi, G., Chemaitelly, H., & Abu-Raddad, L. J. (2022). The role of cognitive impairment in vaccination decision-making among older adults. *Aging Med (Milton), 5*(1), 46–55.
Khubchandani, J., Sharma, S., Price, J. H., et al. (2021). COVID-19 vaccination hesitancy in the United States: A rapid national assessment. *Journal of Community Health, 46*(2), 270–277.
Kulenkampff, M., Schwartzman, J. S., & Wilson, J. (1974). Neurological complications of pertussis inoculation. *Archives of Disease in Childhood, 49*, 46–49.
Larson, H. J., Clarke, R. M., Jarrett, C., et al. (2018). Measuring trust in vaccination: A systematic review. *Human Vaccines & Immunotherapeutics, 14*(7), 1599–1609.
Larson, H. J., de Figueiredo, A., Xiahong, Z., Schulz, W. S., Verger, P., Johnston, I. G., et al. (2016). The state of vaccine confidence 2016: Global insights through a 67-country survey. *eBioMedicine, 12*, 295–301.
Larson, H. J., Jarrett, C., Schulz, W. S., et al. (2015). Measuring vaccine hesitancy: The development of a survey tool. *Vaccine, 33*(34), 4165–4175.
Lazarus, J. V., Ratzan, S. C., Palayew, A., et al. (2021). A global survey of potential acceptance of a COVID-19 vaccine. *Nature Medicine, 27*(2), 225–228.
Liang, J. L., Tiwari, T., Moro, P., et al. (2018). Prevention of pertussis, tetanus, and diphtheria with vaccines in the United States: Recommendations of the advisory committee on immunization practices (ACIP). *MMWR – Recommendations and Reports, 67*(RR-2), 1–44.
Lu, P., O'Halloran, A., Williams, W. W., et al. (2015). Racial and ethnic disparities in vaccination coverage among adults in the United States. *Vaccine, 33*(48), 6454–6461.
Lynch, J. B. (2024). Vaccine mandates for health care workers—an effective policy tool for past and future pandemics. *JAMA Network Open, 7*(8), e2426820.
MacDonald, N. E., & Dubé, E. (2022). Unpacking vaccine hesitancy among healthcare providers. *Nature Human Behaviour, 6*, 1434–1435.
Macias, A. E., McElhaney, J. E., Chaves, S. S., et al. (2021). The disease burden of influenza beyond respiratory illness. *Vaccine, 39*(Suppl 1), A6–A14.
McLaughlin, J. M., Khan, F., Pugh, S., et al. (2024). Respiratory syncytial virus vaccination in older adults: Policy considerations and implementation challenges. *Vaccine, 42*(5), 856–864.
Mello, M. M., et al. (2022). Effectiveness of vaccination mandates in improving uptake of COVID-19 vaccines in the USA. *The Lancet, 400*(10351), 535–538.
Michie, S., & West, R. (2020). Behavioural, environmental, social, and systems interventions against COVID-19. *BMJ, 370*, m2982.
Naghavi, M., et al. (2024). Global burden associated with 85 pathogens in 2019: A systematic analysis for the global burden of disease study 2019. *The Lancet Infectious Diseases, 24*(8), 868–895.
Okpani, A. I., Lockhart, K., Barker, S., Grant, J. M., & Yassi, A. (2024). Did the health care vaccine mandate work? An evaluation of the impact of the COVID-19 vaccine mandate on vaccine uptake and infection risk in a large cohort of Canadian health care workers. *American Journal of Infection Control, 52*(9), 1065–1072.
Opel, D. J., Heritage, J., Taylor, J. A., et al. (2013). The architecture of provider-parent vaccine discussions at health supervision visits. *Pediatrics, 132*(6), 1037–1046.

Porter, D., & Porter, R. (1988). The politics of prevention: anti-vaccination and public health in 19th century England. *Medical History, 32*, 231–252.

Quinn, S. C., Jamison, A. M., Freimuth, V. S., An, J., Hancock, G. R., & Musa, D. (2017). Exploring racial influences on flu vaccine attitudes and behavior: Results of a national survey of African Americans. *Vaccine, 35*(8), 1167–1174.

Quinn, S. C., Parmer, J., Freimuth, V. S., Hilyard, K. M., Musa, D., & Kim, K. H. (2017). Exploring racial influences on flu vaccine attitudes and behavior: Results of a national survey of African Americans. *Vaccine, 35*(8), 1167–1174.

Razai, M. S., Osama, T., McKechnie, D. G. J., & Majeed, A. (2021). COVID-19 vaccine hesitancy among ethnic minority groups. *BMJ, 372*, n513.

Report of the SAGE Working Group on Vaccine Hesitancy. (2014).

Roozenbeek, J., Schneider, C. R., Dryhurst, S., et al. (2020). Susceptibility to misinformation about COVID-19 around the world. *Royal Society Open Science, 7*(10), 201199.

MacDonald NE, SAGE Working Group on Vaccine Hesitancy. Vaccine hesitancy: definition, scope and determinants. Vaccine 2015;33(34):4161–4164.

Santini, Z. I., Jose, P. E., Cornwell, E. Y., et al. (2020). Social disconnectedness, perceived isolation, and symptoms of depression and anxiety among older Americans (NSHAP): A longitudinal mediation analysis. *The Lancet Public Health, 5*(1), e62–e70.

Savulescu, J. (2021). Good reasons to vaccinate: Mandatory or payment for risk? *Journal of Medical Ethics, 47*, 78–85.

Schmid, P., Rauber, D., Betsch, C., Lidolt, G., & Denker, M. L. (2017). Barriers of influenza vaccination intention and behavior—a systematic review of influenza vaccine hesitancy, 2005–2016. *PLoS One, 12*(1), e0170550.

Schwarzinger, M., Luchini, S., Alla, F., et al. (2021). COVID-19 vaccine hesitancy in a representative working-age population in France: A survey experiment based on vaccine characteristics. *The Lancet Public Health, 6*(4), e210–e221.

Shapiro, G. K., Tatar, O., Dube, E., et al. (2018). The vaccine hesitancy scale: Psychometric properties and validation. *Vaccine, 36*(5), 660–667.

Shattock, A. J., et al. (2024). Contribution of vaccination to improved survival and health: modelling 50 years of the expanded programme on immunization. *The Lancet, 403*(10441), 2307–2316.

Van Bavel, J. J., Baicker, K., Boggio, P. S., et al. (2020). Using social and behavioural science to support COVID-19 pandemic response. *Nature Human Behaviour, 4*(5), 460–471.

Williams, S. N., Armitage, C. J., Tampe, T., & Dienes, K. (2020). Public perceptions and experiences of social distancing and social isolation during the COVID-19 pandemic: A UK-based focus group study. *BMJ Open, 10*(7), e039334.

Williamson, S. (1984). Anti-vaccination leagues. *Archives of Diseases in Childhood, 59*, 1195–1196.

Wilson, S. L., & Wiysonge, C. (2020). Social media and vaccine hesitancy. *BMJ Global Health, 5*, e004206.

World Health Organization. (2019). *Ten threats to global health in 2019*. WHO. Available from: https://www.who.int/news-room/spotlight/ten-threats-to-global-health-in-2019. Accessed June 1, 2025

World Health Organization. (2021). *Immunization agenda 2030: a global strategy to leave no one behind*. WHO. Available at: https://cdn.who.int/media/docs/default-source/immunization/strategy/ia2030/ia2030-draft-4-wha_b8850379-1fce-4847-bfd1-5d2c9d9e32f8.pdf?sfvrsn=5389656e_69&download=true. Accessed June 1, 2025

Yaqub, O., Castle-Clarke, S., Sevdalis, N., & Chataway, J. (2014). Attitudes to vaccination: A critical review. *Social Science & Medicine, 112*, 1–11.

Zarocostas, J. (2020). How to fight an infodemic. *Lancet, 395*(10225), 676.

Zimmerman, R. K., Nowalk, M. P., Lin, C. J., et al. (2017). Challenges in vaccinating older adults in primary care. *Journal of the American Geriatrics Society, 65*(5), 1023–1030.

Telemedicine as a Response to the Shortage of Skilled Personnel in Home Care: An Integration Server for Remote Consultations as a Practical Model for Elderly Care

Zdislav Dolecek and Michal Štýbnar

1 Introduction: Ageing Population and Challenges in Czech Home Care

Current demographic data in the Czech Republic, as well as across Europe, clearly indicate a **rapidly ageing population** characterized by a declining birth rate and increasing life expectancy. This trend is associated with an increasing number of clients who will need social and health services directly in their own homes (home care). This development is further compounded by a shortage of staff in these services. The Czech Republic, mirroring broader European trends, exemplifies this demographic imperative, experiencing a notable increase in its elderly population coupled with growing pressures on its social and healthcare workforce. This report focuses primarily on health services and explores how digital health and telemedicine are emerging as critical catalysts for innovation in addressing these challenges within the Czech context. It delves into the evolving policy landscape, highlights pioneering initiatives, particularly in the Olomouc Region, and examines the transformative potential of advanced digital solutions, including artificial intelligence (AI), in enhancing home-based care for the elderly. By analysing the benefits and persistent implementation challenges, this document aims to provide a comprehensive framework for building a more resilient, efficient, and patient-centred healthcare system for an ageing society. This situation places significant demands on the healthcare and social care system, which is already struggling with a **shortage of**

Z. Dolecek (✉)
University Hospital Olomouc, Olomouc, Czech Republic
e-mail: zdislav.dolecek@fnol.cz

M. Štýbnar
National Telemedicine Center, Olomouc, Czech Republic
e-mail: michal.stybnar@fnol.cz

A. Ricciardelli, L. Mercurio (eds.), *Building Innovation in Ageing and Health Policy*, Springer Series in Healthcare Management and Innovation,
https://doi.org/10.1007/978-3-032-09163-5_6

qualified personnel in field care. A critical imbalance is thus emerging between the rising demand for home care and the limited capacity of healthcare staff, necessitating the search for **effective tools** to ensure rapid expert support remotely.

The shortage of specialized medical professionals in hospitals is also expected to have a direct impact on the structure of healthcare in the Czech Republic. To maintain quality of care with fewer specialists, it will likely be necessary to consolidate resources, leading to a reduction in the number of hospitals and, consequently, hospital beds across the country. This shift will further emphasize the importance of robust home care services and remote medical support to ensure that patients can still access necessary care outside of traditional hospital settings.

In this context, **telemedicine** emerges as a key strategy for maintaining the quality and accessibility of care. Traditional models of care, based on the physical presence of a doctor or specialist, are becoming increasingly unsustainable given these demographic and personnel challenges. The aim of this chapter is to present a specific innovative solution—an **integrated telemedicine server**, developed by the UHO in cooperation with the Olomouc Region. This solution represents a practical model that seeks to respond to the deteriorating availability of qualified personnel in health home care. We will describe its implementation, operational mechanisms, and benefits in detail, with an emphasis on elderly care and wound management, and long-term venous access management, among other areas.

In the Czech Republic, the topic of **wound photo documentation** and other clinical conditions in home care is still a relatively new field, but its importance is growing. Until now, there has been a lack of unified standards and integrated platforms that would enable efficient and secure exchange of this sensitive data between field workers and hospital specialists. The UHO integration server project thus becomes a pioneer in this area on the national level, as it offers a centralized system for clinical consultations from the field, which are transmitted to specialized departments via a **secure digital platform**. Its design and implementation are aligned with the nationally recognized guideline *Návod k fotodokumentaci ran* (Šeflová et al., 2024), approved by the Ministry of Health of the Czech Republic, which defines standardized procedures for wound imaging and monitoring. The integration server operationalizes these recommendations and extends their use from hospital settings into routine home care practice.

The pilot testing of this solution was carried out in cooperation with the home care agency called **eSestřička** (eNurse) and focused on managing complications related to wounds, invasive inputs, and other nursing procedures for elderly patients. This project not only demonstrates technological innovation but also **inter-institutional cooperation** and the ability to respond to practical needs in the field, which is crucial for creating a sustainable and scalable model of care.

The established network of home health agencies, such as eSestřička, provides a crucial existing infrastructure for the rapid and widespread adoption of digital health innovations like ZUNI application for mobile devices. Project with eSestřička (e-sestricka.cz), with its 29 branches across the Czech Republic, offers comprehensive domestic health and social care, including specialized services like wound care, blood draws, injections, ostomy care, and assistance with daily activities. These services are often covered by public health insurance, making them accessible to a broad patient base. The services provided by agencies like eSestřička, particularly wound care, directly align with the capabilities of digital tools such as ZUNI, which specializes in digital wound documentation. This existing network of home care providers presents a significant opportunity for scaling digital health innovations by integrating them into established workflows. Instead of building new digital health delivery channels from scratch, leveraging widespread home care networks means innovations can be integrated into established patient relationships and logistical frameworks, significantly accelerating deployment and acceptance by all involved.

The patient-centric approach inherent in-home care, emphasizing personal comfort, individualized care plans, and family involvement, aligns perfectly with telemedicine's core value proposition. Telemedicine allows patients to remain in their familiar home environment, fostering feelings of security and connection with healthcare professionals. This philosophical and practical alignment between traditional home care services and telemedicine creates a powerful combination that enhances the patient experience, potentially leading to better health outcomes and more sustainable care models. This alignment fosters greater patient satisfaction and adherence, which are critical for successful long-term care outcomes, especially for the elderly.

2 Theoretical Framework and Context of Telemedicine in Home Care

The Czech National eHealth Center (NTMC), co-founded by the UHO and the Faculty of Medicine and Dentistry of Palacky University in Olomouc in 2012 and later integrated into the UHO, is the first centre in the Czech Republic comprehensively focused on clinical research in telemedicine. Its primary mission is to unify the numerous fragmented eHealth activities currently present in the Czech Republic under a single organizational structure. This mission to unify fragmented eHealth activities and its in-depth approach to clinical research, education, and international knowledge dissemination directly addresses the systemic need for structured innovation and capacity building within the Czech healthcare system, moving beyond isolated digital initiatives. Key objectives of the NTMC include exploring new directions and procedures in the field, verifying and implementing innovations and principles into practice, and developing and using modern methods for both undergraduate and postgraduate education. The NTMC aims to leverage telemedicine for preventive treatment, enhancing patient comfort, saving physicians' time, and improving overall care effectiveness through information and communication technologies. It also seeks to streamline healthcare for the elderly population not only through technology but also by advocating for governmental measures that promote the dissemination of good practices from abroad and the implementation of integrated care within the Czech healthcare system. Meanwhile, telemedicine has been integrated as a study subject at the Faculty of Medicine and Dentistry at Palacký

University in Olomouc. This integration enables students and academic staff to undertake study stays, professional internships, and internships at foreign institutions and companies dealing with eHealth issues, such as hospitals, technology, and development companies, or research centres. The NTMC aims to obtain top know-how from international entities and experts and disseminate it to other professional workplaces throughout the Czech Republic, thereby training new experts in telemedicine. NTMC within UHO has also received the title Reference Site of European Partnership for Active and Healthy Ageing (EIP on AHA) three times for its innovative care practices. We are aware that telemedicine, in its broadest sense, represents the **provision of healthcare services remotely through information and communication technologies (ICTs)**. Its history dates back to the mid-twentieth century, but with the development of digital technologies and the Internet, it has gained significance in recent decades, especially in connection with the **ageing population** and the need for a more efficient healthcare system.

In the context of **home care**, telemedicine becomes a key tool for **ensuring continuity of care** and supporting patients in their home environment. Current home care systems face several significant challenges:

- **Shortage of qualified personnel:** As mentioned, this is a nationwide and European problem that places enormous pressure on existing healthcare professionals.
- **Geographical fragmentation of care:** Especially in rural areas, the physical availability of specialists may be limited.
- **Need for rapid response:** A rapid deterioration of a patient's condition, especially in the elderly, requires immediate expert assessment, which may not always be available through traditional means.
- **Ensuring quality and safety:** With the increasing number of home care providers, it is necessary to ensure uniform standards and oversight of the quality of care provided.

Telemedicine has the potential to bridge these gaps. It provides **effective tools** that enable **rapid expert support remotely** without the need for the physical presence of a doctor or specialist. Key benefits include **reducing the number of patient transports** to the hospital, **optimizing the time of healthcare personnel** (both field nurses and specialists), and **strengthening the clinical confidence** of field workers.

Legislative and ethical aspects of telemedicine in the Czech Republic and the EU are still evolving. It is necessary to ensure the **security and protection of personal data** of patients in accordance with GDPR, minimize the scope of personal data accessible to mobile applications, ensure **secure data encryption** on mobile devices and during transmission, and monitor user access to patients' personal data for audit purposes. At the same time, issues of responsibility, ethical boundaries, and communication security need to be addressed. The UHO project therefore focuses on **implementing a strong password policy**, **secure session management**, and **regular security audits** of authentication processes. Emphasis is placed on **standardization of data formats** and **regular API updates and maintenance**.

The operational and workforce challenges in home healthcare are not isolated but form an interconnected web, where issues like inaccurate documentation and limited oversight are exacerbated by the independent nature of home visits, leading to compromised patient safety, reduced efficiency, and increased burden on nurses.

- **Documentation and workflow inefficiencies**: Traditional methods for wound measurement and documentation are often inaccurate, incomplete, and highly time-consuming. Nurses spend significant time at the bedside and then additional hours entering wound information into electronic health record systems, impacting patient outcomes and potentially leading to reimbursement denials.
- **Limited oversight and expertise**: Home health nurses operate independently in the field, making it challenging for agencies to enforce compliance with care protocols and best practices. There is a lack of direct oversight and specialized wound expertise, particularly for complex wounds in patients discharged early from hospitals, posing a significant challenge for home health clinicians.
- **Patient non-compliance and resource scarcity**: Challenges include patient non-compliance, often due to misunderstandings about instructions or personal health decisions. Unlike hospital settings, home environments may have limited access to necessary equipment and medication. Assessing patient progress can also be more difficult without the frequent tests and observations common in hospital environments.
- **Communication difficulties**: Misunderstanding or ambiguity in communication with patients, their caregivers, and the clinical team can compromise patient safety and the quality of care. A lack of family or caregiver support further exacerbates these issues, placing additional pressure on nurses who often have to fill these gaps.
- **Safety concerns and environmental hazards**: Home health nurses face considerable risks from unsafe working conditions, including unsanitary homes, extreme temperatures, or hostile pets. They are also exposed to bloodborne pathogens (e.g. from needlesticks) and biological hazards like regulated medical waste. Ergonomic hazards from lifting or transporting patients without assistive equipment are also a concern, with numerous reported injuries among home healthcare aides. Managing invasive lines, such as central lines, at home requires meticulous care to prevent infection, dislodgement, or damage, with limited immediate support available in emergencies.

3 UHO Integration Server: Design and Implementation

The UHO integration server project is a concrete response to the above-mentioned challenges in home care. The primary purpose of the server is to **facilitate consultations regarding patient wound treatment procedures** and to serve as a **central hub for wound documentation**, for example pressure ulcers, for patients across the entire region. This significantly contributes to **improving the quality of care during patient transfers** between different healthcare facilities, it helps to decide about hospitalization, changings in treatment etc.

3.1 Target Group and Pilot Testing

The pilot project was tested in collaboration with the home care agency **eSestřička and the patients themselves**. The target group included **seniors and other patients** (such as those in wheelchairs) receiving home care, with a focus on managing complications related to wounds, invasive inputs, and other nursing procedures. The aim was the **possible use of multiple applications**, all of which had to meet predetermined conditions. For those who didn't have their own application, such as **the patients themselves, we utilized the ZUNI application**.

The ZUNI application exemplifies a modern solution for digital wound documentation and care. Designed for healthcare professionals in hospitals, clinics, and home care settings, ZUNI offers comprehensive documentation, tracking wound healing over time, and recording procedures. The application is designed to work even with minimal IT infrastructure and ensures data security through encryption and biometric authentication, meeting all security standards for handling sensitive health data.

3.2 System Architecture and Communication Process

The integration server is designed with a **simple yet robust architecture** that ensures **secure communication** between UHO's information systems and other healthcare facilities or home care agencies. The key components of the system and their interactions are as follows:

Role of the ZUNI Application for Field Workers

The **ZUNI application** is intended for field healthcare professionals and is available for Android devices (smartphones, tablets) via **Google Play**. It is used for:

- **Taking photos of clinical problems:** For example, a wound or an invasive input. To ensure the quality and comparability of images, it is crucial to follow the **wound photo documentation guide**, which specifies guidelines for photographing patients, the environment, and the use of a ruler.
- **Adding a brief report:** A text description of the medical issue is attached to the photo.
- **Sending a consultation request:** The request is sent to a specialist at UHO and can also be sent directly to the hospital ICT system or a system for displaying medical imaging data.

Principles of Quality Wound Photo Documentation: A Guide

To ensure the maximum informational value and comparability of acquired images, a detailed **wound photo documentation guide** was developed and implemented. This guide provides simplified methodological instructions for all healthcare professionals who capture photographic records of wounds and skin/tissue damage, aiming to unify requirements for recording and improving their quality. Key principles include:

- **Patient and privacy**:
  - The **patient's health condition is paramount**; photographs are only taken after their condition is stable.
  - The patient must be **informed**, and verbal consent must be obtained. For clear identification from a photograph (e.g. face), written informed consent is required.
  - **Respecting patient privacy and dignity** is crucial; intimate areas and identifiable body parts should be covered.
  - The **patient's position** should be comfortable for both the patient and the photographer. The bed and its functions (grab bar, positioning aids) are used for optimal positioning.
  - **Documentation over time:** Photo documentation is performed at the beginning of care, during its course (when wound status or treatment changes), and upon completion (during transfer, discharge, or end of treatment).
  - **Patient empowerment and access**: Telehealth empowers patients to manage their illness, improves their quality of life, and enhances access to home-based primary care services, allowing them to remain in their familiar home environment. It significantly reduces burdens such as transportation costs, long waiting times, and the fear of infections associated with hospital visits. Patients frequently report feelings of security, safety, and closeness with healthcare professionals, finding the technology user-friendly and beneficial.
- **Environment and lighting**:
  - **Environment preparation:** The background and surroundings of the photographed area should be clean and tidy, ideally with a solid-coloured background (ideally white pad).
  - **Lighting:** It is crucial to adjust room lighting and eliminate distorting factors such as shadows or reflections. It is recommended to use **only one type of light source** (e.g. ceiling light) and avoid flash.
- **Camera and its use**:
  - **Consistency:** Always use the **same device** provided by the employer (mobile phone, tablet).
  - **Cleanliness:** The lens should be kept clean.
  - **Stability:** Hold the camera with both hands for stability and avoid excessive tilting, which can lead to distortion.

  - **Zoom:** Do not use digital zoom, as it reduces photo quality.
  - **Quality control:** Immediately after taking the photo, check the sharpness and overall quality of the image.
- **Use of a ruler**:
  - **Standardization:** The ruler is an essential technical tool for **objective wound assessment** (size, sharpness, orientation). It should always be placed consistently, approximately 2 cm from the wound, without covering it, and as close as possible to the photographed surface, perpendicular to the wound.
  - **Ruler type:** A right-angled, disposable ruler with a colour scale and an **ArUco marker** (e.g. ID 3) is recommended for image calibration and dimension measurement. The paper weight should be 300 g/m^2 to minimize deformation.
  - **Orientation:** Orientation symbols (figure, heart, clock) on the ruler indicate the direction of photography and should point towards the patient's head (cranial/proximal).
  - **Description:** The ruler should be labelled with the patient's initials, year of birth, and date of image acquisition.

Functions of the Integration Server and Its Security

The Integration Server:

- **Primary purpose:** To facilitate consultations regarding patient wound treatment procedures.
- **Central hub:** The goal is to become a central hub for wound documentation, particularly pressure ulcers, for patients across the entire Olomouc region.
- **Open architecture:** The server is designed to allow simple connection of any third-party system. It supports data transfer in **HL7 FHIR** format, although its own format is preferred in the first phase due to the lack of national standards.
- **Technical solution:** It is written in **Java** for maximum portability. It runs as a service under the UHO domain user on server APP177 at **https://konzultacni-is.fnol.cz**.
- **Data storage:** For internal data, it uses a Microsoft SQL Server Express operational database running on the same server. Authentication to this database is via **Windows Authentication (Kerberos)**.
- **Interface:** The IS exposes an **HTTPS interface for API and Browser**. The HTTPS certificate is stored in Local Machine Certificate Storage.
- **Access:** External information systems (EIS) or users access the integration server via a **Firewall**, which terminates the SSL certificate signed by a public certification authority.
- **Patient registry access:** The IS accesses the Patient Registry on SQL24-CLS in the ZUNI database. Authentication to this database is also via Windows Authentication (Kerberos).

Remote Consultation Process and the Role of the UHO Portal

The **UHO Portal** is a system accessible to relevant specialists at UHO. The consultation process includes the following:

1. **Consultation Request:** An External Healthcare Facility initiates a consultation in ZUNI or within its information system. EIS system collects image documentation and data about the consulted situation (e.g. wound) and then sends the consultation request to UHO.
2. **Verification and Request Transfer:** The integration server receives and verifies patient information (UHO only provides consultations for patients registered in its patient base) and forwards the request to the UHO Portal.
3. **Specialist Assessment:** Specialists at UHO assess the situation and, at their discretion, provide a consultation either within their own system or by phone.
4. **Feedback and Record:** Specialists can immediately contact the field nurse by phone, provide recommendations, and record the solution in the system. After the phone consultation, a note is added to the portal to inform others that the consultation has taken place.
5. **Sending Contribution from UHO:** When a contribution to a consultation is created in the UHO Portal, this contribution is sent to the integration server. Communication back to the EIS occurs via a "pull" system.
6. **Notifications:** If the EIS has a registered WebHook address, the integration server sends a notification about the new contribution. If no WebHook exists, the EIS must periodically query for contributions awaiting on the integration server. The EIS then stores these contributions and confirms their processing back to the integration server.

Request and Task Processing Model

Upon receiving a request, the integration server always processes it and creates tasks necessary for its successful execution. Tasks are performed asynchronously relative to their creation. When tasks are completed, the server retains a log of their execution for potential error state analysis by the operator.

There are three types of tasks:

- **Transfer to portal:** This task is generated when a request is received from the EIS. When executed, the contribution is transferred to the UHO Portal.
- **WebHook call to EIS:** This task is generated when a request is received from the UHO Portal. When executed, the WebHook EIS is called (if defined). At any given time, only one task of this type can exist for a single client in the IN_PROGRESS state.
- **Transfer to EIS:** This task is also generated when a request is received from the UHO Portal. Its execution is ensured by a call from the EIS, which retrieves the corresponding message and confirms its receipt. The integration server thus does not actively perform this task but waits for its completion by the EIS.

Schema

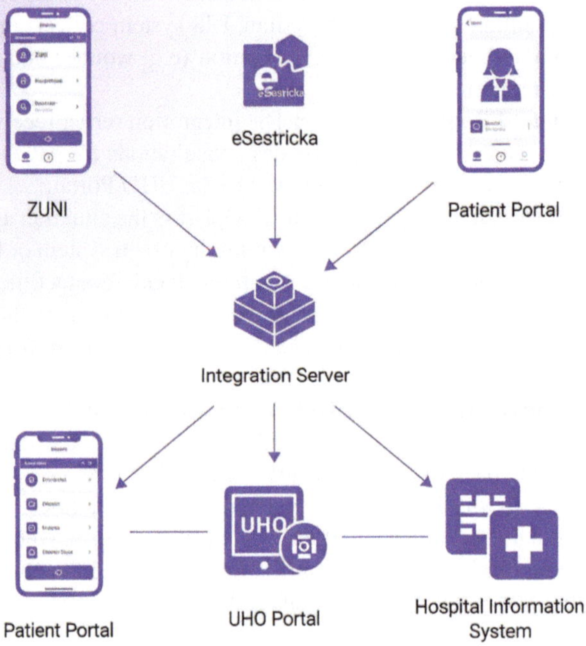

4 Practical Impacts and Benefits of the Integration Server

The implementation of the integration server brings about a series of **fundamental shifts** in home care practice, manifesting in several key areas:

4.1 Operational Efficiency and Cost Savings

- **Reduced patient transports to hospital:** The possibility of remote consultation lessens the need for physical doctor visits or patient transport to the hospital, leading to time and cost savings for both patients and the healthcare system.
- **Optimized healthcare personnel time:** Efficient use of time for field nurses and specialists, who can provide care remotely.
- **Savings for healthcare facilities:** Reduced administrative burden and logistical costs associated with traditional care models.

4.2 Improved Quality of Patient Care

- **Ensured continuity of care:** The system supports seamless care and rapid access to expert assessment, which is crucial for early detection and resolution of complications.
- **Reduced isolation of field workers and strengthened clinical confidence:** Field nurses feel less isolated and have immediate access to expert support, which enhances their decision-making capabilities.
- **Improved decision-making processes:** Less experienced personnel receive expert support for their decision-making processes.
- **Timely detection and management of complications:** The system enables rapid resolution of problems with wounds, invasive inputs, and other nursing procedures.

4.3 Educational Potential and Professional Development

- **Immediate and factual feedback:** Field nurses receive prompt and professionally grounded feedback, contributing to their **education and professional growth**. The detailed **wound photo documentation guide** plays a key role here, as it ensures that feedback is based on standardized and quality image data, maximizing the educational effect.
- **Building an image database:** The system allows for the creation of a **time-distributed image database** for educational purposes or clinical studies. This database, enriched with standardized photographs according to the "wound photo documentation guide", can be used to monitor the progression of conditions over time and the response of wounds to treatment, opening the door for future applications of **artificial intelligence**.
- **Easier triage in case of hospitalization:** Photographs of patients' wounds at home, when transferred to the hospital, can facilitate triage in the emergency department without the need to physically expose the wound, as the doctor can view it beforehand. Standardized photo documentation increases the relevance of these images for clinical decision-making.

5 Operational Workflow with Home Care Agencies

The core of our system involves a seamless communication process between field healthcare workers and hospital specialists. As we mentioned, a home care agency like eSestřička plays a crucial role as an existing infrastructure for adopting digital health innovations.

In practice, the workflow typically unfolds as follows:

- **Field data collection**: A field healthcare worker from a home care agency, such as eSestřička, identifies a clinical problem, often related to wounds or invasive inputs. While the sources state that the ZUNI application is widely used by field healthcare workers for digital wound documentation on Android devices. eSestřička has developed its own application which integrates wound photography capabilities that transmit to your integration server. This collected image documentation, and a brief text report of the clinical issue are sent as a consultation request. It is critical that photos adhere to a wound photo documentation guide to ensure quality and comparability, specifying guidelines for photographing patients, their environment, and using a ruler for objective assessment.

- **Data transmission and verification**: The consultation request is sent to the UHO integration server via a secure digital platform. The integration server receives and verifies patient information, ensuring that only patients registered in the UHO patient base receive consultations.
- **Specialist review and consultation**: The verified request is then forwarded to the UHO Portal, which is accessible to relevant specialists at University Hospital Olomouc. These specialists, often wound nurses or doctors, assess the situation in real-time.
- **Feedback and documentation**: The specialist can immediately contact the home care nurse in the field by phone to provide recommendations. The solution and any advice given are then recorded in the system, with a note added to the portal to confirm the consultation. Contributions from UHO are sent back to the integration server, and if the external information system (EIS) has a registered WebHook address, it receives a notification about the new contribution. This model supports continuity of care and provides decision-making support for less experienced staff.

This process significantly reduces the isolation of individual providers, strengthens clinical confidence, saves time and costs, and contributes to the education of field workers through immediate, factual, and professionally grounded feedback.

5.1 Illustrative Patient Cases and Experiences

To highlight the system's practical impact, consider presenting a few anonymized use cases, elaborating on the patient's condition, how the system was utilized, and the benefits achieved. This directly addresses your request for specific examples.

Here are a few examples, formatted as case studies:

Case Study 1: Remote Monitoring of a Non-Healing Decubitus Ulcer

- **Patient profile:** Mr. N., born in 1975, was a male patient paralysed after a severe car accident, living at home and requiring intensive home care. He developed a persistent decubitus ulcer on his buttocks that was proving difficult to heal.
- **Challenge:** Regular hospital visits for wound assessment and treatment were significantly complicated due to his paralysis and mobility issues, placing a considerable burden on him and his family.

- **System utilization**: To overcome this, Mr. N., with the assistance of a family member, regularly used the ZUNI application on a mobile device to document the wound's progression. High-quality photographs, adhering to the wound photo documentation guide with proper lighting and ruler placement, were captured and accompanied by brief clinical reports. These data were securely transmitted to the UHO integration server and then forwarded to the UHO Portal.
- **Outcome**: A specialized wound nurse at UHO could remotely review the images and reports, providing timely and precise recommendations for wound care directly to Mr. N's family member or the home care nurse. This eliminated the need for frequent, difficult physical transports to the hospital. Through this regular remote consultation, the wound's condition was closely monitored; initial reports indicated significant redness and a larger wound area, but subsequent consultations documented a noticeable improvement, with reduced redness and a decrease in both the content and circumference of the wound. Mr. Novák reported feeling more secure and connected to his healthcare professionals, valuing the user-friendly technology. This case exemplifies how telemedicine ensures continuity of care and provides expert support remotely, significantly improving the patient's quality of life.

Case Study 2: Managing Complications with Long-Term Venous Access

- **Patient profile**: Mrs. D, an elderly female patient receiving home care, had a long-term venous access line in place. The skin around the insertion site was frequently red and presented with dermatitis.
- **Challenge**: Such complications require careful monitoring to prevent infection and ensure the access line remains viable for treatment, but direct hospital visits for every observation can be inconvenient and resource intensive.
- **System utilization:** Her home care nurse utilized the system (e.g. via the agency's integrated application) to regularly photograph the venous access site and its surrounding area, noting any changes in redness, swelling, or skin condition. These observations were then sent to the UHO specialists for remote consultation.
- **Outcome**: Specialists at UHO could provide prompt advice on managing the dermatitis and ensuring proper care for the venous access, such as recommending specific emollients or adjusting dressing protocols. This proactive remote monitoring allowed for timely interventions, preventing the condition from escalating and reducing the need for emergency hospital visits. The consistent, expert feedback to the field nurse also contributed to their professional development and strengthened their clinical confidence in managing complex cases at home. The patient's condition showed marked improvement, with reduced redness and healthier skin around the venous access.

Case Study 3: Proactive Monitoring of Venous Access in a Senior Care Facility

- **Patient profile**: Mrs. B., an elderly female resident in a senior care home had a long-term venous access line inserted in the hospital for nutritional support.
- **Challenge**: Residents in senior care facilities often have multiple comorbidities, making frequent hospital transfers for routine checks challenging and potentially risky. Ensuring the integrity and cleanliness of such invasive inputs is paramount to prevent serious complications like infection.
- **System utilization:** The care staff at the senior home periodically documented the condition of the venous access site using the telemedicine system, capturing images and providing brief descriptive reports. These digital consultations were transmitted to the UHO specialists.
- **Outcome**: This enabled continuous, proactive monitoring of the venous access line without requiring the patient to be transported to the hospital for routine checks. The UHO specialists could confirm the stable condition of the access, or advise on minor adjustments to care, ensuring the line remained functional and free from complications. This not only improved the patient's comfort by allowing her to remain in her familiar environment but also optimized the time of both the home care staff and hospital specialists, demonstrating a more efficient model of care. In case there is a change, and for example a hospital visit or an urgent transfer has been arranged, the triage will be performed on the basis of the image, and it will not be necessary to uncover the wound during the triage and then leave the patient waiting in the waiting room.

These use cases demonstrate how the integration server supports the goal of maintaining quality and accessibility of care in the face of a shortage of qualified personnel and a rapidly ageing population. They highlight the system's ability to facilitate rapid expert support remotely, reduce patient transports, and enhance the clinical confidence of field workers. By providing such detailed narratives, your chapter will offer a more compelling and relatable understanding of the system's transformative potential.

6 Discussion and Future Directions

Although the pilot project of the UHO integration server has demonstrated significant benefits, it is essential to discuss the challenges and potential future directions for the development of this solution.

6.1 Challenges and Limitations of the Pilot Project and Their Solutions

The implementation of telemedicine systems brings with it a number of risks that must be managed and minimized. The integration server documentation thoroughly analyses potential risks and proposes corresponding measures.

- **Server overload risk:** The server can handle a limited number of concurrent transactions (up to 100), but unexpectedly high load can lead to performance degradation.
  - **Measures:** Connecting to a higher-capacity database, increasing the maximum number of database connections, and increasing the number of concurrently running server instances. Load testing showed that 90% of requests were processed within 1650 ms, averaging 1148 ms, and no requests were rejected. Image transfers were processed within 1124 ms (averaging 1000 ms) for 90% of requests.
- **Data loss risk:** Hardware or software failures can lead to the loss of sensitive and critical data.
  - **Measures:** Implementation of robust backup and recovery mechanisms, utilization of transaction logs for data recovery to a consistent state, and use of highly available databases.
- **Authentication mechanism and authorization abuse risk:** Weak passwords, inadequate session security, or errors in authentication implementation can lead to unauthorized access to sensitive data and system functions. Users or processes may gain access to more information or functions than necessary for their roles.
  - **Measures:** Implementation of a strong password policy (password generation), secure session management, regular security audits, introduction of the principle of least privilege, and regular reviews of access rights with detailed audit logs.
- **Input vulnerability risk:** Unsanitized inputs to the application can be exploited for injection attacks (SQL injection, script injection).
  - **Measures:** Implementation of strict rules for input validation and sanitization, use of secure libraries for database operations, and regular security testing.
- **Data transmission security breach risk:** Data transmitted between client and server or between server components can be intercepted or modified.
  - **Measures:** Use of **encryption (TLS/SSL)** for all data transmissions and regular updates and configuration of security certificates.
- **Insufficient scalability and compatibility risk:** With an increasing number of users and data volume, the current infrastructure may become insufficient. The integration server may not be compatible with various external information systems.
  - **Measures:** Implementation of cloud technologies for better scalability, capacity planning, and infrastructure redundancy. Standardization of data formats, regular API updates and maintenance.
- **Software bug and hardware failure risk:** The possibility of bugs in the software or hardware component failures can affect the system's functionality and security.
  - **Measures:** Thorough testing before deployment, continuous maintenance and software updates, establishment of processes for rapid bug fixes. Use of redundant systems and hardware, preventive maintenance, and reliability testing.

- **Non-compliance with regulatory and legal requirements risk:** Failure to comply with current legal and regulatory requirements in the field of health information protection and cybersecurity.
  - **Measures:** Regular reviews of legal requirements, establishment of compliance processes, and employee training.
- **Increased burden on hospital specialists:** As the number of consultations grows, there's a significant risk of overwhelming existing specialists in hospitals. This could lead to a decline in the quality of care, longer waiting times, and burnout among staff.
  - **Measures:** Establish and operate a specialized online clinic—creating a dedicated virtual clinic would allow for more efficient resource allocation and reduce the direct burden on hospital departments. This clinic would leverage telemedicine tools to provide consultations and advice.
  - **Standardize processes and utilize artificial intelligence (AI):** Implementing clear triage protocols (patient prioritization) and employing/utilizing AI for pre-screening of inquiries or automating routine tasks (e.g. generating answers to frequently asked questions) could significantly decrease administrative load and time consumption.
  - **Staff training and education:** Providing regular training for medical personnel in telemedicine, digital communication, and efficient time management within an online environment.
  - **Optimize digital tools**: Ensuring that the systems used are user-friendly and minimize the need for manual data entry, thereby reducing the time burden on specialists. Integrate the online clinic with existing hospital systems for seamless information exchange.

6.2 Potential for System Expansion and Integration with Other Tools

The system is designed with an open architecture, allowing its **easy expansion** to other areas of home care. This may include:

- Remote monitoring of vital signs of patients.
- **Integration with pharmacies** for drug delivery or pharmacist consultations.
- **Expansion to other specialties** and types of consultations, such as nutritional counselling.

6.3 Future Use of Artificial Intelligence in the Project

As mentioned, the full potential of the integration server will be realized with the future involvement of **artificial intelligence (AI)**. Potential applications include:

- **Development of a "suggestion tool":** A tool that, based on analysed image data and clinical reports, could in some cases replace a specialist for initial consultations, providing basic recommendations and triage. The use of high-quality and standardized images from the "wound photo documentation guide" is crucial for training such an AI model.
- **Predictive analytics:** AI could monitor the progression of conditions over time and predict potential complications based on the image database and clinical records.
- **Improved triage in emergency admissions:** Photographs of patients' wounds at home, when transferred to the hospital, can facilitate triage in the emergency department without the need to physically expose the wound. Standardized photo documentation increases the relevance of these images for clinical decision-making.

6.4 Role of Policy and Funding in Supporting and Scaling Telemedicine Solutions

The sustainability and scalability of telemedicine solutions, such as the UHO integration server, depend significantly on **support from health policy and the availability of funding**. It is crucial that the regulatory framework keeps pace with technological developments and supports innovations that can improve the accessibility and quality of care.

7 Conclusion

The integration server developed by the University Hospital Olomouc represents a **significant step forward in the digitalization and modernization of home care** in the Czech Republic. This project, co-financed by the Olomouc Region, is a **functional and scalable model** for maintaining and improving care, especially for the elderly, in the context of a growing shortage of qualified personnel.

The combination of **digital tools** (ZUNI application, integration server, UHO Portal), **interdisciplinary cooperation** (UHO, eSestřička, Olomouc Region), and **practical needs** in the field demonstrates how to effectively respond to structural changes in society and the distribution of the workforce. The system not only **improves the quality and accessibility of care** but also contributes to the **professional development and education** of healthcare workers in the field, which is crucial for long-term sustainability. In this context, the **wound photo documentation guide** is an invaluable tool that ensures the collection of high-quality data, essential for the efficiency of the entire telemedicine system and its future development.

Moving forward, building a truly innovative ageing and health policy requires a holistic and integrated approach. This involves not only continued investment in cutting-edge digital technologies but also a concerted effort to refine regulatory frameworks, secure sustainable funding mechanisms, and cultivate a digitally competent and interdisciplinary workforce. By addressing these interconnected challenges strategically, the Czech Republic can leverage the full potential of digital health and telemedicine to create a healthcare system that is better equipped to meet the complex needs of its ageing population, ensuring high-quality, accessible, and sustainable care for generations to come.

The vision of telemedicine as a **standard part of home care** is much closer to reality with this project. The future integration of advanced technologies, such as **artificial intelligence**, will further enhance the system's capabilities and enable more efficient and personalized care. The UHO integration server is thus an exemplary case of how **innovation and technology** can transform healthcare and ensure **sustainable care** for the ageing population.

Reference

Šeflová, L., Stanke, L., Habáňová, J., Baslarová, B., Tichá, J., et al. (2024). *Návod k fotodokumentaci ran*. Univerzita Palackého v Olomouci. ISBN 978-80-244-6422-0.

Digital Social Innovation for Active Aging: TrentinoSalute+, a Case Study of Participatory Health Promotion

Diego Conforti, Martina Dell'Eva, and Diego Ponte

1 Introduction

The progressive aging of the global population is an unprecedented phenomenon in human history. According to Eurostat data, over 21.3% of the European Union's population was over 65 in 2023, with projections estimating this figure will exceed 30% by 2050 (Eurostat, 2023). This demographic shift accompanies an increased incidence of chronic diseases and evolving healthcare needs. Indeed, while increased life expectancy is a civilizational achievement, it also leads to a need for long-term care, placing significant pressure on healthcare systems (Buyl et al., 2020). This trend presents governments and health authorities with one of the most complex and urgent challenges: ensuring excellent quality of life and good health for this growing demographic. As highlighted by the World Health Organization (WHO), over 70% of premature deaths are attributable to modifiable behaviors (WHO, 2021), underscoring the urgent need for tools that incentivize healthy lifestyles. This demands an efficient healthcare response and a rethinking of governance models, prevention strategies, and civic participation.

D. Conforti
Office of Innovation and Research, Department of Health and Social Policies, Autonomous Province of Trento, Executive Committee of TS4.0 Digital Health Competence Center, Trento, Italy
e-mail: diego.conforti@provincia.tn.it

M. Dell'Eva (✉)
TS4.0 Digital Health Competence Center, Fondazione Bruno Kessler, Trento, Italy
e-mail: mdelleva@fbk.eu

D. Ponte
Department of Economics and Management, University of Trento, Trento, Italy
e-mail: diego.ponte@unitn.it

A. Ricciardelli, L. Mercurio (eds.), *Building Innovation in Ageing and Health Policy*, Springer Series in Healthcare Management and Innovation,
https://doi.org/10.1007/978-3-032-09163-5_7

The concept of healthy aging, promoted by the WHO, centers public policies on individuals' ability to live autonomous, active, and healthy lives for as long as possible (WHO, 2020a, 2020b). In this context, public policies have a crucial opportunity to leverage digital tools as a strategic means to support and improve the health of older adults (Stokes et al., 2017).

Digitalization in health—the set of processes that use digital technologies to improve individual and collective health—represents a strategic leverage to address the challenges associated with aging (Husebø et al., 2021).

The application of digital technologies to social challenges to produce innovative and inclusive solutions is linked to digital social innovation (Certomà & Corsini, 2021; Cosimato et al., 2024). Digital social innovation (DSI) in healthcare can be found in a wide range of solutions: from telemedicine and teleassistance to remote monitoring systems, e-health platforms for the management of electronic health records, apps for well-being, and dedicated social networks that promote inclusion (Batko, 2023). These innovations promise to optimize access to care, reduce the need for hospital admissions, promote the autonomy of older adults, and facilitate their active participation in society (Alruwaili et al., 2023). For example, using smart sensors for fall detection or wearable devices for monitoring vital signs can enable proactive care and timely intervention, contributing to "healthy aging" in the home environment (Nautiyal et al., 2022).

Scientific literature shows that the effective realization of DSI does not happen in isolation; instead, it thrives within complex and interconnected ecosystems. These DSI ecosystems comprise a dynamic network of actors collaborating, sharing resources, and co-creating solutions.

However, despite the potential, empirical evidence on the long-term effectiveness and large-scale impact of these digital solutions in promoting the well-being of older adults remains conflicting and requires further research, especially for rural and mountainous areas (Fahmi & Arifianto, 2022; Zerrer & Sept, 2020). This paper intends to reduce this gap by presenting the TrentinoSalute+ DSI initiative, a research and development project transforming the healthcare system for older adults towards a digital one in the Autonomous Province of Trento in northern Italy. In particular, the paper focuses on the efforts the local DSI ecosystem made to develop and foster *Salute+*, an app aiming to offer innovative health and well-being services for older adults in line with the World Health Organization principles.

This paper is organized as such. Section 2 introduces the concept of digital social innovation. Section 3 describes the methodology used for the case study. Section 4 describes the case study. Sections 5 and 6 discuss and conclude this paper.

2 Background

DSI is a powerful paradigm where digital technologies are collaboratively harnessed to address pressing societal challenges and foster collective well-being. It involves strategically deploying digital tools to develop and implement innovative products, services, processes, and business models to enhance societal well-being, primarily resolving social and environmental challenges (Eckhardt et al., 2017). It is fundamentally a form of collaborative innovation where innovators, users, and communities leverage the inherent network effects of the Internet to co-create knowledge and solutions for a broad spectrum of social needs (Misuraca & Pasi, 2019). More specifically, DSI involves the strategic deployment of digital tools to develop and implement innovative products, services, processes, and business models to enhance society's well-being.

DSI manifests in various forms, including digital citizenship projects, civic crowdsourcing platforms, fab labs, and maker spaces that foster bottom-up innovation and the use of big data to analyze and solve complex problems. These approaches are often driven by communities, nonprofit organizations, and social startups, leveraging connectivity and knowledge sharing to create innovative and inclusive solutions. The key to DSI lies in its ability to mobilize resources, facilitate participation, and accelerate the dissemination of ideas while promoting a more open and distributed innovation model.

2.1 Key Elements of Digital Social Innovation

Beyond the technological and "openness" dimensions introduced above, scientific literature highlights additional key elements characterizing DSI:

- *Social Impact Orientation:* The primary aim of DSI is not profit, but rather the resolution of social and environmental challenges, often aligning with the United Nations Sustainable Development Goals (SDGs). This perspective is crucial for distinguishing DSI from other forms of digital innovation (Bria et al., 2015; Murray et al., 2010).
- *Bottom-Up Collaboration and Participation:* DSI is frequently driven by communities, citizens, civil society organizations, and smaller stakeholders. Innovation is not top-down but emerges from shared needs and ideas, emphasizing the role of co-creation and citizen empowerment (Leadbeater & Winhall, 2022; Von Hippel, 2005).
- *Iterative and Flexible Process:* DSI solutions evolve through cycles of experimentation, feedback, and adaptation, reflecting the complexity of the social problems they aim to address. This agile, nonlinear approach is characteristic of social and digital innovation (Bason, 2010; Mulgan, 2006).
- *Scalability and Replicability:* Many DSI projects seek to develop solutions that can be adopted and adapted across diverse contexts, maximizing their potential impact. The ability to "scale up" innovation is vital for tackling broad social challenges (Phills et al., 2008).
- *Open and Inclusive Governance Models:* The management and development of DSI initiatives often reflect values of openness and participation, involving diverse stakeholders in decision-making processes. This fosters transparency and enhances the acceptance of solutions (Ansell & Gash, 2008; Emerson et al., 2012; Tapscott & Williams, 2008).

- *Sustainability (Economic and Social):* While not profit-driven, DSI initiatives must establish sustainable models to maintain operations and generate impact over time. This includes seeking diversified funding, engaging volunteers, and building resilient networks (Nicholls, 2009; Pol & Ville, 2009).

2.2 The Role of the Ecosystem

While DSI holds immense promise at conceptual, practical, and pragmatic levels for addressing social issues, understanding this complex and rapidly evolving phenomenon is still nascent, especially considering the multifaceted and interconnected ecosystem needed to support it. DSI ecosystems are comprised of a dynamic network of actors—including individuals, communities, civil society organizations, social enterprises, tech startups, research institutions, local and national governments, and foundations—who collaborate, share resources, and co-create solutions. Their effectiveness hinges on accessible digital infrastructures, supportive policies encouraging open innovation and collaboration, and flexible funding mechanisms.

The strength of a DSI ecosystem lies in its ability to lower barriers to innovation, amplify the social impact of digital initiatives, and support the replicability and scalability of solutions through intersectoral and transdisciplinary collaboration (Carayannis & Campbell, 2012).

While these DSIs show potential, the available empirical evidence regarding their sustained effectiveness and broader impact on older adult health remains mixed and warrants additional research. This paper contributes to this literature by presenting the case study of TrentinoSalute+ DSI initiative and the *Salute* + app, which aims to offer innovative health and well-being services for older adults.

3 Methodology

We adopted a case study approach to understand and analyze the implementation of the TrentinoSalute+ project as an example of DSI in health and healthy-lifestyle promotion. The primary goal of the TrentinoSalute+ project is the design, implementation, and real experimentation of the *Salute* + app to offer innovative health and well-being services for older adults, focusing on guiding users through self-assessment, awareness-building, and adoption of healthy lifestyles. At the same time, the project strategically targets younger cohorts who, while currently not in need of healthcare services, represent future users of digital health systems. By familiarizing them early with digital health promotion and lifestyle monitoring tools, TrentinoSalute+ aims to cultivate digital health literacy and preventive habits from a young age. This early engagement is crucial to ensure that, if and when they face chronic conditions later in life, they will be more inclined and better equipped to adopt digital solutions such as health apps and telemedicine services proactively and informally.

The project unfolds in the TrentinoSalute4.0 (TS4.0) Competence Center (PAT, 2016), a strategical alliance among the Autonomous Province of Trento (PAT) as decision/policy-maker, the local Healthcare Trust (APSS) as health service provider, and the Bruno Kessler Foundation (FBK) as internationally-known research institute in the area of technological innovation, coordinated by an inter-institutional steering committee. We analyzed the development of the TrentinoSalute+ project, investigating:

- The project's organizational architecture (PAT, FBK, APSS, and TS4.0).
- The participatory governance logic of the steering committee.
- The technical and organizational implementation of the *Salute* + mobile app.

The analysis delved into the roles of the TS4.0 Competence Center, the associations involved in promoting local health and healthy lifestyle initiatives, the networks of actors activated within the territory (municipalities, project managers, community nurses, voluntary organizations, private businesses, individual citizens), and the characteristics of the app as an enabling technological and digital tool.

A pilot project was launched in the Val di Sole Valley, a rural area in Trentino with approximately 12,000 residents, more than 20% of whom are over 65 years old, making it a particularly relevant context for experimenting with digital health tools for aging populations. This small-scale, community-based implementation allowed the project team to test the app's effectiveness in a real-world setting characterized by demographic aging, geographic dispersion, and limited access to health services, while also engaging local stakeholders in a participatory and iterative innovation process. The choice of Val di Sole was also strategically motivated by the fact that the area had been designated as the second "inner area" in the Province of Trento within the National Strategy for Inner Areas (SNAI), a national policy for territorial cohesion aimed at counteracting marginalization and demographic decline in remote areas of Italy. Within this framework, TrentinoSalute+ was identified as a key intervention aligned with one of the pillars of the strategy, specifically related to services for health, well-being, and personal development, and focused on primary prevention and the promotion of healthy lifestyles, through the deployment of e/mHealth tools such as the *Salute* + app.

We employed a qualitative approach based on:

- Informal discussions with key institutional informants (e.g., members of PAT, FBK, healthcare professionals, representatives of local associations) to explore governance dynamics and the perceived impact of the project.
- Direct observation during workshops, steering committee meetings, and field activities in Val di Sole, to understand co-design practices, user involvement, and the app's impact on increased individual awareness and community activation.
- Documentary analysis of provincial resolutions, project materials, and internal reports provided by the TS4.0 Center.

This methodological design allowed for the triangulation of information, enabling a comprehensive reconstruction of the conception, experimentation, and consolidation processes of the TrentinoSalute+ project, situating it within the theoretical framework of DSI.

4 The Case Study

The Autonomous Province of Trento offers a unique environment for piloting innovative public health models. Despite being a mountainous region with a relatively elderly population (over 22% aged 65+, Istat, 2024) and uneven demographic distribution, the province stands out for its institutional and technological innovation capacity, bolstered by special autonomy and excellent research centers. These conditions enabled the adoption of a 2015–2025 Health Plan, which emphasizes an intersectoral approach, lifelong well-being promotion, and a One Health perspective (PAT, 2015).

Within this strategic framework, TrentinoSalute+ was launched in 2018 (PAT, 2018) and re-launched in 2023 (PAT, 2023b) as a strategic project for the macro-objective "More Years of Healthy Life." The project addresses evolving health needs driven by an aging population and the rising incidence of chronic diseases, which demand more proactive, effective, and accessible prevention models. This project marks a strategic shift from conventional health promotion as it aims to provide the entire Trentino population with personalized action plans, designed to foster healthier lifestyles. The approach focuses on citizen empowerment, utilizing cutting-edge eHealth technologies and a sophisticated and diverse incentive system. This system integrates various nonpublic stakeholders, ensuring a comprehensive and collaborative drive towards improved public health outcomes.

TrentinoSalute+ is designed as a participatory project that aligns with DSI principles. It aims to generate social impact and collective well-being. The central objective is to foster citizen empowerment, enabling individuals to make informed health choices through personalized digital pathways that combine education, motivation, and tangible rewards. The *Salute* + app, the project's technological core, is an app that allows users to engage in many activities. Three key activities are:

1. Self-assessment:

The user experience with the *Salute* + app begins with a structured self-assessment phase, crucial for fostering initial awareness and engagement. Through a validated digital questionnaire, users are guided to reflect on their daily lifestyle about key behavioral risk factors: physical activity, nutrition, alcohol consumption, and smoking. The app processes these responses to generate a personalized user profile, the starting point for defining a tailored improvement path.

Based on this profile, users are invited to undertake one or more "health challenges." These challenges are designed according to behavioral design principles (Fogg, 2009) and digital behavior change interventions (Michie et al., 2017). Each challenge lasts 28 days and is crafted to stimulate small, incremental, and realistic changes, considering individual characteristics and adequate margins for improvement.

Users receive regular notifications, dynamic feedback, and micro-educational content during the challenges to support them on a continuous learning and change journey. The approach is based on noncoercive, persuasive logic, aiming to strengthen self-efficacy and intrinsic motivation, avoid blame, and foster control and autonomy. Every progress made is recognized and valued, contributing to building a positive and rewarding self-care experience. In this way, the self-assessment phase is not just an initial measurement tool; it triggers a dynamic journey of awareness, motivation, and change, where the user becomes an active protagonist in their health.

2. App usage, incentive systems, and funding of other social projects:

A distinguishing and innovative feature of the *Salute* + app is its dual incentive system. This system is designed to foster individual engagement and activate the creation of shared value within the community. This mechanism operates on two interconnected levels:

1. Individual Incentives (Receiving): These consist of vouchers, discounts, or gifts that the project's partner companies offer for goods and services related to health and a healthy lifestyle. These incentives are awarded to users who consistently use the app and monitor their healthy lifestyle progress. These tangible benefits strengthen personal motivation and create a sense of accomplishment, aligning with behavioral science principles that suggest small, immediate rewards can sustain long-term change.
2. Social Incentives (Giving): These introduce a collective and civic dimension of motivation. As users advance on their health journeys, they accumulate "social points" that can be donated to support projects proposed by nonprofit organizations. These projects focus on innovative or experimental activities promoting healthy lifestyles and social inclusion. Once a predetermined threshold is reached, the selected project receives public funding. This creates a participatory circuit where individual actions contribute to shared outcomes, embodying a shared social value logic (Porter & Kramer, 2011).

This second dimension proves particularly effective in promoting civic responsibility, collective accountability, and interdependence between individuals and communities. It aligns personal well-being with collective benefit, transforming daily health actions into tangible support for the local ecosystem. Through consistent app usage, three innovative initiatives promoted by local associations have been funded, showcasing the project's potential to generate local engagement and create both socio-health and economic value. The funded initiatives offer concrete examples of this impact:

- "La mia valle" ("My Valley") is an inclusive audiovisual workshop that engages individuals with physical and mental disabilities in the collaborative creation of a short film. Beyond promoting digital creativity and providing expressive skills, the project fostered emotional expression, social inclusion, and self-esteem among participants. This initiative demonstrated how health encompasses relational, emotional, and psychological dimensions. The project was a tangible opportunity to raise community awareness about inclusion and valuing diversity. It promoted a culture of respect, participation, and recognizing people with disabilities as active resources. The workshop, therefore, became a space for cohesion and change, strengthening the social fabric and stimulating collective reflection on the centrality of accessibility and participation for everyone's well-being.
- "Un orto da 0 a 99" ("A Garden from 0 to 99") is a community-managed urban garden initiative that brought together children, seniors, and volunteers. This project was designed as a collaborative effort to promote health, nutritional education, and social integration. The activities aimed to provide participants with access to information and resources for adopting a balanced and healthy diet, with particular attention to the nutritional needs of children, seniors, and residents of the involved nursing home. Beyond its educational aspects, the garden served as a gathering place for generations, fostering interaction among diverse community groups and helping to combat social isolation. Through hands-on work and theoretical learning sessions, participants deepened their understanding of health, nutrition, and environmental care. The experience was further enriched by outdoor walks and nature activities, which encouraged mobility and physical-mental well-being, strengthening participants' connection to the environment and their sense of community belonging.
- "Insieme a tavola" ("Together at the Table"), this initiative combined nutritional education with conviviality through a series of activities involving local senior clubs. It included interactive meetings with a nutritionist and culminated in a festive social dinner. A chef and the nutritionist co-designed the menu to demonstrate how it is possible to combine flavor and health, promoting the idea that a balanced diet does not mean giving up the pleasure of food. The evening also became a moment of cultural and intergenerational exchange: participants shared traditional local recipes, which were reinterpreted in a healthier and more contemporary way. By blending scientific guidance with shared experiences, the initiative fostered greater awareness of healthy eating habits and reinforced social bonds, while celebrating the culinary heritage of the community.

This outcome reflects a virtuous cycle initiated by the app that begins with individual behavioral change, extends to the empowerment and activation of the local community, and ultimately contributes to shaping a health-conscious culture that benefits future generations. *Salute* + thus operates as a digital health tool and a catalyst for long-term, community-driven transformation.

3. Health pathways and valorization of local heritage:

Among the most original features of the *Salute* + app is its "health geocaching pathways," which are mapped and integrated into the tool. These pathways combine physical activity, local exploration, and well-being promotion. Conceived as genuine "treasure hunts," these itineraries invite users to explore their surroundings, engage in outdoor movement, and rediscover significant, often undervalued, local landmarks. The place-based model strengthens users' sense of community belonging and encourages healthy behaviors. This aligns with research highlighting that geographically contextualized interventions are more effective in promoting lasting lifestyle changes (Marmot, 2010; OECD, 2020). The objective is twofold: first, to foster a culture of health through education and information; second, to provide concrete opportunities to combat sedentary lifestyles by promoting daily movement in an engaging and accessible manner. These pathways cater to both residents and tourists, and they are enriched with anecdotes, memories, and local curiosities gathered from the community, transforming the experience into a collective narrative of the territory. In close collaboration with hospitality partners, this app feature can also become a tool to promote a sustainable and healthy tourism offering, integrating health, culture, and hospitality.

Regarding indirect effects, the presence of information desks in Val di Sole municipalities, managed by local project managers, has helped build trust in the social-health system and disseminate basic digital skills, especially among the older population. Consistent interaction with operators and community nurses has created a bidirectional channel between citizens and institutions, fostering a prevention alliance that stands as one of the project's most promising elements.

4.1 Challenges

Despite positive outcomes, TrentinoSalute+ has encountered significant challenges that must be addressed for future development and model expansion. One primary barrier is the generational digital divide: even with a simplified app interface, many seniors' lack of fundamental digital skills limits autonomous use, requiring constant initial support from project managers and local health operators. This highlights the importance of complementing technological innovation with systematic digital literacy programs recommended by the European Commission to reduce inequalities (European Commission, 2019). A second challenge involved maintaining engagement over time: some users showed reduced app interaction after initial enthusiasm. Experience suggests that motivation must be continuously nourished through periodic updates, new challenges, dynamic content, and personalized interactions, consistent with digital behavior change theories emphasizing the need for constant reinforcement to foster lasting healthy behaviors (Michie et al., 2017).

Managing the incentive system organizationally demands significant administrative effort to select deserving social initiatives, monitor social points, and convert them into funding. Without adequate resources and digital management tools, this aspect risks slowing processes and reducing the effectiveness of community incentives. Strategically, a key challenge relates to scalability: replicating the model in other provincial geographic areas requires available funding, expertise, and multi-level governance capable of adapting interventions to diverse territorial contexts. A lack of structured planning for territorial and organizational expansion risks confining the initiative to a local experiment without ensuring long-term sustainability (Pol & Ville, 2009).

In summary, the challenges confirm that while technology is a powerful enabler, it is insufficient without an ecosystem of actors capable of fostering continuous engagement strategies, providing adequate organizational resources, and designing long-term strategies to scale the techno-organizational model.

5 Discussion

Literature on DSI emphasizes the importance of iterative and co-creative processes to generate effective solutions for complex problems, and TrentinoSalute+ is a fitting example of how co-design with local actors and citizens leads to innovation that addresses territorial specificities. The project's architecture demonstrates how digital innovation can serve as a leverage for a value-based system centered on individuals and the community, fostering dynamics of empowerment, collaboration, and inclusion:

- *Social Impact Orientation:* The project aims to foster a healthy lifestyle in older adults via digital solutions.
- *Bottom-up Participation:* The project is co-designed with public stakeholders, local associations, and citizens, who contribute ideas and feedback for the continuous evolution of the app and territorial initiatives.
- *Iterative and Flexible Process:* TrentinoSalute+ evolves through constant monitoring and adaptation based on emerging territorial needs, as demonstrated in the "Vivere la Salute" lab in Val di Sole, part of the National Strategy for Inner Areas (PAT, 2023a), where the app was enriched with geolocated physical activity and local discovery paths.
- *Scalability and Replicability:* The app's modularity, adaptability of pathways, and ability to integrate new content make the model exportable to other geographical and social contexts, maximizing potential impact.
- *Open and Inclusive Governance:* Coordination is entrusted to the TrentinoSalute4.0 Competence Center, which brings together the Province, APSS, and FBK into an institutional platform capable of uniting diverse actors under a collaborative governance model.
- *Sustainability*: The project aims to integrate public funds, partnerships with local businesses, and the engagement of community social capital, building a resilient ecosystem for ongoing activities.

We believe the project confirms that behavioral design techniques can be successfully applied in public contexts to incentivize healthy behaviors without resorting to coercive models, instead focusing on a persuasive and motivational approach.

The ability of TrentinoSalute+ to integrate personalized awareness and change pathways, feedback mechanisms, and a reward system linked to individual and community benefit enriches the debate on the evolution of "nudge" in health policies, shifting the focus from the individual to the collective value generated.

From a health management perspective, the project proposes a replicable model of collaborative governance: the centralized yet flexible coordination, ensured by the TrentinoSalute4.0 Competence Center, allows for integrating public entities, healthcare, associations, and businesses within an open and participatory architecture. This governance setup aligns with the collaborative governance framework (Ansell & Gash, 2008; Emerson et al., 2012) and offers operational insights for other regions intending to develop citizen-centric digital health interventions.

A further implication concerns the importance of the territorial component: the success of activities in Val di Sole demonstrates that adaptation to local needs and resources is a key element for intervention effectiveness. This implies activating local stakeholder networks, investing in social capital, and combining technological and relational dimensions, as recommended by OECD place-based strategies (2020).

Looking ahead, TrentinoSalute+ presents numerous opportunities for evolution to strengthen its impact and sustainability. One possibility involves integrating some components of the *Salute* + app with the provincial digital health ecosystem, allowing for a continuum between prevention, monitoring, and care. This would pave the way for personalized medicine pathways, where behavioral and lifestyle information informs shared therapeutic plans between patients, general practitioners, and community nurses. Another strategic direction is using artificial intelligence to develop even more accurate personalized suggestions, based on predictive analysis of individual behaviors and adaptive models that evolve with user preferences and performance. Such functionalities could help maintain high motivation and improve the effectiveness of behavioral change interventions. In terms of scalability, a key objective is to extend the pilot to the entire provincial territory and subsequently to other Italian geographical areas, replicating the model in contexts characterized by low population density and difficulty accessing services. This will require significant investment in financial resources, widespread digital skills, and institutional leadership capable of coordinating multiple administrative and healthcare levels. Development prospects include forging new public-private partnerships with companies promoting health and sustainability. Involving economic actors can expand the incentive system and strengthen economic sustainability, aligning with shared value models (Porter & Kramer, 2011). Simultaneously, it will be crucial to consolidate networks with associations, schools, pharmacies, and third-sector organizations to embed the project within social fabrics and encourage the participation of at-risk groups. Finally, a crucial perspective involves impact evaluation, which must evolve towards integrated metrics capable of measuring not only individual outcomes but also effects on social cohesion, institutional trust, and collective well-being. Developing specific assessment frameworks for Digital Social Innovation in healthcare will be a fundamental step towards making digital prevention a stable and replicable leverage for public health.

6 Conclusions

The TrentinoSalute+ project in the Autonomous Province of Trento is a compelling case study illustrating how DSI can effectively address population aging and promote healthy lifestyles within a real-world context. The project's success is rooted in a participatory organizational model that involves close collaboration between public institutions, local health authorities, multidisciplinary professionals, the third sector, and citizens, emphasizing co-creation and active involvement of local associations for rooting and sustainability. TrentinoSalute+ promotes healthy lifestyles through several key mechanisms:

- *Personalized Pathways and Behavior Change:* The *Salute +* app offers a gradual path for users to increase awareness of their lifestyle quality and improve it by pursuing personalized goals. It utilizes "health challenges" built on behavioral design principles and digital behavior change interventions, integrating notifications, feedback, and personalized educational content to boost user motivation.
- *Dual Incentive System for Shared Social Value:* A distinctive feature is its dual incentive system, offering both individual rewards (vouchers, discounts) and "social points" that the users can allocate to community projects. This mechanism activates a system of shared social value, fostering local engagement and generating socio-health and economic value for the community.
- *Strengthening Social and Community Dimensions:* The project significantly strengthens social support networks, particularly in rural and mountain contexts. Funded initiatives like "La mia valle," "Un orto da 0 a 99," and "Insieme a tavola" exemplify how DSI can foster social inclusion, intergenerational interaction, nutrition education, and community bonds. Furthermore, the app's health pathways combine physical activity with valorizing local heritage, encouraging the discovery of significant locations, and enhancing a sense of belonging. This strengthens motivation and the sustainability of health practices, aligning with place-based intervention literature.
- *Digital Literacy and Trust Building:* Recognizing the "digital divide" as a significant obstacle for older populations, TrentinoSalute+ has actively worked to disseminate basic digital skills, especially among seniors, through information desks and interaction with local project managers and community nurses. This continuous interaction builds trust in the healthcare system and establishes a bidirectional channel between citizens and institutions, fostering a prevention alliance.

Despite its positive outcomes and innovative approach, TrentinoSalute+ has encountered significant challenges pertinent to broader DSI implementation. The generational digital divide remains a primary barrier, as many seniors lack the basic digital skills for autonomous app use, necessitating continuous initial support. This underscores the critical need for complementary systematic digital literacy programs alongside technological innovation. Another challenge lies in maintaining user engagement over time, suggesting that motivation requires continuous nourishment through periodic updates, new challenges, and personalized interactions. Organizationally, managing the incentive system is administratively intensive, demanding adequate resources and digital management tools to prevent process slowdowns and maintain effectiveness. Strategically, scalability and replicability are key concerns, requiring significant investment in funding, expertise, and multi-level governance to adapt interventions to diverse territorial contexts and avoid remaining a localized experiment. These challenges confirm that while technology is a powerful enabler, its impact is limited without accompanying training actions, continuous engagement strategies, adequate organizational resources, and a long-term strategic design for scaling the techno-organizational model.

The TrentinoSalute+ project contributes to the theoretical discussion on DSI applied to public health, specifically socio-health prevention and healthy lifestyle promotion. It demonstrates how DSI can evolve from abstract theory to concrete practice capable of mobilizing citizens, institutions, and communities towards common well-being objectives. The project's co-design with local actors and citizens exemplifies the importance of iterative and co-creative processes for developing effective solutions to complex problems and addressing territorial specificities. Furthermore, its centralized yet flexible collaborative governance model, coordinated by the TrentinoSalute4.0 Competence Center, offers operational insights for other regions developing citizen-centric digital health interventions. The success in Val di Sole also highlights that adaptation to local needs and resources, activating local stakeholder networks, and investing in social capital are crucial for intervention effectiveness, emphasizing the combination of technological and relational dimensions.

Looking ahead, opportunities for evolution include integrating the app with the provincial digital health ecosystem for personalized medicine pathways and exploring the use of artificial intelligence for more accurate personalized suggestions. Scaling the pilot to the entire provincial territory and other Italian geographical areas, particularly those with low population density and service access difficulties, remains a key objective, necessitating significant investment and institutional leadership. Forging new public-private partnerships and consolidating networks with associations, schools, pharmacies, and third-sector organizations are vital for long-term economic and social sustainability, aligning with shared value models. Ultimately, continuous evolution in impact evaluation frameworks will be fundamental to establishing digital prevention as a stable and replicable leverage for public health.

References

Alruwaili, M. M., Shaban, M., & Elsayed Ramadan, O. M. (2023). Digital health interventions for promoting healthy aging: A systematic review of adoption patterns, efficacy, and user experience. *Sustainability, 15*(23), 16503.

Ansell, C., & Gash, A. (2008). Collaborative governance in theory and practice. *Journal of Public Administration Research and Theory, 18*(4), 543–571.

Bason, C. (2010). *Leading public sector innovation*. Policy Press. ISBN 978-1447324270.

Batko, K. (2023). Digital social innovation based on Big Data Analytics for health and well-being of society. *Journal of Big Data, 10*(1), 171.

Bria, F., Gascó, M., & Kresin, F. (2015). Growing a digital social innovation ecosystem for Europe. In *Digital social innovation final report*. European Union. ISBN: 978-92-79-45603-9.

Buyl, R., Beogo, I., Fobelets, M., Deletroz, C., Van Landuyt, P., Dequanter, S., et al. (2020). e-Health interventions for healthy aging: A systematic review. *Systematic Reviews, 9*, 1–15.

Carayannis, E. G., & Campbell, D. F. J. (2012). Mode 3 knowledge production in the fourth helix of mode 2 to make innovation pervasive: Digital innovation ecosystems. *Journal of Innovation and Entrepreneurship, 1*(1), 1–20.

Certomà, C., & Corsini, F. (2021). Digitally-enabled social innovation. Mapping discourses on an emergent social technology. *Innovation: The European Journal of Social Science Research, 34*(4), 560–584.

Cosimato, S., Di Paola, N., & Vona, R. (2024). Digital social innovation: How healthcare ecosystems face Covid-19 challenges. *Technology Analysis & Strategic Management, 36*(8), 1763–1778.

Eckhardt, J., Kaletka, C., & Pelka, B. (2017). Inclusion through digital social innovations: modelling an ecosystem of drivers and barriers. *In International Conference on Universal Access in Human-Computer Interaction* (pp. 67–84). Cham: Springer International Publishing.

Emerson, K., Nabatchi, T., & Balogh, S. (2012). An integrative framework for collaborative governance. *Journal of Public Administration Research and Theory, 22*(1), 1–29.

European Commission. (2019). *The digital skills gap in Europe*. European Commission Report.

Eurostat. (2023). Ageing Europe—statistics on population developments. https://ec.europa.eu/eurostat/statistics-explained/index.php?title=Ageing_Europe_-_statistics_on_population_developments

Fahmi, F. Z., & Arifianto, A. (2022). Digitalization and social innovation in rural areas: A case study from Indonesia. *Rural Sociology, 87*(2), 339–369.

Fogg, B. J. (2009, April). A behavior model for persuasive design. In *Proceedings of the 4th international conference on persuasive technology* (pp. 1–7).

Husebø, A. M. L., Storm, M., Ødegård, A., Wegener, C., Aakjær, M., Pedersen, A. L., et al. (2021). Exploring social innovation (SI) within the research contexts of higher education, healthcare, and welfare services—A scoping review. *Nordic Journal of Social Research, 12*(1), 72–110.

Istat. (2024). Indicatori demografici per provincia. In *Anno 2023*. Istituto Nazionale di Statistica.

Leadbeater, C., & Winhall, J. (2022). Reframe and transform: Resourcing systems innovation. The Rockwool Foundation.

Marmot, M. (2010). *Fair society, healthy lives*. Leo Olschki. ISBN: 9788822262516.

Michie, S., Atkins, L., & West, R. (2017). *The behaviour change wheel: A guide to designing interventions*. Silverback Publishing.

Misuraca, G., & Pasi, G. (2019). Landscaping digital social innovation in the EU: Structuring the evidence and nurturing the science and policy debate towards a renewed agenda for social change. *Government Information Quarterly, 36*(3), 592–600.

Mulgan, G. (2006). The process of social innovation. *Innovations, 1*(2), 145–162.

Murray, R., Caulier-Grice, J., & Mulgan, G. (2010). *The open book of social innovation* (Vol. 24). Nesta. ISBN 978-1848750715.

Nautiyal, S., Shrivastava, A., Deka, C., & Chauhan, P. (2022). Role of digital healthcare in the well-being of elderly people: A systematic review. In *Proceedings of the 13th Indian conference on human-computer interaction* (pp. 30–41).

Nicholls, A. (2009). 'We do good things, don't we?': 'Blended value accounting' in social entrepreneurship. *Accounting, Organizations and Society, 34*(6–7), 755–769.

OECD. (2020). A territorial approach to the sustainable development goals: Synthesis report. In *OECD urban policy reviews*. OECD Publishing.

PAT. (2015). *Deliberazione della Giunta provinciale n. 2389 del 18 dicembre 2015—Piano per la Salute 2015–2025*. Provincia autonoma di Trento.

PAT. (2016). *Deliberazione della Giunta provinciale n. 2412 del 20 dicembre 2016—Istituzione TrentinoSalute4.0*. Provincia autonoma di Trento.

PAT. (2018). *Deliberazione della Giunta provinciale n. 535 del 29 marzo 2018—TrentinoSalute+*. Provincia autonoma di Trento.

PAT. (2023a). Deliberazione della Giunta provinciale n. 600 del 6 aprile 2023—Progetto "Vivere la salute" in Val di Sole. Provincia autonoma di Trento.

PAT. (2023b). *Deliberazione della Giunta provinciale n. 674 del 21 aprile 2023—Ripresa TrentinoSalute+*. Provincia autonoma di Trento.

Phills, J. A., Jr., Deiglmeier, V., & Miller, D. T. (2008). Rediscovering social innovation. *Stanford Social Innovation Review, 6*(4), 34–43.

Pol, E., & Ville, S. (2009). Social innovation: Buzz word or enduring term? *The Journal of Socio-Economics, 38*(6), 878–885.

Porter, M., & Kramer, M. (2011). *The Big Idea: Creating Shared Value; How to reinvent capitalism—and unleash a wave of innovation and growth*. Harvard Business Review.

Stokes, M., Baeck, P., & Baker, T. (2017). *What next for digital social innovation*. European Union. ISBN: 978-1-84875-160-6.

Tapscott, D., & Williams, A. D. (2008). *Wikinomics: How mass collaboration changes everything*. Penguin.

Von Hippel, E. (2005). *Democratizing innovation*. MIT Press.

WHO. (2020a). *Decade of healthy ageing 2020–2030*. World Health Organization.

WHO. (2020b). *Noncommunicable diseases: Key facts*. World Health Organization.

WHO. (2021). *Noncommunicable diseases*. World Health Organization.

Zerrer, N., & Sept, A. (2020). Smart villagers as actors of digital social innovation in rural areas. *Urban Planning, 5*(4), 78–88.

Falls Prevention: A Multidimensional and Intersectoral Approach—The AGE-IT Approach

Antonio Picone, Angela Palomba, Rossana Gnasso,
Ayda Tavakkolifar, and Carlo Ruosi

1 Background

Italy, like many other developed nations, faces a rapidly aging population. This demographic shift increases the prevalence of age-related health conditions. One of the most important elderly-related health issues is sarcopenia (Cruz-Jentoft & Sayer, 2019; Rosenberg, 1997).

Sarcopenia is a degenerative loss of skeletal muscle mass and its function. The term sarcopenia (from the Greek sarx = flesh and penia = loss) was first introduced by Rosenberg et al. in 1989 to describe the age-related progressive loss of muscle mass. Since then, the definition has evolved to include declines in muscle strength and physical performance. Age-related muscle strength reduction contributes to functional impairment and is linked to increased morbidity and mortality through mechanisms such as falls, reduced quality of life, depression, and hospitalization (Cruz-Jentoft et al., 2019; Cruz-Jentoft & Sayer, 2019; Invernizzi et al., 2018; Rosenberg, 1997).

With the global rise in life expectancy and the growing elderly population, sarcopenia and its comorbidities have become more significant due to their disabling impact. Early definitions focused solely on muscle mass loss, but more recent updates—especially from the European Working Group on Sarcopenia in Older People (EWGSOP2)—highlight muscle strength as the primary diagnostic marker, complemented by reductions in muscle quantity and physical performance (Cruz-Jentoft et al., 2019).

A. Picone (✉) · A. Palomba · R. Gnasso · A. Tavakkolifar · C. Ruosi
Department of Public Health, University of Naples Federico II, Naples, Italy
e-mail: antonio.picone@unina.it; angela.palomba@unina.it; rossana.gnasso@unina.it; tavakkolifar.ayda@unina.it; carlo.ruosi@unina.it

A. Ricciardelli, L. Mercurio (eds.), *Building Innovation in Ageing and Health Policy*, Springer Series in Healthcare Management and Innovation,
https://doi.org/10.1007/978-3-032-09163-5_8

Pathophysiologically, sarcopenia involves both quantitative and qualitative degeneration of muscle tissue (Brown et al., 2016).

Clinically, patients experience muscle weakness, fatigue, slow gait, poor balance, and a tendency to fall, all of which increase the risk of fractures, immobility, and subsequent hospitalization. Sarcopenia is also closely linked with osteoporosis, as the muscle-bone interaction—known as the "bone-musk unit"—is crucial for maintaining skeletal integrity. Muscle deterioration disrupts mechanical bone remodeling, raising fragility and fracture risk.

After age 40, a healthy adult loses about 8% of muscle mass every 10 years, reaching an overall reduction of around 24% by age 70. This rate accelerates by 15% each decade afterward. However, lifelong physical activity can lessen this decline, highlighting the role of exercise in preventing or delaying sarcopenia. Sedentary lifestyles, inactivity, or immobilization are not inevitable parts of aging but modifiable risk factors.

The EWGSOP2 diagnostic algorithm, widely used in Italy, recommends a stepwise approach called F-A-C-S:

- F (Find cases): Use of the SARC-F questionnaire or clinical suspicion to identify at-risk individuals.
- A (Assess): Measure muscle strength through grip strength (<27 kg in men; <16 kg in women) or the chair stand test (>15 s for five repetitions).
- C (Confirm): Confirm sarcopenia by measuring low muscle mass with DXA (cutoffs: <7.0 kg/m^2 in men; <6.0 kg/m^2 in women).
- S (Severity): Assess severity using functional performance tests:

  Gait speed (<0.8 m/s)
  Short Physical Performance Battery (SPPB) (<8 points)
  Time Up and Go (TUG) test (≥20 s)
  4-Min Walk Test (>6 min)

While several imaging methods—such as bioelectrical impedance analysis (BIA), dual-energy X-ray absorptiometry (DEXA), CT, and MRI—are used to evaluate muscle mass, none are currently considered definitive gold standards due to variable sensitivity and specificity.

Lastly, EWGSOP2 proposes a three-tier classification of sarcopenia based on combinations of reduced muscle mass and physical impairment to guide diagnosis and treatment planning. One of the most significant consequences of sarcopenia is an increased risk of falls, which can lead to functional decline, hospitalization, and reduced quality of life.

The incidence of fall-related injuries, especially proximal femoral fractures (FFP), is rising steadily in Italy. These injuries predominantly affect individuals over 65 years old, with 84.9% of cases occurring in those over 75, reflecting increased prevalence of osteoporosis and age-related frailty.

Falls not only increase the risk of mortality in older adults but also, like sarcopenia, cause a significant decline in function and loss of autonomy, leading to increased rates of institutionalization.

2 Proximal Femur Fractures and the 2021 Guidelines Issued by the Italian Society of Orthopedics and Traumatology

Proximal femur fractures (PFFs) are among the most significant health challenges in geriatric orthopedics, especially in countries with aging populations like Italy. These injuries often result from low-energy trauma, usually falls, and are closely linked to conditions such as osteoporosis and sarcopenia. The incidence of PFFs increases sharply with age, particularly among postmenopausal women (https://siot.it/lineeguida-fratturafemore2021/).

Based on epidemiologic data from the general population, the risk of fractures is projected to rise significantly by 2050. This demographic trend intensifies the clinical and economic burden of PFFs, impacting hospitalizations, long-term care, mortality, and healthcare resource allocation (Luo, 2025).

In response, Italian Society of Orthopedics and Traumatology (SIOT) published comprehensive national guidelines in 2021 for diagnosing, surgically managing, and providing postoperative care for elderly patients with PFFs. These guidelines aim to standardize care, reduce variability in clinical practice, and improve outcomes through a multidisciplinary, evidence-based approach.

Prompt and accurate diagnosis is essential for effective fracture management. According to SIOT guidelines, initial imaging should include anteroposterior and axial X-rays of the hip. In certain cases, MRI is also recommended. If MRI is unavailable, a CT scan may be an alternative.

Timely surgical intervention is strongly emphasized by SIOT guidelines. Patients should ideally undergo surgery within 24–48 h of hospital admission. Early surgery is associated with lower mortality rates, fewer pressure ulcers, better pain control, and higher chances of regaining pre-fracture functional status. Clinical delays are only justified if there are correctable medical conditions, such as severe anemia or other critical health issues.

Based on the SIOT guideline, pain management is a crucial aspect of care for PFF patients. The guidelines recommend a multimodal approach, integrating both systemic and regional analgesia. Peripheral nerve blocks (PNBs), such as femoral nerve block and fascia iliaca block, are preferred due to their effectiveness in reducing pain at rest and during movement, without the systemic side effects commonly associated with opioids.

A defining feature of the SIOT guideline is its endorsement of the orthogeriatric model, which involves coordinated care among orthopedic surgeons, geriatricians, anesthesiologists, nurses, physiotherapists, and social services. This approach improves the management of comorbidities, reduces complications, shortens hospital stays, and enhances functional outcomes.

It is important to note that the SIOT 2021 guideline and the AGE-IT project are complementary strategies aimed at addressing the challenges posed by Italy's rapidly aging population. While the SIOT provides evidence-based clinical protocols for managing fragility fractures, the AGE-IT project offers a broader framework to promote healthy aging, focusing more on predicting fall and fracture risks and encouraging technological innovations (such as digital fall risk screening) to strengthen community resilience. In our AGE-IT project, we will focus on a group of individuals who have experienced a fall but without fractures, as this project emphasizes prediction and prevention of falls.

3 SUNFRAIL+: A Digital Multidimensional Model for Early Frailty Detection in Older Adults

The SUNFRAIL+ protocol represents a significant advancement in proactive management of frailty among older adults, especially those living in the community. Developed as an ICT-supported, multidimensional assessment tool, SUNFRAIL+ is designed to identify early signs of pre-frailty by screening across biological, psychological, and social health domains. Its digital platform allows healthcare professionals to conduct structured assessments that generate specific alerts linked to validated follow-up scales, enabling timely and targeted interventions (De Luca et al., 2023).

Central to SUNFRAIL+ is its ability to support early risk screening and stratification in individuals aged 65 and older, even before overt disability appears. The protocol includes a short nine-item questionnaire that can be administered during the initial contact with the healthcare system—usually by a family nurse, general practitioner, or social care professional. Based on the responses, the system activates domain-specific assessments (e.g., nutritional status via MNA, cognitive function via GPCOG, physical performance via SPPB), facilitating an efficient and comprehensive cascade of evaluations. This enables early identification of vulnerable individuals and supports preventive strategies before more severe outcomes such as falls, hospitalization, or institutionalization occur.

A key element of the SUNFRAIL+ model is its alignment with person-centered, multidisciplinary care planning. The tool not only helps identify at-risk individuals but also guides integrated care pathways tailored to each person's needs and preferences. The active involvement of the Infermiere di Famiglia e di Comunità (IFeC)—a crucial figure in Italy's evolving primary care landscape—ensures effective coordination of services, follow-up, and patient empowerment within the community. The IFeC functions both as a clinical operator and a navigator of services, bridging health and social care through ongoing relationships with patients and families (Bernardo et al., 2022).

Moreover, SUNFRAIL+ is strategically aligned with Italy's broader efforts to reform territorial healthcare services and supports European goals for active and healthy aging. Its deployment across multiple regional reference sites—many of which participate in the European Innovation Partnership on Active and Healthy

Ageing (EIP on AHA)—demonstrates its scalability and potential to reduce health disparities. By integrating technology with human-centered practice, SUNFRAIL+ stands as a replicable model for preventive, equitable, and sustainable elderly care in modern health systems.

To address the aforementioned elderly-related conditions, the AGE-IT project proposes a multidisciplinary intervention rooted in collaboration between public institutions and private entities. This project addresses the issues with a proactive strategy by integrating biomedical, psychological, and environmental interventions. Our goal is to create a person-centered model that supports elderly patients, especially those with sarcopenia, in maintaining independence and quality of life.

4 SUNFRAIL+ and the AGE-IT: A Comparison Between the Two Projects

The SUNFRAIL+ protocol and the AGE-IT project represent two synergistic initiatives that embody a shared vision for promoting healthy aging through early, multidimensional, community-based care models.

At their core, both programs leverage Information and Communication Technology (ICT) to support proactive identification and management of frailty and sarcopenia among older adults. SUNFRAIL+, in particular, functions as a validated digital platform designed to detect early signs of vulnerability across bio-psycho-social domains, using a structured yet adaptable framework suitable for integration within primary care and community settings (De Luca et al., 2025).

AGE-IT, on the other hand, extends this framework by offering a comprehensive model of personalized interventions that include physical rehabilitation, nutritional support, motivational strategies, and environmental risk mitigation.

One of the most compelling intersections between the two initiatives lies in their commitment to early screening of pre-frailty, especially among community-dwelling older adults who may otherwise go undetected until a significant health event occurs. SUNFRAIL+ provides a scalable, user-friendly screening tool that enables frontline health professionals to flag risks early and activate more specialized assessments or interventions.

The main aim of the AGE-IT project is to develop a scalable model for fall prevention among sarcopenic elderly individuals, which aligns with broader goals of promoting healthy aging, reducing healthcare costs, and improving quality of life through inclusive, technologically supported strategies. It is important to highlight that the main objectives of the project are: (1) raising awareness of the importance of prevention; (2) identifying and evaluating risk factors and determinants of frailty, such as nutrition and physical function; (3) recognizing and implementing realistic and effective interventions; and (4) integrating rehabilitation programs with APA or adapted physical activity and current nutrition.

5 Methods and Materials

The assessment of elderly patients affected by sarcopenia within the AGE-IT framework uses a multidimensional, technology-supported evaluation approach designed to inform personalized, evidence-based rehabilitation plans. This method is based on combining several standardized and innovative tools that examine the structural and functional impacts of muscle loss, allowing for the creation of a personalized "Person Blueprint"—a dynamic clinical profile used to guide tailored interventions plans (Gentile et al., 2022; Scott et al., 2018).

In this study, we used different assessment tools and instruments to help elderly people with sarcopenia and fall prevention (Frontera, 2018). The project framework has a very specific structure. The fall prevention model was developed under Task 3.2 of the AGE-IT project, which includes: 1—Characterization of the at-risk elderly population; 2—Identification and application of innovative solutions; 3—Development and implementation of preventive interventions; 4—Clinical-functional evaluation of their efficacy; and 5—Economic-health data analysis to support sustainable models.

The target population of this project is sarcopenic elderly patients. As we mentioned before, Sarcopenia, as defined by the European Working Group on Sarcopenia in Older People (EWGSOP2), involves both decreased muscle strength and muscle mass, leading to increased vulnerability to falls. The project includes a Use Case analysis, where individual patient profiles (age, social context, comorbidities) are used to tailor interventions. We used many diverse tools and personalized instruments for this study. The Person Blueprint Tool was used to define individual needs, aligning rehabilitation with personalized goals and capacity. Upon conclusion of treatment, patients are directed toward Adapted Physical Activity (APA) programs to sustain gains (Guralnik et al., 1994).

The model utilizes a robust set of evaluation tools to assess sarcopenic elderly patients and design personalized interventions:

- Isokinetic Testing: Isokinetic dynamometry is used to objectively measure muscle strength, power, and endurance, especially during knee flexion and extension, which are essential for walking and daily activities. This method is considered the gold standard for evaluating muscle performance in clinical and research environments, offering reliable and consistent measurements that can identify subtle weaknesses often missed in manual testing (Radaelli et al., 2025; Tarantino et al., 2024; Zhang et al., 2024).
- Muscle Ultrasound: Muscle ultrasound (US) provides a noninvasive and accessible method for assessing muscle structure and trophism. It analyzes parameters such as muscle thickness, pennation angle, and echogenicity to identify structural changes related to sarcopenia, like atrophy and infiltration of noncontractile tissue. Its use is increasingly favored in geriatric assessment due to its high diagnostic value, especially when access to more costly techniques (e.g., MRI, DXA) is limited. This method evaluates muscle trophism and the structural effects of sarcopenia.

- Strength Platform: The strength platform (or force plate) is used to assess lower limb power output during tasks like sit-to-stand or jump tests. These metrics are important indicators of dynamic muscle function and are strongly linked to fall risk, functional capacity, and rehabilitation prognosis in older adults. Force-time curves generated by the platform provide valuable data on both the amplitude and velocity of force production. It mainly assesses force output during physical activity.
- Dynamometer that measures grip and limb strength accurately. Handheld and fixed dynamometry, including grip strength assessment, remains a fundamental part of sarcopenia evaluation, supported by international guidelines such as EWGSOP2. Grip strength acts as a surrogate marker for overall muscle strength and has predictive value for morbidity, disability, and mortality in elderly populations. When combined with limb-specific dynamometry, it provides a more detailed understanding of regional strength deficits achieved.
- Balance and Gait Analysis identifies deficits in stability. Balance and gait analysis systems, including instrumented walkways (also called Walker View) and wearable inertial sensors, provide quantitative evaluations of postural control, stride parameters, and gait variability. These tools are essential for identifying compensatory patterns and instability, which are hallmarks of sarcopenic progression and key contributors to fall-related injuries (Gnasso et al., 2023).
- Virtual Reality Rehabilitation Systems: Incorporating virtual reality (VR)-based rehabilitation platforms creates an interactive, adaptive, and motivating environment that boosts patient engagement while enabling real-time monitoring of performance metrics. VR applications have proven effective in improving balance, motor planning, and cognitive-motor integration, making them especially suitable for older adults with frailty or mild cognitive impairment. VR enhances engagement and outcomes in elderly rehabilitation. This personalized evaluation feeds into a Person Blueprint, used to determine specific needs, goals, and obstacles (Gnasso et al., 2023).

One of the main features of this study is its multidomain intervention strategies. In the next paragraph, we will explore other important interventions implemented in the AGE-IT project.

6 Personalized Interventions in Sarcopenia Management

Within the AGE-IT framework, developing personalized interventions for sarcopenic patients follows a multidomain approach that combines nutritional, physical, psychological, environmental, and pharmacological strategies.

These interventions align with current international guidelines and are tailored to each patient's clinical profile created through the Person Blueprint model, ensuring both precision and effectiveness in treatment planning.

Nutritional support focuses on increasing protein intake, especially essential amino acids like leucine, along with calcium, vitamin D, and omega-3 supplements to stimulate protein synthesis and reduce muscle loss. Adequate nutrition, particularly protein intake of about 1.2–1.5 g/kg/day, is fundamental in managing sarcopenia.

The model emphasizes a high-protein diet with attention to essential amino acids, especially leucine, due to its anabolic effects on muscle protein synthesis via the mTOR pathway. Vitamin D supplementation is recommended because deficiencies are common among older adults and impair muscle function. Calcium supports bone health, and omega-3 fatty acids, with their anti-inflammatory properties, may help decrease muscle breakdown and improve functional outcomes. Incorporating nutritional counseling into rehabilitation ensures that dietary advice is personalized, practical, and sustainable within the patient's socio-economic context.

Physical activity includes personalized programs with aerobic exercise, muscle strengthening, balance, and resistance training. Physical activity remains the key component in treating sarcopenia. The AGE-IT approach develops tailored training plans combining resistance exercises (to boost muscle mass and strength), aerobic workouts (to improve cardiovascular and metabolic health), balance exercises (to lower fall risk), and functional mobility tasks (to maintain independence). These programs are based on initial physical assessments and are regularly adjusted to match the patient's changing abilities. Additionally, assistive technologies, wearable sensors, and tele-rehabilitation platforms are used to support adherence and provide monitoring, enabling remote supervision and real-time feedback (Frontera, 2018).

Motivational interviewing (psychological domain) aims to boost engagement and long-term adherence to rehab routines. Motivational interviewing (MI) is a collaborative, person-centered counseling method designed to enhance an individual's internal motivation to change by resolving ambivalence and aligning treatment goals with personal values. In the AGE-IT framework, MI is integrated into standard clinical visits and delivered by trained professionals, which enhances outcomes in dietary compliance, physical activity participation, and overall health behavior changes among older adults. It's a collaborative, person-centered approach to promote behavioral change and ensure treatment adherence.

Environmental risk assessment uses questionnaires and educational materials to identify indoor and outdoor hazards. Environmental hazards, both inside and outside, significantly contribute to falls and injuries in frail seniors. The AGE-IT model incorporates structured environmental risk assessments using validated questionnaires and checklists to identify modifiable hazards like poor lighting, loose rugs, inaccessible stairs, and uneven walking surfaces. Educational efforts—delivered via printed materials, digital apps, and caregiver training—aim to raise awareness and encourage proactive safety modifications in homes and community settings.

Polypharmacy management focuses on reviewing medications, especially FRIDs (Fall-Risk Increasing Drugs), using established protocols. Because polypharmacy is common among older adults, the AGE-IT model includes a thorough medication review process, emphasizing Fall-Risk Increasing Drugs (FRIDs), such as sedatives, antihypertensives, and anticholinergics. Periodic medication reviews are conducted by clinical pharmacists and geriatricians following protocols like STOPP/

START, with the goal of deprescribing unnecessary drugs and optimizing therapy. This approach reduces fall risk and helps prevent adverse drug reactions, cognitive decline, and hospitalizations.

The abovementioned personalized interventions represent a comprehensive, interdisciplinary approach to managing sarcopenia that goes beyond traditional clinical care. By addressing biological, functional, behavioral, and environmental factors, the AGE-IT model offers a scalable and replicable example for promoting healthy aging and reducing disability in frail older adults.

7 Discussion and Conclusions

The AGE-IT project establishes a strong example for a multidisciplinary, evidence-based approach to fall prevention among older adults with sarcopenia. By integrating personalized interventions, technology-assisted assessment, and behavioral support techniques, the model provides a comprehensive and forward-looking view of aging care—shifting emphasis from reactive treatment to proactive prevention.

Fundamentally, the AGE-IT framework connects clinical care with public health by creating an integrated, person-centered model that is both scalable and adaptable. Its focus on early detection of risk factors—whether physiological, behavioral, or environmental—enables timely, targeted actions that do more than just treat symptoms; they address the root causes of frailty and falls.

Preliminary pilot data show promising results in patient adherence, functional recovery, and fall risk reduction. If these outcomes can be replicated on a larger scale, the public health impact could be substantial: fewer hospital stays, lower healthcare costs, and a better quality of life for millions of older adults. The model is designed with regional flexibility, making it suitable for gradual implementation across Italy's national health system and adaptable to similar aging populations across Europe.

A major strength of the AGE-IT approach is its multidisciplinary structure. By combining rehabilitation, nutrition, psychological support, and environmental safety into a single care plan, the model recognizes that fall risk isn't just about muscle loss or balance issues—it's also influenced by medication use, home hazards, behavioral habits, and a person's sense of control. In this context, motivational interviewing plays a crucial role, not only improving treatment adherence but also empowering older adults to actively participate in their health, bolstering self-efficacy and resilience.

However, significant challenges remain. Expanding implementation will require harmonizing healthcare services across regions, providing interprofessional training in person-centered care models, and sustained investment to maintain interventions beyond the pilot stage. Bridging these gaps is vital to unlock the full potential of this innovative model—not just as a clinical protocol but as a blueprint for healthy, dignified aging in a rapidly changing demographic landscape (Korkmaz Yaylagul et al., 2022).

Table 1 An approach to the sarcopenic patient at risk of falling

	Current clinical task	Functionalities of the supportive digital solutions
Nutritional support	Healthcare professionals suggest a standard nutritional scheme and re-valuate the patient after 1 month	A mHealth app with personalized information (weight, height, measurements, BMI), a specific nutritional plan based on patient needs and taste, suggestions and recipes for meal preparation
Psychological support	Patients are suggested to comply with medical prescriptions, nevertheless there is no specific control on what they do or how they do	Digital platforms for on-line consultations, with the possibility of remotely monitoring patients progress through everyday questions and tasks
Physical activity	Patients are suggested to start doing physical activities, nevertheless there is no specific control on what they do or how they do	Adapted physical activity, prescribed directly by a healthcare professional. A mHealth app with a videolibrary device for patient monitoring
Polypharmacy management	Health professional draw up a personalized treatment plan on taking medications which is communicated orally to the patient and printed on a paper	Shared therapeutic plan, which can be updated remotely, with alerts on drug intake times and connected via Bluetooth to a smart pill box, which allows the patient to take the right drug, at the correct time and in the correct doses
Environment	Patient receives specific questionnaires and information leaflets on environmental risk factors	Patients are guided through an app to be aware of risks and to find safe solutions

The next and final step is to create digital solutions to improve the approach to the sarcopenic patient at risk of falling (Table 1).

References

Barrea, L., de Alteriis, G., Muscogiuri, G., Vetrani, C., Verde, L., Camajani, E., Aprano, S., Colao, A., & Savastano, S. (2022). Impact of a very low-calorie ketogenic diet (VLCKD) on changes in handgrip strength in women with obesity. *Nutrients, 14*(19), 4213. https://doi.org/10.3390/nu14194213

Bernardo, J., Apóstolo, J., Loureiro, R., Santana, E., Yaylagul, N. K., Dantas, C., Ventura, F., Duque, F. M., Jøranson, N., Zechner, M., Staalduinen, W. V., De Luca, V., Illario, M., & Silva, R. (2022). eHealth platforms to promote autonomous life and active aging: A scoping review. *International Journal of Environmental Research and Public Health, 19*(23), 15940. https://doi.org/10.3390/ijerph192315940

Brown, J. C., Harhay, M. O., & Harhay, M. N. (2016). Sarcopenia and mortality among a population-based sample of community-dwelling older adults. *Journal of Cachexia, Sarcopenia and Muscle, 7*(3), 290–298.

Cruz-Jentoft, A. J., & Sayer, A. A. (2019). Sarcopenia. *Lancet, 393*, 2636–2646.

Cruz-Jentoft, A. J., et al. (2019). Writing Group for the European Working Group on Sarcopenia in Older People 2 (EWGSOP2), and the Extended Group for EWGSOP2. Sarcopenia: Revised European consensus on definition and diagnosis. *Age and Ageing, 48*(1), 16–31.

De Luca, V., Donnoli, C., Formosa, V., Carnevale, E., Bisogno, M., Patumi, L., Leonardini, L., Obbia, P., Palummeri, E., Ruatta, M., Basso, A. M., Minichini, M., Adamo, D., Bruzzese, D., Mercurio, L., Virgolesi, M., Toccoli, S., Sforzin, S., Denisi, F., Borgioli, M., Dell'Acqua, M., Cacciapuoti, V., Iaccarino, G., Liotta, G., & Illario, M. (2025). Preliminary results of a multidimensional approach to screen for frailty in community-dwelling older adults of eight Italian regions: the SUNFRAIL+ study. *Frontiers in Public Health, 13*, 1543724. https://doi.org/10.3389/fpubh.2025.1543724

De Luca, V., Femminella, G. D., Leonardini, L., Patumi, L., Palummeri, E., Roba, I., Aronni, W., Toccoli, S., Sforzin, S., Denisi, F., Basso, A. M., Ruatta, M., Obbia, P., Rizzo, A., Borgioli, M., Eccher, C., Farina, R., Conforti, D., Mercurio, L., Salvatore, E., Gentile, M., Bocchino, M., Sanduzzi Zamparelli, A., Viceconte, G., Gentile, I., Ruosi, C., Ferrara, N., Fabbrocini, G., Colao, A., Triassi, M., Iaccarino, G., Liotta, G., & Illario, M. (2023). Digital health service for identification of frailty risk factors in community-dwelling older adults: The SUNFRAIL+ study protocol. *International Journal of Environmental Research and Public Health, 20*(5), 3861. https://doi.org/10.3390/ijerph20053861

Frontera, W. R. (2018). In S. Masiero & U. Carraro (Eds.), *Physical activity and rehabilitation in elderly in rehabilitation medicine for elderly patients*. Springer International Publishing. Edition 1, Series ISSN 2509-6060.

Gentile, M., De Luca, V., Patalano, R., Laudisio, D., Tramontano, G., Lindner-Rabl, S., Mercurio, L., Salvatore, E., Farrell, J., Roller-Wirnsberger, R., Kubitschke, L., Triassi, M., Colao, A., Illario, M., & Vigour Consortium. (2022). Innovative approaches to service integration addressing the unmet needs of irritable bowel syndrome patients and new approaches for the needs of IBS patients. *Frontiers in Medicine (Lausanne), 9*, 998838. https://doi.org/10.3389/fmed.2022.998838

Gnasso, R., Palermi, S., Picone, A., Tarantino, D., Fusco, G., Messina, M. M., & Sirico, F. (2023). Robotic-assisted rehabilitation for post-stroke shoulder pain: A systematic review. *Sensors (Basel), 23*(19), 8239. https://doi.org/10.3390/s23198239

Guralnik, J. M., Simonsick, E. M., Ferrucci, L., et al. (1994). A short physical performanc battery assessing lower extremity function: Association with self-reported disability and prediction of mortality and nursing home admission. *Journal of Gerontology, 49*(2), M85–M94.

Invernizzi, M., Baricich, A., & Cisari, C. (2018). In S. Masiero & U. Carraro (Eds.), *Sarcopenia and aging in rehabilitation medicine for elderly patients*. Springer International Publishing. Edition 1, Series ISSN 2509-6060.

Korkmaz Yaylagul, N., Kirisik, H., Bernardo, J., Dantas, C., van Staalduinen, W., Illario, M., De Luca, V., Apóstolo, J., & Silva, R. (2022). Trends in telecare use among community-dwelling older adults: A scoping review. *International Journal of Environmental Research and Public Health, 19*(24), 16672. https://doi.org/10.3390/ijerph192416672

Luo, Y. (2025). Hip fractures: Clinical, biomaterial and biomechanical insights into a common health challenge. *Bioengineering (Basel), 12*(6), 580. https://doi.org/10.3390/bioengineering12060580

Radaelli, R., Rech, A., Molinari, T., Markarian, A. M., Petropoulou, M., Granacher, U., Hortobágyi, T., & Lopez, P. (2025). Effects of resistance training volume on physical function, lean body mass and lower-body muscle hypertrophy and strength in older adults: A systematic review and network meta-analysis of 151 randomised trials. *Sports Medicine, 55*(1), 167–192. https://doi.org/10.1007/s40279-024-02123-z

Rosenberg, I. H. (1997). Sarcopenia: Origins and clinical relevance. *The Journal of Nutrition, 127*, 990S–991S.

Scott, R. A., et al. (2018). Assistive technologies to overcome sarcopenia in ageing. *Maturitas, 112*(78), 84.

Tarantino, D., Forte, A. M., Picone, A., Sirico, F., & Ruosi, C. (2024). The effectiveness of a single hyaluronic acid injection in improving symptoms and muscular strength in patients with knee osteoarthritis: A multicenter, retrospective study. *Journal of Personalized Medicine, 14*(8), 784. https://doi.org/10.3390/jpm14080784

Zhang, X., Jiang, W., Chen, Z., Yang, G., & Ren, Z. (2024). Effects of Yi Jin Jing on enhancing muscle strength and physical performance in older individuals: A systematic review and meta-analysis. *Frontiers in Medicine (Lausanne), 11*, 1441858. https://doi.org/10.3389/fmed.2024.1441858

Motivational Interviewing to Promote Self-Care Behaviors Change: A Framework for Healthy Aging in Clinical Practice

Daniela Lemmo, Fabrizio Mezza, and Maria Francesca Freda

1 Introduction

Over the last century, increased life expectancy and declining birth rates have led to a significant rise in the proportion of older adults worldwide. In parallel, global health patterns have shifted: while infectious diseases remain relevant in certain regions, noncommunicable diseases (NCDs) such as cancer, diabetes, cardiovascular conditions, and neurodegenerative disorders have become increasingly prevalent (Bloom & Luca, 2016). These conditions are not solely the result of individual behaviors, but rather the cumulative outcome of complex interactions between biological vulnerability, social determinants of health, environmental exposures, access to care, and life-course events (Ogugua et al., 2024).

In response, public health strategies have shifted toward a broader vision of prevention and health promotion—one that recognizes individuals not simply as passive recipients of care, but as active participants in shaping their own well-being (Rudnicka et al., 2020). Central to this shift is the concept of Healthy Aging, defined by the WHO as "the process of developing and maintaining the functional ability that enables well-being in older age" (WHO, 2015, p. 13). This ability emerges from the interplay between intrinsic capacity—physical, cognitive, and emotional—and the surrounding environment, which can either foster or limit participation and autonomy (Beard et al., 2016).

Rather than viewing aging as a trajectory of inevitable decline, this perspective sees it as a dynamic and adaptable life phase, shaped by personal resources, cultural contexts, and social opportunities. Mobility, cognition, emotional stability, and

D. Lemmo (✉) · F. Mezza · M. F. Freda
Department of Humanities, University of Naples Federico II, Naples, Italy
e-mail: daniela.lemmo@unina.it; fabrizio.mezza@unina.it; fmfreda@unina.it

A. Ricciardelli, L. Mercurio (eds.), *Building Innovation in Ageing and Health Policy*, Springer Series in Healthcare Management and Innovation,
https://doi.org/10.1007/978-3-032-09163-5_9

relationships are not isolated indicators of health, but interconnected dimensions of a meaningful life in later age.

In this evolving landscape, self-care has emerged as a cornerstone of both policy and clinical action—a means of translating the principles of Healthy Aging into everyday practice. Defined by WHO as "the ability of individuals, families, and communities to promote health, prevent disease, and maintain well-being, with or without the support of a healthcare provider" (WHO, 2022, p. 8), self-care includes a wide range of actions—from managing medications to cultivating supportive relationships or adopting adaptive routines. Far from being a purely individual responsibility, self-care is increasingly understood as a shared and situated process, shaped by education, cultural norms, access to technologies, and systems of social support (Riegel, 2021).

Empowering self-care thus means more than transmitting knowledge: it requires creating environments where people are enabled to act in line with their values and capacities. It also entails acknowledging the structural and emotional barriers—such as poverty, digital exclusion, functional limitations, or loss of social roles—that may hinder motivation and engagement, especially in older adults (WHO, 2024). Effective person-centered interventions for promoting self-care behavior change consistently emphasize: the activation of motivation through empathic human connection; personalized approaches supported by technology and adapted to cultural contexts; social support from caregivers, family, peers, and professionals; facilitated communication between patients and healthcare providers; competency-based methods that build specific self-care skills; and policies that promote the formation of healthy habits in daily life.

2 Understanding Self-Care: A Comparative Overview of Models and Perspectives

The concept of self-care has assumed a central role in contemporary healthcare policies, sparking growing interest in the field of psychology as well. However, the plurality of definitions, models, and theoretical interpretations associated with the term has led to semantic ambiguity, hindering both conceptual integration and practical implementation (Lemmo et al., 2025a; Wilkinson & Whitehead, 2009). A primary challenge lies in the multidimensional nature of the construct: self-care encompasses a wide range of physical, cognitive, emotional, and relational practices, which may vary significantly depending on clinical context, age, and individual circumstances.

A second layer of complexity stems from the multiple disciplines that have addressed self-care—medicine, nursing, public health, psychology, sociology, and educational sciences—each contributing its own theoretical tradition and disciplinary lexicon. In public health, self-care is primarily framed as a strategy to ensure the sustainability of healthcare systems and reduce healthcare costs (El-Osta et al., 2023). Within this framework, Webber et al. (2013) proposed the Seven Pillars of Self-Care (7PSC), a model that identifies key domains of self-care: health literacy, mental well-being, physical activity, healthy eating, risk avoidance, hygiene, and the rational use of health products and services.

Originating in the field of nursing, Dorothea Orem's theory (2001) remains one of the most comprehensive frameworks for understanding self-care. Orem conceptualized self-care as a fundamental regulatory function for maintaining life and well-being, composed of two central elements: self-care agency—referring to the individual's capacity to make informed decisions and perform care-related behaviors—and self-care behaviors, encompassing daily actions (e.g., hygiene, nutrition, physical activity) that promote health and sustain quality of life. This theory emphasizes intentional and learned behaviors, supported by knowledge, decision-making skills, and access to resources. According to the Self-Care Deficit Nursing Theory, nursing becomes necessary when individuals are no longer able to meet their own care needs and thus require professional support.

Other disciplinary perspectives have framed self-care in distinct ways. In sociology, it has been interpreted as a form of responsible action (Levin, 1979), while behavioral medicine has addressed it as a response to symptoms (Dean, 1986), a set of daily health practices, a decision-making process (Haug et al., 1989), or adherence to treatment.

In the context of chronic illness, the concept of self-care has frequently expanded into the broader construct of self-management. While often used interchangeably, the two terms reflect different emphases. Self-care refers to a broad set of proactive, everyday actions undertaken to maintain health and prevent disease. In contrast, self-management is more specific to chronic illness and refers to the individual's ability to manage symptoms, treatment regimens, and lifestyle adjustments in collaboration with healthcare professionals. Self-management entails more advanced decision-making and problem-solving skills and often necessitates tailored support and education (Kitson & Lawless, 2025).

In gerontology, Høy et al. (2007) offered a particularly relevant perspective, describing self-care as a multidimensional construct comprising two interrelated dimensions: self-care as a capability and self-care as a process. As a capability, self-care refers to an individual's potential to take health-related actions that maintain or enhance functional ability, manage illness, and prevent disability in daily life. This includes not only functional capacity but also cognitive and emotional components that enable individuals to recognize their needs, evaluate internal and external resources, and select appropriate behaviors to support well-being and independence. As a process, self-care is understood as a dynamic, lifelong trajectory through which individuals engage with their own health over time. This view emphasizes strategies by which older adults make sense of their experiences, adapt to changing health conditions, and remain engaged with personal and contextual goals. It frames self-care as a developmental pathway encompassing the construction of meaning (life experience process), the acquisition and application of knowledge (learning process), and the integration of internal and external resources into a resilient lifestyle (ecological process).

More recently, self-care has emerged as a key framework in understanding how individuals adapt to NCDs. The Middle-Range Theory of Self-Care of Chronic Illness (Riegel et al., 2012, 2019) defines self-care as a process of maintaining health and managing illness through health-promoting practices. It views self-care as a naturalistic decision-making process shaped by lived experience, motivation, habitual behavior, personal values, environmental resources, and the evolving course of illness. The theory identifies three core components:

1. Self-care maintenance, encompassing behaviors aimed at promoting well-being, preserving health, and maintaining physical and emotional stability. These include lifestyle habits (e.g., healthy eating, stress management) and adherence to medical treatments (e.g., medication use). These behaviors may be self-initiated or agreed upon with healthcare providers and require reflection, vigilance, and ongoing evaluation.
2. Self-care monitoring, referring to the routine and attentive observation of one's body (Dickson et al., 2008). Based on somatic awareness, this process enables early detection of clinically significant changes and timely decision-making. It serves as the link between maintenance and management.
3. Self-care management, which involves evaluating detected changes and deciding how to respond. This includes implementing appropriate treatments and assessing their outcomes. Effective management requires understanding the meaning of symptoms and making informed decisions even in uncertain or complex circumstances.

This theory highlights the evolving nature of self-care as influenced by illness trajectory, values, lived experience, and environmental conditions. It positions individuals as active agents in managing their health, requiring both motivation and practical competence. Section 3 will explore the psychological foundations of self-care, particularly among older adults with chronic conditions, emphasizing the role of motivation and behavior change theories.

3 Core Processes and Psychological Drivers of Self-Care: The Role of Motivation

In recent years, the concept of self-care has gained increasing scientific attention. A growing body of research demonstrates that individuals actively engaged in self-care tend to report better clinical outcomes, enhanced psychological well-being, improved quality of life, greater autonomy, and a stronger sense of control (Jonkman et al., 2016; Schulman-Green et al., 2016; Matarese et al., 2020; Grady & Gough, 2014).

From a psychological perspective, self-care is not a unitary process but a system of interwoven capacities, including self-determination, self-esteem, self-confidence[1] (Ros-Sanchez et al., 2023), awareness, self-control,[2] and self-reliance (Cook-Cottone

[1] Self-confidence is an attitude toward one's own abilities and skills. It means accepting and trusting oneself, and having a sense of control over one's life. It involves knowing your strengths and weaknesses well, maintaining a positive self-image, setting realistic expectations and goals, communicating assertively, and handling criticism effectively.

[2] According to Denyes et al. (2001), self-care is the outcome of a person acting as a unified being, engaging in the regulation and control of oneself and one's emotions. Cook-Cottone et al. (2018) support this view, emphasizing that self-control—understood as self-regulation and self-management—is essential for achieving cognitive approaches to prevention and self-care. Self-control is reinforced by awareness and self-reliance. Self-reliance, translated as self-sufficiency, refers to treatment adherence and reflects a person's resilience and perseverance

et al., 2018). It can be understood as a set of protective mental functions oriented toward self-preservation[3] (Khantzian & Mack, 1983).

In The Middle-Range Theory of Self-Care of Chronic Illness, the authors propose that underlying the self-care components are crucial psychological processes, primarily decision-making and reflection (Riegel et al., 2012). Contrary to classical models of rational choice, decision-making in self-care is often based on naturalistic and intuitive strategies shaped by previous experience, context, and time constraints. Reflection, on the other hand, refers to the individual's ability to interpret signals, evaluate behaviors, and make sense of their health condition over time. Both mechanisms are essential for developing adaptive self-care responses.

To better illustrate the operational components of self-care in chronic illness, Table 1 summarizes the three core components of the Middle-Range Theory of Self-Care of Chronic Illness—maintenance, monitoring, and management—along with illustrative examples and processes underlying self-care.

In relation to the main factors that act as barriers or facilitators of self-care, the literature highlights emotional states (e.g., depression, anxiety), personality traits, social support, and clinical variables all influence the extent and quality of self-care behaviors (Afaya et al., 2023; Fivecoat et al., 2018; Skinner et al., 2014). Other key factors include cognitive and physical functioning, knowledge, habits, previous health experiences, culturally shaped beliefs and values, self-efficacy, supportive relationships with family members, informal caregivers, and healthcare professionals, as well as access to affordable services, treatments, and tools (Martinez et al., 2021; Tulu et al., 2021; Riegel et al., 2019). Engaging in self-care can be especially demanding for older adults living with multiple NCDs. Age-related changes, including physical decline (e.g., muscle loss, reduced mobility, sensory impairments), cognitive deterioration (e.g., memory deficits, attentional difficulties), and psychosocial challenges (e.g., loneliness, depression), further complicate self-care routines. Moreover, the characteristics of the illnesses themselves, such as symptom severity, the presence of comorbid conditions, and the complexity of treatment, tend to fluctuate over time and may be influenced by age-related changes. This makes self-care a dynamic process that requires ongoing decision-making, adaptability, and the implementation of strategies to manage the shifting physical, psychological, and social demands of chronic illness (Alqahtani & Alqahtani, 2022).

---

[3] When self-care is viewed as a developed system of psychic functions (Khantzian & Mack, 1983), it includes the following elements:

- A libidinal investment in caring for or valuing oneself—a sufficiently positive self-esteem to feel worthy of care and protection.
- The ability to anticipate dangerous or risky situations and to respond to the signals that anxiety provides.
- The capacity to control impulses and to forgo pleasures whose consequences are harmful.
- Pleasure in mastering unavoidable risk situations, or in those where dangers are adequately assessed.
- A sufficient knowledge of the external world and of oneself to survive within it.
- The ability to be assertive or aggressive enough to protect oneself.
- Some degree of object-relational competence, particularly the ability to choose others who will ideally enhance one's protection, or at least not endanger one's existence.

Table 1 Core processes of self-care in chronic illness: definitions, examples, and underlying mechanisms

Dimension	Definition	Examples	Underlying processes
Maintenance	Engaging in behaviors—either autonomous or jointly planned with healthcare professionals—aimed at enhancing well-being and maintaining physiological and emotional stability.	Physical activity, regular sleep, medication adherence, stress management	Reflective (utility assessment), Adaptive (adjustment over time), Relational (agreement with professionals), Decisional (active commitment)
Monitoring	Ongoing observation of bodily changes and emotional states to detect early signs or symptoms.	Blood glucose checks, emotional tracking, blood pressure monitoring	Somatic and emotional awareness, Decisional activation, Relational communication
Management	Responding to emerging symptoms through evaluation, adaptation, or seeking help.	Modifying exercise, using medication, consulting healthcare providers	Decisional reasoning, Evaluative judgment, Situational awareness, Professional collaboration

Adapted from Riegel et al. (2012, 2019, 2021)

To better illustrate the key factors that influence self-care in older adults, Table 2 provides a synthesis of the most recent literature highlighting psychological, relational, and contextual dimensions involved in the process.

In particular, among the psychological factors, motivation emerged as a key driver both in initiating self-care and in sustaining it over time, acting as a transversal element that supports and integrates all other components.

Intrinsic motivation, such as engaging in an activity for personal satisfaction, has been shown to be more influential than extrinsic motivation, such as following others' recommendations (Palombi et al., 2023). According to Self-Determination Theory (Deci & Ryan, 2017), behaviors that satisfy basic psychological needs—particularly autonomy—are more likely to be internalized and sustained over time.

An intrinsically motivated behavior brings about feelings of interest, enjoyment, or satisfaction. For instance, individuals are more likely to desire or retain a healthy aging motive (e.g., physical activity) if their basic psychological needs can be satisfied from pursuing that motive, resulting in positive outcomes and well-being (Ng & Abbas, 2020). For many individuals with NCDs, maintaining autonomy stands out as a top priority in the personal goal hierarchy. However, socially driven values, such as social recognition, a sense of responsibility, and adherence to traditions, can also serve as important motivational drivers (Chew et al., 2019; Abotalebidariasari et al., 2016). Sustained motivation for engaging in health-promoting behaviors represents a crucial psychological resource for older adults with multimorbidity. Motivation has become increasingly central in the latest iterations of the Middle-Range Theory of Self-Care of Chronic Illness. Initially described as a factor influencing self-care (Riegel et al., 2012), it is now seen as a driving force behind

Table 2 Key psychological drivers influencing self-care in older adults

Factor	Description	Impact on self-care
Cognitive functioning	Memory, attention, and executive function	Affects decision-making and monitoring of symptoms
Emotional state	Depression, anxiety, mood fluctuations	Can reduce motivation and perceived self-efficacy
Personality traits	Conscientiousness, openness, neuroticism	Influence health behaviors and adaptability
Self-efficacy	Belief in one's ability to perform self-care tasks	Key predictor of adherence and behavioral change
Health literacy	Ability to understand and act on health information	Shapes informed decision-making and autonomy
Social support	Family, caregivers, peer relationships	Buffers stress and enhances adherence
Cultural values and beliefs	Norms about aging, illness, responsibility	Influence motivation, stigma, and willingness to change
Past health experiences	Previous engagement with healthcare and behavioral interventions	Shape trust, expectations, and openness to self-care

goal-directed behaviors—whether activated internally or stimulated by others (Ajzen & Fishbein, 2005). The experience of symptoms can act as a motivational trigger, prompting patients to engage in self-care actions (Auld et al., 2018), whereas depressive symptoms or cognitive fatigue can diminish motivation (Lee et al., 2018; Egede & Osborn, 2010).

In the 2021 revision of the theory, Riegel and colleagues identify two overarching challenges: *behavioral change* and *illness-related factors*. The lack of motivation is cited as a primary barrier to long-term engagement in self-care, along with habitual routines, decision-making difficulties, and the struggle to maintain behavioral changes over time (Chichirez & Purcarea, 2018; Kwasnicka et al., 2016).

Importantly, self-care behaviors that align with personal goals and values are more likely to become sustainable habits (Campoli & Cummings, 2024). However, stress, negative mood, and attentional overload often disrupt motivation and increase reliance on default routines.

Behavioral economics has further illustrated the human tendency toward *future discounting*—giving more weight to immediate discomfort than to long-term benefits (Parthasarathi et al., 2017). This tendency, known as temporal discounting, illustrates how individuals often prioritize short-term comfort over long-term health benefits (Parthasarathi et al., 2017). Behavioral economics has highlighted this natural human bias: people tend to undervalue future outcomes and assign greater importance to immediate experiences. As a result, they may avoid health-related decisions whose benefits are abstract or delayed—such as reducing cardiovascular risk—especially when those decisions involve immediate discomfort, like giving up caloric foods or taking medications with unpleasant side effects.

When the perceived costs of self-care outweigh its anticipated benefits, the likelihood of engaging in health-promoting behaviors significantly decreases (Mohebi et al., 2013). In this context, research grounded in behavior change theory becomes crucial to understanding why, when, and how self-care interventions succeed—and, importantly, how they can be sustained over time (Herber et al., 2018). Without appropriate support, difficulties and barriers that emerge during implementation may erode an individual's self-efficacy and willingness to maintain behavioral change (Bandura, 1986).

4 From Amotivation to Maintenance of Action: Behavioral Change in Older Adults through the Transtheoretical Model

This convergence of self-care theory and behavior change models is exemplified by frameworks such as the Transtheoretical Model of Change and the Motivational Model of Pain Self-Management (Prochaska et al., 2008), both of which place motivation at the core of behavioral change.

Indeed, motivation is commonly defined as the internal drive that propels an individual to act toward a specific goal. Any action undertaken without sufficient motivation is at risk of failure—either immediately or over time. In the perspective of Miller and Rollnick (2012b), motivation is not a static trait but a dynamic process—shaped by goals, values, fears, and fluctuating experiences and reflects the individuals' perceived alignment between a specific behavior and their personal values and goals. Understanding this alignment is key to sustaining engagement and making self-care a meaningful part of everyday life need. This construct allows us to explore what people truly desire, what they reject or fear, how these preferences are translated into goals, how they pursue or abandon them, and how these motivational processes can evolve over time.

The Transtheoretical Model of Change (TTM) provides a dynamic and integrative framework for understanding health behavior change. It is structured around four main components: the stages of change, the processes of change, decisional balance, and self-efficacy. A core tenet of the model is that change unfolds over time, progressing through identifiable stages, and that individuals vary in their readiness to engage with change. Therefore, effective interventions must be tailored to the specific stage each person is in (Prochaska et al., 2009).

The model outlines five sequential stages:

1. Precontemplation—the person is not yet considering change and may be unaware of the problem
2. Contemplation—ambivalence dominates as the person begins to weigh pros and cons
3. Determination—motivation increases and plans for change are made.
4. Action—active implementation of new behaviors
5. Maintenance—consolidation and long-term sustainability of behavioral change

Beyond this temporal structure, TTM integrates several psychological constructs that deepen its explanatory power. One of these is decisional balance—the weighing of perceived costs and benefits of change. Initially, the costs may outweigh the perceived benefits, but as individuals progress through the stages, this balance typically shifts in favor of action. Another essential component is self-efficacy: the belief in one's ability to perform and sustain the change, especially in high-risk or stressful situations. This is complemented by the concept of temptation, or the urge to revert to previous behaviors, which tends to decrease as commitment strengthens.

The model also identifies ten processes of change, divided into experiential (e.g., consciousness raising, self-reevaluation, environmental reevaluation) and behavioral processes (e.g., stimulus control, reinforcement management, helping relationships). The former are more prominent in the early stages, while the latter become essential during action and maintenance, helping to consolidate habits and prevent relapse.

By acknowledging the cyclical, nonlinear nature of the change—and by integrating motivational, cognitive, and affective dynamics—the TTM serves as a powerful theoretical and clinical tool for designing self-care interventions that are both effective and sustainable over time. Drawing upon the construct of readiness to change from the Transtheoretical Model (TTM) developed by Prochaska and colleagues (2008), the Motivational Model of Pain Self-Management posits that motivation is a fundamental prerequisite for initiating, managing, and sustaining self-care behaviors.

Literature shows that in elderly people with chronic conditions, the ambivalence or contemplation stage of the change prevail: they want to improve their health but experience discouragement, low self-efficacy, low perceived value and dysfunctional beliefs (Tang et al., 2025; Wang et al., 2024; Mitzner et al., 2013). Numerous studies have applied the TTM to older adults with chronic conditions, such as interventions aimed at increasing physical activity, improving medication adherence, or supporting cognitive functioning in cases of mild cognitive impairment. These interventions have consistently shown positive results in stage progression, self-efficacy, and sustained behavioral change (Jiménez-Zazo et al., 2020; Wang et al., 2020; Shi et al., 2025). For example, TTM-based physical activity programs have fostered habit formation successfully among older adults, while adherence-focused applications have improved clinical outcomes in chronic disease management. Randomized controlled trials have also demonstrated enhanced cognitive functioning in seniors with MCI. Collectively, these findings support the TTM as a bridge between motivational dynamics and tangible self-care behaviors in aging populations with chronic illness.

Despite its wide application in health promotion, the TTM is not without limitations. Some scholars have argued that its sequential stage structure does not always capture the subjective and fluctuating experience of change, and that transitions between stages are often difficult to measure or observe (West, 2005). Moreover, while the concept of "readiness to change" is central to the model, it can be challenging to assess reliably, as it may vary rapidly depending on contextual or emotional factors.

4.1 Translating Behavior Change Theory into Practice: The Motivational Interviewing Approach

Behavioral change is central to interventions targeting older adults, as most age-related conditions are chronic and strongly influenced by lifestyle factors (Bloom et al., 2015). However, promoting change in this population can be particularly challenging. Older individuals often maintain unhealthy habits—such as smoking, poor diet, and physical inactivity—and may lack intrinsic motivation to modify them (Harvey et al., 2015; Wang et al., 2025; Yannakoulia et al., 2018). Factors like ambivalence, habitual patterns, resistance to change, apathy, depression, fatigue, and disability further complicate engagement with new behaviors (Fernandes et al., 2022; Harrison et al., 2023).

Despite the growing need for behavioral interventions in later life, traditional methods have often shown limited long-term efficacy. Many of these approaches focus on external or environmental factors, neglecting the internal psychological drivers that underpin sustained behavioral change (Fjeldsoe et al., 2011). This gap underscores the importance of clinical methods that can address both the motivational landscape and the relational dimensions of change—especially in older adults.

Motivational Interviewing (MI) offers a person-centered, directive approach specifically designed to strengthen intrinsic motivation by exploring and resolving ambivalence (Miller & Rollnick, 2012b). According to its most mature definition, MI is "a collaborative, goal-oriented style of communication with particular attention to the language of change, designed to strengthen personal motivation and commitment to a specific goal by eliciting and exploring the person's own reasons for change" (Miller & Rollnick, 2012a, p. 29).

MI draws on the humanistic tradition of Carl Rogers, emphasizing empathy, unconditional acceptance, and respect for autonomy. However, it distinguishes itself through its strategic focus on change: it is clinically directive in form, though non-directive in content. This makes MI a unique blend of relational depth and therapeutic direction, capable of adapting to the complex motivational dynamics of aging.

The method unfolds through four interrelated processes:

1. Engaging—establishing a trusting, collaborative relationship
2. Focusing—identifying and clarifying a specific behavioral target
3. Evoking—eliciting the individual's own motivations, values, and reasons for change
4. Planning—co-constructing a feasible action plan aligned with personal goals and resources (Miller & Rollnick, 2012b)

A pivotal contribution to the evolution of MI came from Amrhein et al. (2003), who empirically distinguished between *change talk* (language that supports change) and *sustain talk* (language that favors the status quo). Expressions of desire, ability, reasons, need, commitment, and taking steps have been linked to positive clinical outcomes. Rollnick et al. (2008) further elaborated on motivational architecture through three dimensions—willingness, ability, and readiness—which can be evoked and strengthened using targeted conversational strategies.

Central to MI is the relational climate. Authentic empathy, nonjudgmental listening, and autonomy support are foundational conditions that reduce resistance and enhance self-determination. In this context, change does not result from external persuasion but emerges internally, through the alignment of personal values, goals, and behaviors.

Recent evidence supports MI as an effective intervention for older adults, especially in managing chronic conditions. Studies have shown that MI improves treatment adherence, supports self-management, and fosters engagement in health-promoting behaviors such as physical activity, nutrition, and medication use (Lundahl et al., 2013; Frost et al., 2018). These effects are particularly valuable in geriatric care, where health decisions are often shaped by ambivalence, low motivation, and cumulative vulnerability.

MI has also proven effective in promoting weight loss, mobility improvement, and medication management among older adults. When adapted to this population—by slowing the conversational rhythm, allowing repetitions, and addressing cognitive load (Pietrabissa, 2024)—MI strategies are well received and can lead to behavioral improvements in relatively short timeframes (Cummings et al., 2009). These effects are amplified when MI is embedded within broader health promotion and disease prevention programs (Purath et al., 2014).

Importantly, MI retains its effectiveness even when delivered remotely (e.g., by telephone), which is especially relevant given the mobility limitations often faced by older adults (Kolt et al., 2007; Kreman et al., 2006). This versatility positions MI as not only a clinical technique, but a person-centered philosophy of care—capable of enhancing self-management, reducing healthcare burdens, and fostering autonomy in the aging process. Despite its documented efficacy, the application of Motivational Interviewing in older adults also presents some critical limitations that must be acknowledged.

Cognitive impairment, such as memory deficits or reduced executive function, can compromise the individual's ability to engage in reflective dialogue, track intentions, or follow through on behavioral goals (Chou et al., 2025). Additionally, low health literacy and limited familiarity with therapeutic conversation styles may reduce the accessibility or perceived relevance of MI techniques, particularly in older adults with low educational backgrounds. Motivational Interviewing (MI), despite its strong empirical effectiveness, presents methodological challenges related to standardization, practitioner training, and outcome measurement. The balance between its relational approach and technical structure remains one of the most significant tensions in its clinical application (Hettema et al., 2005). Furthermore, some older individuals may show passive communication styles or deference to authority, which may inhibit the open expression of ambivalence and hinder the collaborative spirit essential to MI.

These factors underscore the importance of adapting MI delivery—by simplifying language, using visual aids, pacing interactions, and reinforcing key messages—to meet the specific cognitive and communicative needs of aging populations.

4.2 An Integrative Framework: Aligning Self-Care, Motivation, and Behavior Change with Motivational Interviewing

In response to the gap between self-care and behavioral change (Riegel et al., 2021)—both theoretically and in applied settings—and to unify conceptual models with clinical practice, we propose an integrative framework called *The Self-Care Motivation Change Framework* (SCMC Framework): a conceptual structure that connects motivation, change processes, and clinical tools such as Motivational Interviewing.

SCMC Framework offers a conceptual and dynamic structure that uses Motivational Interviewing as a clinical method to activate, guide, and sustain the maintenance of behavioral change in self-care among individuals with chronic illness, supporting healthy aging.

In chronic conditions, maintaining self-care behaviors and functional abilities over time requires more than a rational choice: it is necessary to address ambivalence, resistance and relapses. In this framework, Motivational Interviewing is not only a technique for activating change, but a real clinical method capable of accompanying the person through all the phases of change, including the maintenance phase, facilitating the transition between awareness and action. Each MI process can assume a specific function in supporting change. For example, Engaging contributes to building a narrative alliance that reinforces the individual's sense of agency; Focusing supports reflexivity and helps clarify care priorities; Evoking works on ambivalence, promoting commitment and intrinsic motivation; Planning finally supports the consolidation of change and the prevention of relapses. The proposed model thus integrates the decisional and motivational dimension of self-care with a processual vision of change and a relational and transformative method to support it clinically.

Figure 1 synthesizes *The Self-Care Motivation Change Framework* (SCMC Framework) that underpins the application of Motivational Interviewing in promoting self-care change among older adults with chronic illness.

At the center of the model lies intrinsic motivation as a dynamic psychological process with three critical dimensions: willingness (the desire to change), ability (the confidence to act), and readiness (the openness and timing to change). Behavioral change is a transformative process that requires will, ability, and readiness. Willingness refers to the internal desire to change one's behavior to achieve personal goals or improve the quality of life. Ability indicates the practical, cognitive, and emotional resources needed to implement such a change. Readiness represents the subjective moment in which the individual feels able to act, after having processed the ambivalence, recognized the need, and understood the meaning of the change.

Rather than fixed subcomponents, these dimensions reflect the qualitative nature and functional capacity of motivation at a given point in the change process. These dimensions, that is, the motivational components and the stage of change, which we will call from now on motivational profiles.

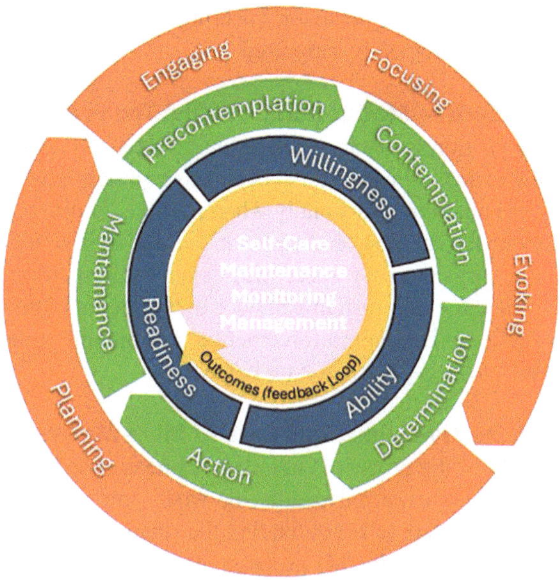

Fig. 1 The self-care motivation change framework (SCMC framework)

Motivational Profile → MI: Activating the Change Talk About Self-Care

Motivation serves as the inner engine that prepares the psychological ground for change. However, it requires a relational method to be activated and channeled. This is where Motivational Interviewing enters: it functions as a structured and empathic method that draws upon this inner energy, fostering the emergence of change talk and guiding ambivalence toward resolution. The directionality here is vertical and functional: a higher-level condition (motivation) triggers a strategic process (MI). Notably, MI was originally designed for individuals in the precontemplation and contemplation stages of change, where ambivalence is predominant and motivational readiness is often fragile or unclear. In these stages, the *Evoking* and *Engaging* processes are central—working to enhance discrepancy, reinforce personal values, and elicit intrinsic motivation.

MI → Self-Care: Translating Intention into Action

Through its four core processes—*engaging*, *focusing*, *evoking*, and *planning*—MI offers a set of relational and strategic tools to transform motivational energy into concrete action. These include open-ended questions, affirmations, reflections, and summaries, all of which help the individual articulate goals, manage ambivalence, and define specific behavioral targets.

As individuals progress through the preparation and action stages, the *Planning* process becomes especially relevant, helping to operationalize self-care intentions into structured behaviors (e.g., establishing routines, managing barriers, setting realistic goals). The directionality here is instrumental: MI guides the transition from intention to behavior, ensuring that the path to self-care is tailored, feasible, and psychologically supported.

Self-Care → Motivational Profile: The Feedback Loop

Once action is taken—such as initiating a physical activity routine or adhering to medication—the individual begins to experience the concrete outcomes of self-care. These outcomes, especially when positive, reinforce self-efficacy, competence, and autonomy, thereby feeding back into the motivational system. This forms a feedback loop, whereby successful experiences reinforce the underlying motivational architecture and sustain behavior over time. In clinical terms, this mechanism activates a motivation reinforcement cycle, making it more likely that the person continues to engage in self-care behaviors.

A Reflective Loop: Self-Care → MI → Motivational Profile

However, the process is not always linear or successful. When self-care efforts fail to produce expected results, or when ambivalence re-emerges, individuals may express sustain talk—defending the status quo or expressing doubt. Here, the clinician re-engages the MI process, returning to unresolved motivational material and co-constructing new goals or behavioral adjustments. This reflective loop—from self-care outcomes back to MI and motivation—illustrates the adaptive and recursive nature of the framework, where each phase informs and reshapes the others in an ongoing cycle.

This integrative model shows that effective self-care promotion does not rely solely on education or behavioral prescriptions. Rather, it emerges from the meaningful alignment between:

- Why: the motivational drivers that sustain change
- How: the relational and strategic processes that guide it (MI)
- What: the tasks of self-care

The SCMC does not limit itself to describing self-care as a series of actions, but conceives it as a transformative process in which the identity, values and motivation of the individual are reorganized. In this perspective, promoting self-care means supporting change in all its phases, recognizing that each person goes through blocks, ambivalences, relapses and moments of insight that must be welcomed as part of the process. By situating Motivational Interviewing at the intersection of these levels, the framework links theory and practice, offering clinicians a flexible and responsive structure for supporting change across different stages of readiness. It highlights MI not just as a set of techniques, but as a dynamic method whose processes must be tailored to the individual's motivational profile and stage of change—from awakening ambivalence to sustaining long-term behavioral adherence.

Importantly, this framework conceptualizes behavior change as an iterative and adaptive process (Lemmo et al., 2025b). Each new self-care behavior or health goal reactivates the motivational cycle, requiring renewed alignment between psychological readiness, relational support, and behavioral tasks. Rather than a one-time shift, self-care may be sustained through a dynamic feedback loop, in which motivation is re-engaged and reshaped over time as individuals navigate new challenges and transitions. What makes the SCMC framework original is its recursive integration of three dimensions: the motivational dynamics of behavioral change, the relational structure of MI, and the multidimensional nature of self-care. Unlike existing models (e.g., COM-B, PHE), it emphasizes not only readiness and capability, but also the emotional alignment and narrative construction needed to sustain change in later life.

This triadic integration highlights that effective self-care promotion does not stem from education alone, but from a meaningful alignment between individual goals, relational guidance, and structured behavioral support—revisited and renewed at every stage of the health journey.

5 Applying SCMC Framework for Healthy Aging in Clinical Practice

The integration of Motivational Interviewing (MI) into clinical practice represents a promising approach to enhance self-care among older adults living with chronic illness. Given the evolving nature of self-care—comprising maintenance, monitoring, and management (Riegel et al., 2012, 2019, 2021)—MI offers a flexible, relationally grounded method to address both psychological barriers and behavioral challenges specific to this population.

MI does not treat ambivalence as a dysfunction to be corrected, but as a starting point for engagement. Through empathetic listening and the amplification of small openings toward change, MI helps individuals integrate conflicting inner voices and build a coherent and empowering narrative of care.

In the self-care maintenance, MI strengthens commitment to consistent health behaviors—such as physical activity, medication adherence, and dietary regulation—by connecting these practices with the person's deeply held values and long-term goals. Through the technique of *evocation*, clinicians help older adults explore what truly matters to them, anchoring motivation in meaning (Resnicow et al., 2002).

In the self-care monitoring, MI supports bodily and emotional awareness by encouraging reflection on fatigue, pain, or emotional states. This awareness promotes timely decision-making and helps prevent complications by fostering early recognition of warning signs.

In the self-care management, MI enhances self-efficacy and problem-solving skills, empowering individuals to respond to new or worsening symptoms without panic or passivity. By supporting autonomy and confidence, MI helps older adults regain a sense of control and authorship over their health journey.

The relational dimension of MI—rooted in empathy, collaboration, and non-judgment—makes it especially suited to older populations, who often value trust, continuity, and personal connection in therapeutic settings. The narrative tools embedded in MI allow clinicians to facilitate meaning-making processes, supporting identity continuity and psychological adaptation in the face of aging and illness (Freda et al., 2023).

Clinical evidence confirms the effectiveness of MI in improving key outcomes such as medication adherence, glycemic control, and physical rehabilitation among older adults (Lundahl et al., 2013; Hardcastle et al., 2017; O'Halloran et al., 2014). These benefits are not limited to in-person delivery: remote MI interventions (e.g., via phone) have shown comparable results, making MI an accessible and adaptable strategy even when physical mobility is limited (Kolt et al., 2007; Kreman et al., 2006).

Promoting self-care necessarily involves reflecting on the environmental and sociocultural constraints that influence the ability to adopt healthy behaviors. In many older adults living with noncommunicable disease, factors such as low educational attainment, poverty, social isolation, digital illiteracy, and unequal access to services constitute structural barriers to self-care. Furthermore, internalized cultural norms (e.g., passivity, distrust of change, gender roles) may diminish motivation or reinforce a sense of resignation. In this context, motivational interviewing assumes a crucial role as a dialogical space for acknowledging such constraints, valuing latent resources, and co-constructing sustainable and realistic pathways to change.

Within the Age.it project, Motivational Interviewing was adopted as a core strategy to support older adults—specifically those living with hypertension—in developing personalized self-care practices related to adapted physical activity. This population often faces both physical and psychological barriers to adopting new behaviors (Tang et al., 2025; Wang et al., 2024; Mitzner et al., 2013) making the nuanced, person-centered approach of MI particularly suitable.

A key feature of the intervention involved an initial assessment of the: (a) Self-care of chronic illness and (b) Motivational profile as individual's stage of motivational readiness to change about self-care behavior target, based on the Transtheoretical Model (Prochaska & DiClemente, 1983), and motivational components influencing the motivation to change in the subdimensions of (1) *Discrepancy* (DI): it reflects dissatisfaction and concern to the present situation, need for change, and the perceived importance of change; (2) *Importance* (IM): it is the value given to correct behavior for reaching the well-being; (3) *Self-Efficacy* (SE): it reflects the perceived confidence in attaining and maintaining the predefined goals of change; (4) *Temptation* (TE): it defines the attraction by unhealthy behaviors as those that characterized the old lifestyle; (5) *Readiness to Change* (RTC): it is the degree of the problem recognition and the willingness degree to change a behavior; (6) *Stabilization of Change* (ST): it is the acquisition degree of the new lifestyle.

This profiling allowed for the identification of a self-care habits and motivational profile for each participant, which informed the tailoring of subsequent MI sessions. Rather than identifying only the motivational phase for change, the SCMC allows us to identify motivational profiles for self-care (e.g., unmotivated, ambivalent, engaged, active, sustaining). These profiles are not fixed, but dynamic: people can advance, regress or remain in a phase for a long time. The model also includes a transversal phase of crisis or relapse, in which the change stops, but can represent a transformative resource if managed consciously. In the SCMC, each phase is associated with specific motivational needs, barriers, decision-making processes and relational strategies. This allows healthcare professionals, coaches or therapists to personalize interventions based on the motivational phase, working more effectively on engagement, awareness, evocation, planning and maintenance support.

Following the assessment, each participant engaged in a cycle of individual MI sessions, conducted by trained clinicians. These sessions were structured to align with the participant's motivational stage, fostering reflective dialogue and exploring personal goals, fears, and perceived discrepancies between current behaviors and desired health outcomes.

In addition to evaluating perceived effectiveness in enhancing engagement with adapted physical activity, the sessions were audio-recorded and transcribed for a systematic analysis of the dialogic process.

To assess the effectiveness of the motivational pathway in the Age.it project,[4] a suite of psychometric instruments was administered in a pre–post design to evaluate several domains:

1. Readiness to Change—measured using instruments derived from the Transtheoretical Model (TTM).
2. Motivational Profile—assessed via a validated self-report scale.
3. Engagement in Adapted Physical Activity—quantified through logs of participation frequency and intensity.
4. Types of Self-Care—determined by identifying domains in which participants actively engaged.
5. Program Participation and Retention—tracked via attendance rates and completion statistics.
6. Psychological Well-Being & Perceived Health—measured through standardized self-reported well-being and health-status instruments.

In parallel, the Motivational Interviewing Skill Code (MISC)—a validated system for coding therapist and client utterances during a motivational interview—was applied to audiotaped sessions, enabling the qualitative coding of linguistic patterns, specifically distinguishing change talk from sustain talk to identify markers of motivational evolution. This mixed-methods, multilevel framework combines quantitative psychometric data with qualitative discourse analysis to detect improvements in: (1) Engagement in self-care behavior as physical activity; (2) Psychological well-being. Together, these indicators lay a robust foundation for future longitudinal analyses exploring the long-term effectiveness of motivational interviewing in promoting healthy aging.

Using the Motivational Interviewing Skill Code (MISC) framework, utterances were coded to identify patterns of change talk (statements indicating desire, ability,

[4] Extended Partnership (EP) Project 8, Age-It "A novel public-private alliance to generate socio-economic, biomedical and technological solutions for an inclusive Italian ageing society" of the Ministry of University and Research (Project number: PE0000015), supported by the National Recovery and Resilience Plan financed by the Next Generation EU program. The project is organized into ten thematic spokes, with Spoke 4 focusing on "Trajectories for active and healthy ageing." Within this spoke, the authors are active contributors to Work Package 1 (Task 1.2) which is dedicated to life course psychological approaches in chronic domains.

reason, or need for change) and sustain talk (language expressing resistance, doubts, or reasons to maintain the status quo).

Beyond its evaluative function, the MISC coding system also serves as a clinical insight tool: it enables practitioners to detect motivational shifts, unresolved ambivalence, and emotional barriers in real time. This granular analysis of patient language allows clinicians to personalize their conversational strategies, calibrating evocation techniques, reframing efforts, and planning interventions based on the motivational profile emerging from the dialogue.

Moreover, MI facilitated the emergence of deep motivational themes, including autonomy, vitality, and legacy, showing how older adults reconnect with values that give meaning to their health journey. The sessions also highlighted how sustain talk, when empathetically explored rather than suppressed, served as a diagnostic lens to access unresolved fears, past failures, or identity-related resistance. In order to provide a tangible example of how the SCMC framework and the MISC-based analysis inform real clinical practice, we now present a clinical vignette conducted within the Age.it project, in the context of clinical settings dedicated to promoting adapted physical activity (Box 1). The example showcases the practical application of the four core MI processes—engaging, focusing, evoking, and planning—and illustrates how the intervention was tailored to the individual's motivational profile assessed during the initial phase and to type of talk, sustain talk.

This structured application of MI demonstrates its dual function: both as an intervention to promote behavioral change and as a clinical tool to analyze motivational dynamics in depth, offering insights that go beyond surface-level adherence. By making space for ambivalence and affirming the person's agency, MI proved to be a valuable method for catalyzing sustainable self-care transformations in older individuals coping with chronic illness.

While the case of L. exemplifies a responsive and engaged trajectory of change, clinical practice frequently encounters older adults for whom motivational interviewing produces more nuanced or partial outcomes. Several contextual and individual variables may moderate the effectiveness of MI in promoting self-care change among this population. Cognitive impairment, particularly deficits in

Box 1 An example of motivational interviewing-based SCMC framework: Supporting self-care change readiness in a case of ambivalence

L. is a 78-year-old retired widow, living alone, with a medical history of chronic low back pain, severe osteoporosis, and hypertension. Despite having a son, she receives minimal daily support and experiences reduced mobility, relying on a shopping trolley for balance when walking outside. She was recently prescribed adapted physical activity (APA) and physiotherapy, but has not yet engaged in any behavioral change. At the initial motivational assessment (T0), L. was in the contemplation stage of the Transtheoretical Model: aware of her health problems and their potential progression, yet ambivalent and hesitant to take action. Psychometrically, she scored high on discrepancy—indicating concern and awareness of the importance of change—but low on readiness, with fears about aggravating pain and a sense of resignation ("I've lived with this pain for too long. I just don't see how it could get better."). From a self-care perspective, L. showed basic engagement in self-care maintenance (e.g., medication adherence, using assistive devices), but limited capacity for self-care monitoring, as she rarely tracks her symptoms or bodily sensations in a structured way. Her self-care management appeared compromised by low confidence and decision fatigue: she expressed difficulty in identifying coping strategies and lacked a concrete plan for health maintenance. Her type of talk, analyzed trough MISC is Sustain talk. The motivational interviewing session focused on:

Engaging: Building trust and affirming her lived experience of vulnerability, pain, and loss of control.

Focusing: Highlighting her intrinsic value of maintaining mobility and autonomy ("Walking means everything to me. If I lose that, I don't know what I'll do.").

Evoking: Exploring both fears and hopes, using reflective listening to validate ambivalence while eliciting values such as vitality, independence, and connection.

Planning: Co-constructing a micro-goal—a low-intensity movement routine, seated or supported, with continuous reassessment to ensure safety and emotional comfort.

After 3 months, L. remained in the contemplation stage but demonstrated a notable increase in self-efficacy, reporting greater belief in her ability to try new behaviors without worsening symptoms. Importantly, she began experimenting with light physical movements and expressed a willingness to continue "if things don't get worse."

This case illustrates the critical role of MI in supporting older adults with low readiness, by gently amplifying motivational discrepancy, restoring agency, and scaffolding action through tailored, empathic dialogue. It also shows how sustain talk—often seen as resistance—can be reframed as a window into unspoken fears, identity disruption, and the deep emotional work required for behavioral change in aging. Follow-up: During the following months, the patient's engagement with adapted physical activity remained stable. However, moments of fatigue and discouragement emerged, requiring further MI-based support. This highlights the importance of sustaining the planning phase with long-term relational strategies to consolidate change and prevent relapse.

executive functioning or working memory, may limit the person's ability to engage in reflective dialogue or retain behavioral goals. Similarly, the absence of familial or social support can reduce the translation of motivation into action, especially when self-care requires logistical help or environmental adaptation. Moreover, severe multimorbidity or chronic pain may introduce competing health demands that drain motivational resources or contribute to ambivalence and sustain talk. These challenges do not invalidate the use of MI but rather highlight the need for flexible, person-centered adaptations—such as shorter sessions, involvement of caregivers, or greater emphasis on values clarification. Beyond the promotion of adapted physical activity, the SCMC framework can be flexibly applied across various domains of chronic disease self-care. For instance, it may support older adults in managing complex medication regimens by fostering adherence through values-based planning and reflective decision-making. Similarly, in caregiving scenarios, MI can be used to enhance caregiver engagement and mitigate emotional overload, promoting sustainable care routines. The framework is also relevant in facilitating dietary adjustments, emotional regulation, or digital health literacy—areas that often require motivational alignment and behavioral adaptation. These examples underscore the potential of SCMC to inform a wide range of personalized, context-sensitive interventions for healthy aging. Recognizing these complexities reinforces the clinical importance of tailoring MI processes to each individual's cognitive, relational, and medical context, maintaining a realistic yet hopeful stance toward change.

6 Conclusions and Future Directions

The convergence between self-care theory, behavior change models and motivational interviewing approach marks a fundamental evolution in how we understand and promote healthy aging. The SCMC framework highlights that the aging with chronic illness is not merely a matter of clinical management. It is a psychological and existential process that calls for adaptability, purpose, and autonomy.

Based on our proposed framework, healthy aging is not simply the result of medical prescriptions or behavioral adherence, but the outcome of a motivational process grounded in personal meaning, emotional congruence, and relational support. The SCMC framework helps to reframe the clinical dialogue as a space for restoring agency, co-constructing values, and sustaining long-term transformation.

This chapter has outlined how Motivational Interviewing (MI) emerges as a dynamic clinical interface between psychological theory and personalized care. MI does not simply prescribe change, it cultivates the internal conditions that make change possible and sustainable. In older adults, whose lives are often shaped by loss, vulnerability, or ambivalence, this approach enables the reactivation of agency, narrative integration, and alignment with personal values.

Motivation is an evolving force that interacts with life goals, emotional defenses, physical limitations, and relational contexts. Interventions aimed at promoting self-care must therefore move beyond education or persuasion. They must diagnose motivational readiness, tailor relational strategies, and nurture emotional alignment with the desired health behaviors.

We propose that the integration of self-care theory, the Transtheoretical Model of Change, and MI provides a translational framework that can effectively inform both research and practice. This model emphasizes: Assessing self-care capacities and identifying motivational barriers; Profiling stage of change and motivational readiness, using tools like MISC; Tailoring MI strategies (evoking, planning) to the individual's psychological and relational context; Embedding MI into multidisciplinary care pathways, including remote or digital delivery; Training professionals in adapted MI communication for older adults.

While the SCMC framework offers a novel and integrated approach to promoting self-care in older adults, several limitations must be acknowledged. First, the theoretical integration of MI, TTM, and self-care theory—although conceptually robust—requires empirical validation through longitudinal and cross-cultural studies. Second, the successful application of SCMC depends on the clinician's ability to flexibly adapt MI techniques to individual motivational profiles, which demands advanced training and reflective skills. Third, the framework may be less effective in cases of severe cognitive impairment, low health literacy, or when environmental barriers (e.g., poverty, lack of access to care) remain unaddressed. Future research should explore the contextual conditions that facilitate or hinder the effective use of SCMC, as well as potential adaptations for underserved or highly vulnerable populations.

For future research, key directions include: Evaluating long-term effects of MI on self-care adherence and quality of life; Developing digital MI interventions for digital self-care; Identifying motivational subtypes in older populations to personalize interventions. Nonetheless, the application of this framework requires adequate training, clinical adaptability, and ongoing assessment to ensure its effectiveness across diverse populations.

Ultimately, promoting self-care in aging is more than a clinical task—it is an ethical and cultural imperative. It means recognizing older adults as active agents of change, capable of reclaiming meaning, navigating ambivalence, and sustaining transformation through empathic, supportive relationships. As the global population continues to age, the MI offers a personalized and sustainable path to change and further research should explore how MI can be adapted across diverse healthcare settings and cultural contexts to foster health, autonomy, and meaning in later life.

References

Abotalebidariasari, G., Memarian, R., Vanaki, Z., Kazemnejad, A., & Naderi, N. (2016). Self-care motivation among patients with heart failure: a qualitative study based on Orem's theory. *Research and Theory for Nursing Practice, 30*(4), 320–332. https://doi.org/10.1891/1541-6577.30.4.320

Afaya, R. A., Bam, V., Lomotey, A. Y., & Afaya, A. (2023). Clinical factors influencing knowledge and self-care practice among adults with type 2 diabetes mellitus. *Nursing open, 10*(4), 2492–2500. https://doi.org/10.1002/nop2.1506

Ajzen, I., & Fishbein, M. (2005). The influence of attitudes on behavior. In D. Albarracín, B. T. Johnson, & M. P. Zanna (Eds.), *The handbook of attitudes* (pp. 173–221). Lawrence Erlbaum Associates.
Alqahtani, J., & Alqahtani, I. (2022). Self-care in the older adult population with chronic disease: Concept analysis. *Heliyon, 8*(7), e09991. https://doi.org/10.1016/j.heliyon.2022.e09991
Amrhein, P. C., Miller, W. R., Yahne, C. E., Palmer, M., & Fulcher, L. (2003). Client commitment language during motivational interviewing predicts drug use outcomes. *Journal of Consulting and Clinical Psychology, 71*(5), 862–878. https://doi.org/10.1037/0022-006X.71.5.862
Auld, J. P., Mudd, J. O., Gelow, J. M., Hiatt, S. O., & Lee, C. S. (2018). Self-care moderates the relationship between symptoms and health-related quality of life in heart failure. *The Journal of Cardiovascular Nursing, 33*(3), 217–224. https://doi.org/10.1097/JCN.0000000000000044
Bandura, A. (1986). *Social foundations of thought and action: A social cognitive theory.* Prentice-Hall.
Beard, J. R., Officer, A., de Carvalho, I. A., Sadana, R., Pot, A. M., Michel, J.-P., et al. (2016). The world report on ageing and health: A policy framework for healthy ageing. *Lancet, 387*(10033), 2145–2154. https://doi.org/10.1016/S0140-6736(15)00516-4
Bloom, D. E., & Luca, D. L. (2016). The global demography of aging: Facts, explanations, future. In J. Piggott & A. Woodland (Eds.), *Handbook of the economics of population aging* (Vol. 1, pp. 3–56). North-Holland. https://doi.org/10.1016/bs.hespa.2016.06.002
Bloom, D. E., Canning, D., & Lubet, A. (2015). Global population aging: Facts, challenges, solutions & perspectives. *Daedalus, 144*(2), 80–92.
Chew, H. S. J., Sim, K. L. D., Cao, X., & Chair, S. Y. (2019). Motivation, challenges and self-regulation in heart failure self-care: A theory-driven qualitative study. *International Journal of Behavioral Medicine, 26*(5), 474–485. https://doi.org/10.1007/s12529-019-09798-z
Chichirez, C. M., & Purcărea, V. L. (2018). Interpersonal communication in healthcare. *Journal of Medicine and Life, 11*(2), 119–122.
Chou, C. C., Chen, H. F., Liao, Y. M., Chen, C. W., Liu, P. C., & Yeh, A. Y. (2025). Specific cognitive functions associated with self-care behaviors in older adults with type 2 diabetes and mild cognitive impairment. *Western Journal of Nursing Research, 47*(7), 605–612. https://doi.org/10.1177/01939459251331857
Cook-Cottone, C. P., & Guyker, W. M. (2018). The development and validation of the Mindful Self-Care Scale (MSCS): An assessment of practices that support positive embodiment. *Mindfulness, 9*(1), 161–175. https://doi.org/10.1007/s12671-017-0759-1
Campoli, J., & Cummings, J. A. (2024). "Becoming a person who does self-care": How health care trainees naturalistically develop successful self-care practices. *Journal of Medical Education and Curricular Development*, 11. https://doi.org/10.1177/23821205231223321
Cummings, S. M., Cooper, R. L., & Cassie, K. M. (2009). Motivational interviewing to affect behavioral change in older adults. *Research on Social Work Practice, 19*(2), 195–204. https://doi.org/10.1177/1049731508320216
Ryan, R. M., & Deci, E. L. (2017). *Self-determination theory: Basic psychological needs in motivation, development, and wellness* (p. 398). Guilford Press. https://doi.org/10.1521/978.14625/28806
Dean, K. (1986). Lay care in illness. *Social Science & Medicine, 22*(2), 275–284. https://doi.org/10.1016/0277-9536(86)90076-6
Denyes, M. J., Orem, D. E., & Bekel, G. (2001). Self-care: A foundational science. *Nursing science quarterly, 14*(1), 48–54. https://doi.org/10.1177/089431840101400113
Dickson, V. V., Deatrick, J. A., & Riegel, B. (2008 Sep). A typology of heart failure self-care management in non-elders. *European Journal of Cardiovascular Nursing, 7*(3), 171–181. https://doi.org/10.1016/j.ejcnurse.2007.11.005
Egede, L. E., & Osborn, C. Y. (2010). Role of motivation in the relationship between depression, self-care, and glycemic control in adults with type 2 diabetes. *The Diabetes Educator, 36*(2), 276–283. https://doi.org/10.1177/0145721710361389

El-Osta, A., Sasco, E. R., Barbanti, E., Webber, I., Alaa, A., Karki, M., et al. (2023). Tools for measuring individual self-care capability: A scoping review. *BMC Public Health, 23*(1), 1312. https://doi.org/10.1186/s12889-023-16194-6

Fernandes, A. P. G., Cardoso, V. R., Dos Santos, K. C., Migliaccio, M. M., & Pinto, J. M. (2022). Factors related to the accumulation of healthy behavior among older adults attending primary health care. *Journal of Population Ageing, 15*(3), 677–690.

Fivecoat, H. C., Sayers, S. L., & Riegel, B. (2018). Social support predicts self-care confidence in patients with heart failure. *European Journal of Cardiovascular Nursing, 17*(7), 598–604. https://doi.org/10.1177/1474515118762800

Fjeldsoe, B., Neuhaus, M., Winkler, E., & Eakin, E. (2011). Systematic review of maintenance of behavior change following physical activity and dietary interventions. *Health psychology, 30*(1), 99. https://doi.org/10.1037/a0021974

Freda, M. F., Lemmo, D., Auriemma, E., De Luca, P. R., & Martino, M. L. (2023). From sense to meaning: Narrative Function Coding System for the experience of illness. *Qualitative Research Journal, 23*(1), 41–61. https://doi.org/10.1108/QRJ-06-2022-0081

Frost, H., Campbell, P., Maxwell, M., O'Carroll, R. E., Dombrowski, S. U., Williams, B., et al. (2018). Effectiveness of motivational interviewing on adult behaviour change in health and social care settings: A systematic review of reviews. *PLoS One, 13*(10), e0204890. https://doi.org/10.1371/journal.pone.0204890

Grady, P. A., & Gough, L. L. (2014). Self-management: A comprehensive approach to management of chronic conditions. *American Journal of Public Health, 104*(8), e25–e31. https://doi.org/10.2105/AJPH.2014.302041

Hardcastle, S. J., Fortier, M., Blake, N., & Hagger, M. S. (2017). Identifying content-based and relational techniques to change behaviour in motivational interviewing. *Health Psychology Review, 11*(1), 1–16. https://doi.org/10.1080/17437199.2016.1190659

Harrison, F., Mortby, M. E., Mather, K. A., Sachdev, P. S., & Brodaty, H. (2023). Apathy as a determinant of health behaviors in older adults: Implications for dementia risk reduction. *Alzheimer's & Dementia: Diagnosis, Assessment & Disease Monitoring, 15*(4), e12505.

Harvey, J. A., Chastin, S. F. M., & Skelton, D. A. (2015). How sedentary are older people? A systematic review of the amount of sedentary behavior. *Journal of Aging and Physical Activity, 23*(3), 471–487. https://doi.org/10.1123/japa.2014-0164

Haug, M. R., Wykle, M. L., & Namazi, K. H. (1989). Self-care among older adults. *Social Science & Medicine, 29*(2), 171–183. https://doi.org/10.1016/0277-9536(89)90165-2

Herber, O. R., Atkins, L., Störk, S., Wilm, S., & Bücker, B. (2018). Enhancing self-care adherence in patients with heart failure: a study protocol for developing a theory-based behaviour change intervention using the COM-B behaviour model (ACHIEVE study). *BMJ Open, 8*(9), e025907. https://doi.org/10.1136/bmjopen-2018-025907

Hettema, J., Steele, J., & Miller, W. R. (2005). Motivational interviewing. *Annual Review of Clinical Psychology, 1*, 91–111. https://doi.org/10.1146/annurev.clinpsy.1.102803.143833

Høy, B., Wagner, L., & Hall, E. O. C. (2007). Self-care as a health resource of elders: An integrative review of the concept. *Scandinavian Journal of Caring Sciences, 21*(4), 456–466. https://doi.org/10.1111/j.1471-6712.2006.00491.x

Jiménez-Zazo, F., Romero-Blanco, C., Castro-Lemus, N., Dorado-Suárez, A., & Aznar, S. (2020). Transtheoretical model for physical activity in older adults: Systematic review. *International Journal of Environmental Research and Public Health, 17*(24), 9262. https://doi.org/10.3390/ijerph17249262

Jonkman, N. H., Westland, H., Groenwold, R. H. H., Ågren, S., Atienza, F., Blue, L., et al. (2016). Do self-management interventions work in patients with heart failure? An individual patient data meta-analysis. *Circulation, 133*(12), 1189–1198. https://doi.org/10.1161/CIRCULATIONAHA.115.018006

Khantzian, E. J., & Mack, J. E. (1983). Self-preservation and the care of the self: Ego instincts reconsidered. *The Psychoanalytic Study of the Child, 38*(1), 209–232.

Kitson, A. L., & Lawless, M. T. (2025). Why we need to think differently about self-care and self-management. *Nursing Inquiry, 32*(2), e70013. https://doi.org/10.1111/nin.70013

Kolt, G. S., Schofield, G. M., Kerse, N., Garrett, N., & Oliver, M. (2007). Effect of telephone counseling on physical activity for low-active older people in primary care: A randomized, controlled trial. *Journal of the American Geriatrics Society, 55*(7), 986–992. https://doi.org/10.1111/j.1532-5415.2007.01203.x

Kreman, R., Yates, B. C., Agrawal, S., Fiandt, K., Briner, W., & Shurmur, S. (2006). The effects of motivational interviewing on physiological outcomes. *Applied Nursing Research, 19*(3), 167–170. https://doi.org/10.1016/j.apnr.2005.10.004

Kwasnicka, D., Dombrowski, S. U., White, M., & Sniehotta, F. (2016). Theoretical explanations for maintenance of behaviour change: a systematic review of behaviour theories. *Health Psychology Review, 10*(3), 277–296. https://doi.org/10.1080/17437199.2016.1151372

Lee, C. S., Bidwell, J. T., Paturzo, M., Alvaro, R., Cocchieri, A., Jaarsma, T., Strömberg, A., Riegel, B., & Vellone, E. (2018). Patterns of self-care and clinical events in a cohort of adults with heart failure: 1-year follow-up. *Heart & Lung, 47*(1), 40–46. https://doi.org/10.1016/j.hrtlng.2017.09.004

Lemmo, D., Bianco, R., & Freda, M. F. (2025a). Motivazione e cura di sé nell'invecchiamento: una revisione sistematica della letteratura. *Psicologia dela Salute, 2*, 52–72. https://doi.org/10.3280/PDS2025-002004

Lemmo, D., Martino, M. L., Bianco, R., Donizzetti, A. R., Freda, M. F., & Caso, D. (2025b). Iterative situated engagement perspective: Meaning-making challenges across cancer screening phases. *Cancers (Basel), 17*(12), 2007. https://doi.org/10.3390/cancers17122007

Levin, L. S. (1979 Oct). Self-care: New challenge to individual health. *Journal of the American College Health Association, 28*(2), 117–120. https://doi.org/10.1080/01644300.1979.10392909

Lundahl, B., Moleni, T., Burke, B. L., et al. (2013). Motivational interviewing in medical care settings: A systematic review and meta-analysis of randomized controlled trials. *Patient Education and Counseling, 93*(2), 157–168. https://doi.org/10.1016/j.pec.2013.07.012

Martínez, N., Connelly, C. D., Pérez, A., & Calero, P. (2021). Self-care: A concept analysis. *International Journal of Nursing Sciences, 8*(4), 418–425. https://doi.org/10.1016/j.ijnss.2021.08.007

Matarese, M., Clari, M., De Marinis, M. G., & Barbaranelli, C. (2020 Mar). The self-care in chronic obstructive pulmonary disease inventory: Development and psychometric evaluation. *Evaluation & the Health Professions, 43*(1), 50–62. https://doi.org/10.1177/0163278719856660

Miller, W. R., & Rollnick, S. (2012a). Meeting in the middle: motivational interviewing and self-determination theory. *International Journal of Behavioral Nutrition and Physical Activity, 9*, 25. https://doi.org/10.1186/1479-5868-9-25

Miller, W. R., & Rollnick, S. (2012b). *Motivational interviewing: Helping people change* (3rd ed., p. 482). Guilford Press.

Mitzner, T. L., McBride, S. E., Barg-Walkow, L. H., & Rogers, W. A. (2013). Self-management of wellness and illness in an aging population. *Reviews of Human Factors and Ergonomics, 8*(1), 277–333. https://doi.org/10.1177/1557234X13492979

Mohebi, S., Azadbakht, L., Feizi, A., Sharifirad, G., & Kargar, M. (2013 Jul). Structural role of perceived benefits and barriers to self-care in patients with diabetes. *Journal of Education Health Promotion, 2*(1), 37. https://doi.org/10.4103/2277-9531.115831

Ng, B., & Abbas, D. (2020). Self-determination theory: Attributes of healthy aging. In B. Ng & G. Ho (Eds.), *Self-determination theory and healthy aging. Comparative contexts on physical and mental well-being*. Springer.

Ogugua, J. O., Olorunsogo, T. O., Muonde, M., Maduka, C. P., & Omotayo, O. (2024). Developing countries' health policy: A critical review and pathway to effective healthcare systems. *International Journal of Science and Research Archive, 11*(1), 371–382. https://doi.org/10.30574/ijsra.2024.11.1.0069

O'Halloran, P. D., Blackstock, F., Shields, N., Holland, A., Iles, R., Kingsley, M., et al. (2014). Motivational interviewing to increase physical activity in people with chronic health conditions: A systematic review and meta-analysis. *Clinical Rehabilitation, 28*(12), 1159–1171. https://doi.org/10.1177/0269215514536210

Orem, D. E. (2001). *Nursing: Concepts of practice* (6th ed., p. 542). Mosby.

Palombi, T., Lucidi, F., Chirico, A., Alessandri, G., Filosa, L., Tavolucci, S., et al. (2023). Is the behavioral regulation in exercise questionnaire a valid measure in older people? *Healthcare (Basel), 11*(20), 2707. https://doi.org/10.3390/healthcare11202707

Parthasarathi, T., McConnell, M., Luery, D., & Kable, J. W. (2017). The vivid present: Visualization abilities are associated with steep discounting of future rewards. *Frontiers in Psychology, 8*, 289. https://doi.org/10.3389/fpsyg.2017.00289

Pietrabissa, G. (2024). Aspetti teoretici e funzionali della motivazione negli anziani. In F. Morganti & G. Castelnuovo (Eds.), *Psicologia dell'invecchiamento. Ambiti, prospettive, interventi.* Franco Angeli.

Prochaska, J. O., & DiClemente, C. C. (1983). Stages and processes of self-change of smoking: Toward an integrative model of change. *Journal of Consulting and Clinical Psychology, 51*(3), 390–395. https://doi.org/10.1037/0022-006X.51.3.390

Prochaska, J. O., Redding, C. A., & Evers, K. E. (2008). The transtheoretical model and stages of change. In K. Glanz, B. K. Rimer, & K. Viswanath (Eds.), *Health behavior and health education: Theory, research, and practice* (4th ed., pp. 97–121). San Francisco, CA: Jossey-Bass.

Prochaska, J. O., Johnson, S., & Lee, P. (2009). The transtheoretical model of behavior change. In S. A. Shumaker, J. K. Ockene, & K. A. Riekert (Eds.), *The handbook of health behavior change* (3rd ed., pp. 59–83). Springer.

Purath, J., Keck, A., & Fitzgerald, C. E. (2014). Motivational interviewing for older adults in primary care: A systematic review. *Geriatric Nursing, 35*(3), 219–224. https://doi.org/10.1016/j.gerinurse.2014.02.002

Resnicow, K., Dilorio, C., Soet, J. E., Borrelli, B., Hecht, J., & Ernst, D. (2002). Motivational interviewing in health promotion: It sounds like something is changing. *Health Psychology, 21*(5), 444–451. https://doi.org/10.1037/0278-6133.21.5.444

Riegel, B., Jaarsma, T., Lee, C. S., & Strömberg, A. (2019). Integrating symptoms into the middle-range theory of self-care of chronic illness. *Advances in Nursing Science, 42*(3), 206–215. https://doi.org/10.1097/ANS.0000000000000237

Riegel, B., Jaarsma, T., & Strömberg, A. (2012). A middle-range theory of self-care of chronic illness. *ANS: Advances in Nursing Science, 35*(3), 194–204. https://doi.org/10.1097/ANS.0b013e318261b1ba

Riegel, B., Westland, H., Iovino, P., Barelds, I., Bruins Slot, J., Stawnychy, M. A., et al. (2021). Characteristics of self-care interventions for patients with a chronic condition: A scoping review. *International Journal of Nursing Studies, 116*, 103713. https://doi.org/10.1016/j.ijnurstu.2020.103713

Rollnick, S., Miller, W. R., & Butler, C. C. (2008). *Motivational interviewing in health care: Helping patients change behavior* (p. 210). Guilford Press.

Ros-Sanchez, T., Lidon-Cerezuela, M. B., Lopez-Benavente, Y., & Abad-Corpa, E. (2023). Promoting empowerment and self-care in older women through participatory action research: Analysis of the process of change. *Journal of Advanced Nursing, 79*(6), 2224–2235. https://doi.org/10.1111/jan.15573

Rudnicka, E., Napierała, P., Podfigurna, A., Męczekalski, B., Smolarczyk, R., & Grymowicz, M. (2020). The World Health Organization (WHO) approach to healthy ageing. *Maturitas, 139*, 6–11. https://doi.org/10.1016/j.maturitas.2020.05.018

Schulman-Green, D., Jaser, S. S., Park, C., & Whittemore, R. (2016). A metasynthesis of factors affecting self-management of chronic illness. *Journal of Advanced Nursing, 72*(7), 1469–1489. https://doi.org/10.1111/jan.12902

Shi, L., Wu, B., Liu, X., Ren, Y., Zhang, C., Wang, X., & Wang, L. (2025). Health changes from transtheoretical model–based education in older adults with mild cognitive impairment: A randomized controlled trial. *International Journal of Nursing Studies, 162*, 104961. https://doi.org/10.1016/j.ijnurstu.2024.104961

Skinner, T. C., Bruce, D. G., Davis, T. M. E., & Davis, W. A. (2014). Personality traits, self-care behaviours and glycaemic control in Type 2 diabetes: The Fremantle Diabetes Study Phase II. *Diabetic Medicine, 31*(4), 487–492. https://doi.org/10.1111/dme.12339

Tang, C., Xiao, L. D., Huang, R., Hu, Y., & Wang, Y. (2025). Older adult's acceptance and uptake of referral after screening for cognitive impairment: A cross-sectional study in China. *BMC Geriatrics, 25*(1), 178. https://doi.org/10.1186/s12877-025-05824-w

Tulu, S. N., Cook, P., Oman, K. S., Meek, P., & Kebede, G. E. (2021). Chronic disease self-care: A concept analysis. *Nursing Forum, 56*(3), 734–741. https://doi.org/10.1111/nuf.12577

Wang, L., Chen, H., Lu, H., Wang, Y., Liu, C., Dong, X., … Shang, S. (2020). Effect of a transtheoretical model–based home exercise intervention on exercise adherence, symptoms, and knee function in older adults with knee osteoarthritis: A cluster randomized trial. Arthritis Research & Therapy, 22, 134. doi: https://doi.org/10.1186/s13075-020-02222-y.

Wang, L. Y., Hu, Z. Y., Chen, H. X., Zhu, H., Zhou, C. F., Zhang, R. X., Tang, M. L., & Hu, X. Y. (2025). Systematic review of longitudinal studies on daily health behavior and activity of daily living among older adults. *Frontiers in Public Health, 13*, 1419279. https://doi.org/10.3389/fpubh.2025.1419279

Wang, T., Ho, M. H., Xu, X., Choi, H. R., & Lin, C. C. (2024). Motivational interviews to enhance advance care plans in older adults: Systematic review. *BMJ Supportive & Palliative Care, 14*(e3), e2293–e2301. https://doi.org/10.1136/spcare-2023-004424

West, R. (2005). Time for a change: Putting the Transtheoretical (stages of change) model to rest. *Addiction, 100*(8), 1036–1039. https://doi.org/10.1111/j.1360-0443.2005.01139.x

Wilkinson, A., & Whitehead, L. (2009). Evolution of the concept of self-care and implications for nurses: A literature review. *International Journal of Nursing Studies, 46*(8), 1143–1147. https://doi.org/10.1016/j.ijnurstu.2008.12.011

World Health Organization. (2015). *World report on ageing and health* (p. 246). World Health Organization. ISBN 978-92-4-156504-2.

World Health Organization. (2022). *WHO guideline on self-care interventions for health and well-being: 2022 revision*. World Health Organization.

World Health Organization. (2024). *Implementation of self-care interventions for health and well-being: Guidance for health systems*. World Health Organization.

Yannakoulia, M., Mamalaki, E., Anastasiou, C. A., Mourtzi, N., Lambrinoudaki, I., & Scarmeas, N. (2018). Eating habits and behaviors of older people: Where are we now and where should we go? *Maturitas, 114*, 14–21. https://doi.org/10.1016/j.maturitas.2018.05.001

Webber, D., Guo, Z., & Mann, S. (2013). Self-Care in Health: We Can Define It, but Should We Also Measure It? *Self-Care Journal*, *4*(5), 101–106

Health Tourism: Beyond the Current Model of Thermal Spa Services

Vincenzo De Luca, Michele Virgolesi, Claudia Vetrani, Sara Cacciapuoti, Stefania Capaldo, Emanuele Boaretto, Bruno Mercurio, Teresa Rea, Maurizio Droli, John Farrell, Regina Roller-Wirnsberger, Annamaria Colao, and Maddalena Illario

1 Introduction

The ageing society needs a paradigmatic shift from reactive disease management towards a more proactive approach to active and healthy living that invests all economic sectors, including tourism and related structures and processes, in order to take advantage of the opportunities for sustainable development supported by the

V. De Luca (✉) · M. Virgolesi · T. Rea
Department of Public Health, University of Naples Federico II, Naples, Italy
e-mail: vincenzo.deluca5@unina.it; michele.virgolesi@unina.it

C. Vetrani
Department of Well-being, Nutrition and Sport, Pegaso Telematic University, Naples, Italy

S. Cacciapuoti · A. Colao
Department of Clinical Medicine and Surgery, Federico II University of Naples, Naples, Italy
e-mail: sara.cacciapuoti@unina.it; colao@unina.it

S. Capaldo · E. Boaretto
Federalberghi Terme, Rome, Italy
e-mail: federalberghi@abanomontegrotto.it

B. Mercurio
Department of Human and Social Sciences, L'Orientale University of Naples, Naples, Italy

M. Droli
Aviano Oncology Reference Center, Scientific Institute for Research Hospitalization and Healthcare (IRCCS), National Cancer Institute, Aviano, Italy

J. Farrell
European Innovation Partnership on Active and Healthy Ageing Reference Site Collaborative Network, Brussels, Belgium
e-mail: johnfarrell@lanuaihc.eu

A. Ricciardelli, L. Mercurio (eds.), *Building Innovation in Ageing and Health Policy*, Springer Series in Healthcare Management and Innovation,
https://doi.org/10.1007/978-3-032-09163-5_10

digital transformation. This also includes an adaptation of services according to the needs of older adults, in the light of accessibility due to an increasing number of tourists with reduced mobility, people with disabilities or those suffering from chronic illnesses, whose needs should be integrated into the provision of tourism services (Vega-Vázquez et al., 2020).

In the document "WHO Traditional Medicine Strategy 2002–2005", the World Health Organization (WHO) established the Pain Management Protocol for pain relief, encouraging the development of access policies, for rational, responsible, safe practice and recommends the development of studies that validate the use of Integrative and Complementary Practices (PICS) in prevention and care (World Health Organization, 2002). The strategy recognizes the effectiveness of balneotherapy, hydrotherapy and chronotherapy as PICS (De Macedo Antunes et al., 2019).

Thermal medicine is currently considered the branch of medicine that utilizes the properties of thermal water for curative and rehabilitative purposes, and there is a huge window of opportunity for future innovation and research in various dysfunctions, from rheumatic (Cozzi et al., 2018; Fioravanti et al., 2010) to skin conditions (Cacciapuoti et al., 2020) and cardiovascular diseases (Oyama et al., 2012). Thermal waters and spas have ancient roots in history and still represent a promising opportunity for health and social well-being (Gianfaldoni et al., 2017). The therapeutic role of mineral elements and other chemical compounds present in spa waters for pain relief and restoration of function has been demonstrated with an impact on quality of life as well (Güleç, 2018; Harzy et al., 2009; Matsumoto, 2018; Morer et al., 2017; Özkuk et al., 2018). The methods of application of thermal treatments may concern immersion in water with the head or parts of the body, drinking, inhalation, irrigation, local application of peloids, or dry peloid therapy (for example with sand), gas baths or local application of gas (Gutenbrunner et al., 2010). The indication for treatments with natural mineral waters, gases and peloids are based both on the chemical and physical properties of the agents. Treatments with natural mineral waters, gases and peloids in many countries is called balneotherapy. The use of natural water for therapy is called hydrotherapy, which uses the physical properties of water, namely temperature, hydrostatic pressure, hydrodynamics, buoyancy, viscosity and electrical conductivity. Climatotherapy includes the medical application of climatic factors for the prevention or treatment of diseases, such as high-altitude climates, marine coastal climates and includes changes in the climatic environment (Gutenbrunner et al., 2010).

R. Roller-Wirnsberger
Research Unit Services for Old Age and Lifelong Health, Department of Internal Medicine, Medical University of Graz, Graz, Austria
e-mail: regina.roller-wirnsberger@medunigraz.at

M. Illario
Department of Public Health, University of Naples Federico II, Naples, Italy
e-mail: illario@unina.it

Thermal spa environments lend themself to supporting a holistic approach to health promotion, integrating spa treatment with exposure to natural open spaces, access to physical activities, physiotherapy and health education opportunities.

According to the study on health tourism carried out by the Directorate General for Internal Policies of the European Parliament (Mainil et al., 2017), the UK, Italy, Germany, Belgium and Croatia were the most frequently involved countries in the case studies that they identified for health tourism, although there are relevant experiences also in Austria (Styria) and Slovenia (Prekmurje) (Lindner et al., 2021).

Italy has a very high number of thermal centres, about 380, recognized by the National Health Service (SSN), whose services are reimbursed by the public budget. Thermal care is included in the essential levels of care (LEA) provided by the SSN to citizens suffering from certain illnesses who can effectively benefit from this type of treatment (Presidency of the Council of Ministers, 2017). Thermal services paid for by the SSN consist of cycles of services for specific diseases and include, in all cases, a medical visit upon acceptance by the thermal centre.

The SSN indicates the list of illnesses that can benefit from thermal cares and the list of services that can be provided (Presidency of the Council of Ministers, 2017). The average duration of treatments is 12 days (Masiero, 2008), which is considered too long by working age users/patients. In fact, they prefer to take multiple but shorter stays, especially considering that thermal treatments are carried out in several instalments. The types of treatment that are most in demand are mud baths and thermal baths, which treat diseases of the musculoskeletal system such as arthrosis and other degenerative forms, and also treatments for the respiratory diseases, which had an important upswing especially after COVID-19 pandemics.

Recent studies by the Global Wellness Institute (Wang et al., 2023) have shown that, after the COVID-19 pandemic, there has been an increased propensity to spend on health/wellness even when travelling. Such increased concern about health has been leading to tourism destination choices based on health and wellness service offer (thermal services, integrative medicine, physiotherapy, physical activity, healthy diet and healthy environment, etc.). This new type of traveller, during a holiday, enjoys leading a healthy lifestyle and taking advantage of health/wellness services (Quirino, 2016). In this perspective, a very important value is assumed by the "healthiness" of the territory and the holistic health and care services in the area that can be integrated with the accommodation and hospitality offer, including culture, nature, gastronomy and other more specific health services.

The Reference Site Collaborative Network for Active and Healthy Ageing (Bousquet et al., 2019), through the establishment of a thematic working group on Health Tourism, is organizing an effort to evaluate continuous and successful examples of tourism offer accessible to older adults and citizens with special health needs.

This article aims to evaluate some existing services and good practices that combine health services and thermal spa treatments, with the tourist offer.

2 An Innovative Model for Thermalism

Different users coexist in the thermal facilities: patients, especially interested in medical treatments, and health tourists interested in an overall well-being experience. These two categories of users have different motivations whose understanding is fundamental not only from an economic perspective, but above all from a medical and organizational point of view.

The current shift towards a proactive approach to health needs, supported by the digital transformation of health and care, represent a "golden" opportunity to integrate healthcare processes with personalized yet sustainable health tourism offers that can reflect in their variety the sociocultural heritage of the different European region, that is unparalleled worldwide.

Innovative thermal services, for example, can exploit the potential of the territories where they are located, in particular the presence of attractive sites for their scenic beauty or archaeological and cultural sites, and the adaptation of local gastronomic offer to specific health needs to attract new users, who wish to combine the travel experience with health and well-being. Such integrated services would be favoured by policies for the simplification of cross-border assistance and better synergies with the galaxy of public and private operators in the sector of tourism provision and promotion at a local level. However, the possibility that a thermal destination realizes effective management of tourist and health flows depends on the identification of the peculiarities that the territory can offer, to prevent the onset of diseases or in response to a specific disease. The enhancement of specific or health-related treatments, which can be applied only in local thermal sites and not in others, due to the properties of the waters, should be supported by the coordination of decision-making, organizational and marketing processes, which go alongside with other services responding to the unmet health needs of users/patients.

2.1 The Psoriasis Use Case

The effect of thermal balneotherapy (TB) on skin diseases (psoriasis, atopic dermatitis, acne vulgaris, lichen planus, etc.) has been widely reported. In particular, TB showed promising results in the management of psoriasis, a chronic skin inflammatory disease whose course may be affected by weather, humidity, temperature and climate factors (Liang et al., 2015).

Despite the introduction of more rapid and effective treatments such as biologic drugs led to the reduction of the use of TB, the minimum risk of side effects makes this treatment a valuable option. However, acute infection, active tuberculosis, cardiac arrhythmias and poorly controlled arterial hypertension contraindicate its use as well as pustular or erythrodermic psoriasis cannot be treated with TB. Of note, TB does not interfere with metabolic comorbidities which often affect psoriasis patients.

Currently, several authors showed that TB can benefit to psoriasis patients, particularly plaque psoriasis, after 3 or 4 weeks of treatment. However, few clinical trials are available. Another interesting use of TB is its combination with natural or artificial ultraviolet defined as balneotherapy (Huang et al., 2018).

Globally, several centres have been recommended for TB for psoriasis, involving several countries such as Italy, Poland, Spain, Germany, Bulgaria, Serbia, and the USA (Kazandjieva et al., 2008).

As regards Italy, TB at Comano spa in Trentino showed to improve psoriasis severity as well as patients' quality of life. Indeed, Comano thermal water seems to reduce the expression of several cytokines involved in psoriasis pathogenesis such as vascular endothelial growth factor-A isoforms, interleukin (IL)-6, IL-8, tumour necrosis factor-α, and cytocheratin-16 (Peroni et al., 2008).

Promising results in terms of psoriasis severity reduction in mild-to-moderate disease have also been reported at the thermal spa sites of Levico and Vetriolo (Trentino Region, Northern Italy) with arsenical-ferruginous spring water (Borroni et al., 2013). Thermal bath plus muds have been shown to reduce psoriasis severity also in Ischia Island, Italy (Delfino et al., 2003).

To sum up, TB showed to reduce scale, inflammation and pruritus in psoriatic patients, suggesting its use as an interesting alternative or adjuvant weapon in psoriasis patients. Moreover, TB could be a valuable option in patients who momentarily discontinued pharmacologic therapies. However, studies investigating the effectiveness of TB on psoriasis are heterogeneous. Therefore, standardized studies are required to better understand the possible role of TB in psoriasis management and its treatment algorithm (Cacciapuoti et al., 2020).

Psoriasis is triggered by a combination of genetic and environmental factors and is often associated with multiple comorbidities. Other diseases strongly contribute to the onset of psoriasis and make more complex pharmacological treatments and management of the psoriatic patient (Camela et al., 2023). Psoriatic arthritis affects about 20–30% of patients and generally affects the pathologies of the fingers and toes but can also affect other joints such as knees and spine (Napolitano et al., 2016). Physical therapy in response to the management of psoriatic arthritis improves general cardiovascular conditions, articular motion and reduces pain (Lubrano et al., 2009). The metabolic syndrome is a frequent comorbidity in people with psoriasis (Lubrano et al., 2020). The control of body weight with a modification of the food plan (Garbicz et al., 2021) and physical exercise (Myers et al., 2019) could be important in the management of psoriasis. There is an increased prevalence of cardiovascular diseases, linked to the presence of chronic inflammation (Polachek et al., 2016). As well as systemic inflammation may adversely influence neurocognitive functions (Chimenti et al., 2019). High prevalence of mental health comorbidities among patients with psoriasis is well recognized (Zhao et al., 2019).

2.2 Digital Solutions and Age-Friendly Environments

Integration of information technologies in general healthcare industry changes health tourists travel options and patterns, particularly for the initial check-up and follow-up phases of the healthcare services they will receive abroad (Wong & Hazley, 2020). Digital solutions enable healthcare professionals to communicate effectively with patients and the delivery of rehabilitation programmes using virtual reality and serious games (Cano Porras et al., 2018).

Mobile apps for telemonitoring, through medical devices connected to mobile phone, allow the patient's progress to be tracked remotely through a shared care plan to be modified in real time.

Prescription of diet and physical activity provided by healthcare professionals are probably the most unattended medical prescriptions. Digital solutions support this adherence, integrating prescription and monitoring of the activities related to these prescriptions. Mobile apps for personalized coaching offer the opportunity for patients to be coached on physical activity, nutrition and other lifestyles in line with personal preferences. Harmful effects (such as intolerances and unwanted food-drug interactions) can be avoided, and the patient can receive comprehensive long-term coaching (De Luca et al., 2019). Similarly, personalized coaching solutions allow instruction in activities to prevent and avoid a sedentary lifestyle and receive useful and comprehensive long-term coaching (Bevilacqua et al., 2020). For instance, Geocaching allows to combine the acquisition of digital skills, a visit to a museum, a city or a nature reserve, with the maintenance of physical and mental well-being, contrasting a sedentary lifestyle. Geocaching is also a means of social relations because it allows to stay informed in a constantly evolving environment as well as to share and strengthen the interest in the historical and artistic heritage of the destination city, as well as the sharing of knowledge and experiences and the felling of intergenerational gaps (Fornasini et al., 2020).

Digital solutions can contribute both to more efficient use of healthcare resources and to better targeted, more integrated, and safer healthcare (Kim et al., 2017; OECD, 2010). To provide services aimed at users with specific accessibility and health needs, built environments and services must be designed with particular attention to the specific needs deriving from their health conditions, so that their fruition can be pleasant.

In recent years, special emphasis is given to smart homes for people suffering from chronic diseases and disabilities and to supporting tools, including robotics, smart living environments and smart communication, to improve formal and informal care, and increase the well-being and active participation of older people (Vimarlund et al., 2021). Lifestyles are the first level of intervention for chronic patients. Digitally supported mapping systems could represent opportunities to give to both one-day-trip visitors and tourists the possibility to locate forest environments by considering their accessibility, attractiveness, and competitiveness (Dodev et al., 2021).

Smart Health Age-Friendly Environments (SHAFE) is a new concept introduced in Europe since 2011 by the European Commission, which combines the concept of Age-Friendly Environments with digital solutions to improve health and disease management of older people (Dantas et al., 2019).

2.3 Gastronomy and Healthy Nutrition

Culinary tourism is one of the most dynamic segments in tourism. It is aimed at discovering the food and wine of a territory and through which the tourist can experience the local culture and acquire a sense of place (Garibaldi, 2022). Nutrition plays a key role in determining population health outcomes and its impact depends on food features and stages of life. The possibility to harness nutritional and functional, thus "nutraceutical" (Stephen & De Felice, 2002) properties of specific foods for human health purposes has been underlined in the last four decades. Nutraceutical have been defined as: "a food (or part of a food) that provides medical or health benefits, including the prevention and/or treatment of a disease" (Brower, 1998). In some cases, this innovation has led to the wrong perception that all natural foods could be good for human health improvement purposes (Heyland, 2001). Nevertheless, despite this obstacle reducing rationality in the usage of healthy and nutraceutical foods as medicines, potentials of nutraceuticals for both human health and sustained socio-economic development have been recently underlined (Sachdeva et al., 2020; Patel et al., 2019). Malnutrition is a serious health problem in the elderly population, as food intake worsens with increasing age (Ferreira et al., 2011; Johansson et al., 2009). Among the reasons why older adults or people with specific diseases are at high risk of malnutrition there are disease-related factors that affect adequate food intake, even when food is qualitatively and quantitatively available and properly prepared. The most serious factors are anorexia, nausea and eating problems due to difficulties in food intake (e.g. muscle weakness, coordination problems), oral problems, difficulties in chewing, tasting or swallowing and problems with motility or absorption (Stratton, 2003; Westergren et al., 2009). Appropriate nutritional intervention can reduce the risk of developing chronic diseases including cardiovascular, neurodegenerative and metabolic syndromes, decreased bone density, muscle mass, immune response and cancer (Di Furia et al., 2016; Di Somma et al., 2017; Milne et al., 2009; Morley, 1997; Pascale et al., 2018; Roberts, 2000; Roberts et al., 1994; Viñas et al., 2011; Vuolo et al., 2012). Gastrological Approach to Malnutrition represents a primary nutritional approach to prevent and treat malnutrition in older adults and in patients suffering from diseases that alter the perception of taste. The approach involves personalized nutritional interventions that use tools, such as taste steering, to assess taste perception and improve patients' food intake and quality of life. A multidisciplinary team of clinicians, nutritionists and chefs interfaces with the patient to create personalized nutritional interventions, which take into account the specificities of the disease, safeguarding taste and quality of the food (Illario et al., 2016). Personalized nutritional interventions require the personnel involved to be properly trained. Chefs will have to be trained on innovative cooking methods aimed at enhancing healthiness and taste, and at promoting food intake (Winters et al., 2022).

2.4 Active Living

Travelling for tourism is always a good opportunity to undertake a more active lifestyle, while hopping from one cultural site to another, or walking a natural trail, a beach and a forest. There are experiences available to support the personalization of these experiences, while measuring their impact on our health (Fornasini et al.,

2020). Especially when combined to dedicated health assessments, such activities can be synergic with adapted physical activity prescriptions and offer a different experience also to travellers with specific health conditions.

Walks and low physical activities at high altitude mountains have positive effects in people suffering from respiratory diseases (Massimo et al., 2013; Vinnikov et al., 2016). The possibility to leverage forest climate potentials for human health purposes has gained attraction in some Asian countries.

In Japan, the term "forest therapy" has been suggested by the Forest Therapy Society, representing a leading organization acting in this research field, to indicate "an evidence-based approach aimed to facilitate the healing of individuals through experiencing forest immersions" (Forest Therapy Society, 2008).

In South Korea, forest therapy has been defined very similarly by law as "immune-strengthening and health-promoting activities utilizing various elements of the forest, such as fragrance and scenic view" (Ochiai et al., 2015).

Although psychological and clinical benefits of forest therapy (FT) have been documented across regions (Hansen et al., 2017; Kamioka et al., 2012; Li, 2022; Rajoo et al., 2020), ambiguities in how FT is defined are emerging among health professionals in countries such as Italy, driven by a proliferation of definitions that are not evidence-based and consequently misleading (Droli, Bašan, & Vassallo, 2022).

Despite these ambiguities, evidence highlights the contribution of healthy forests to human health (FAO, 2020) and the benefits of forest immersions ("forest bathing") for hypertension in older adults (Mao et al., 2012). In addition, low-altitude forest climatic stays may be more effective than high-altitude mountain stays (Droli, Sigura, et al., 2022), and forest therapy can support sustainable tourism development in rural areas (Ohe et al., 2017).

3 Discussion

Health tourism is a growing sector worldwide, and there is an ever-growing attention by travellers about well-being and services with an added value for their health. This is fundamental because, despite the growing interest in the topic of health mobility and related opportunities, there is currently no shared definition of the phenomenon. Several gaps need to be addressed, for example the knowledge about service providers and facilities. Wellness tourism dominates EU health tourism with two-thirds to three-quarters of the total market: we may take advantage of this opportunity and combine it to the digital transformation of health and care through coherent and coordinated investment strategies across the EU for the triple win: improved sustainability of the healthcare systems, improved health outcomes and sustainable development policies (Mainil et al., 2017).

An innovative and integrated health tourism service must take into consideration, in addition to the effect of healthcare treatment, also the potential benefits of an entire health tourism product on the health and quality of life of patients (Prossegger et al., 2019). Thermal spas may represent the forefront of a market offer for health tourism as long as we will manage to engage the diversity of operators in the health tourism supply chain, ranging from service providers, brokers or hotels to certification, accreditation and insurance companies.

It is therefore necessary to initiate regional processes of health tourism development, positioning specific products and service chains for target groups on the market (European Union, 2022). To this purpose, thermal spa represents an excellent candidate to carry out a first definition of a dataset that might allow an assessment exercise to define a methodology to be scaled up further, to other services. Indeed, thermal spa already includes some health services that can be more easily connected to local valuable offers and initiatives through innovative tools, thus defining customizable service offers.

The need emerges to identify, adopt and develop digital solutions that can on the one hand facilitate the connection between patients and key regional and local stakeholders, which encourage the sharing of knowledge about services and local opportunities and experiences; on the other, improving the travel and accommodation experience by supporting the patient in managing their health conditions. Both healthcare and tourism sectors are being revolutionized by digital tools. Cross-sectoral and transnational level digital solutions can support the redefinition of competitiveness in health tourism services and provide better management strategies (Wong & Hazley, 2020).

4 Conclusions

This paper has identified the possibility of integrating the services and products (product portfolio) offered by a balneotherapy tourism destination to include the services and products offered by the agri-food chain, the forestry health tourism chain, and by other supply chains, to promote health and well-being.

Despite this possibility, the expansion of their product portfolio and supply chains requires the expansion of quality controls and certification systems. To encourage harmonious integration between different products and supply chains, it could be useful to identify the "thin-fil-rouge" that will unite all the offers promoted and supply chains integrating the conventional balneotherapy value chain.

This paper suggests the need to identify the elements characterizing all the offers facilitating management initiatives. Those elements could be represented by: (a) the presence of medical evidence to support the activity offered, (b) the presence of certain health objectives (prevention, integration of conventional pharmacological and/or rehabilitation) of some type to be achieved and (c) the difficult duplicability of local offers, i.e. their being based on natural resources characterizing the destination.

Balneotherapy tourism destinations that expand their product portfolio and integrate their respective supply chains by specifying these linking pins will offer a service permanently capable of creating value for their users. Moreover, they could create the conditions for a competitive advantage that can be defended by the competition and therefore more stable and long-lasting over time.

Acknowledgements Not applicable.

DisclosureThe author reports no conflicts of interest in this work.

References

Bevilacqua, R., Casaccia, S., Cortellessa, G., Astell, A., Lattanzio, F., Corsonello, A., D'Ascoli, P., et al. (2020). Coaching through technology: A systematic review into efficacy and effectiveness for the ageing population. *International Journal of Environmental Research and Public Health/ International Journal of Environmental Research and Public Health, 17*(16), 5930. https://doi.org/10.3390/ijerph17165930

Borroni, G., Brazzelli, V., Fornara, L., Rosso, R., Paulli, M., Tinelli, C., & Ciocca, O. (2013). Clinical, pathological and immunohistochemical effects of Arsenical-Ferruginous SPA waters on mild-to-moderate psoriatic lesions: A randomized placebo-controlled study. *International Journal of Immunopathology and Pharmacology, 26*(2), 495–501. https://doi.org/10.1177/039463201302600223

Bousquet, J., Illario, M., Farrell, J., Batey, N., Carriazo, A., Malva, J., Hajjam, J., et al. (2019). The reference site collaborative network of the European innovation partnership on active and healthy ageing. *HAL (Le Centre Pour La Communication Scientifique Directe), 19*, 66–81.

Brower, V. (1998). Nutraceuticals: Poised for a healthy slice of the healthcare market? *Nature Biotechnology, 16*(8), 728–731. https://doi.org/10.1038/nbt0898-728

Cacciapuoti, S., Luciano, M. A., Megna, M., Annunziata, M. C., Napolitano, M., Patruno, C., Scala, E., et al. (2020). The role of thermal water in chronic skin diseases management: A review of the literature. *Journal of Clinical Medicine, 9*(9), 3047. https://doi.org/10.3390/jcm9093047

Camela, E., Potestio, L., Fabbrocini, G., Pallotta, S., & Megna, M. (2023). The holistic approach to psoriasis patients with comorbidities: The role of investigational drugs. *Expert Opinion on Investigational Drugs, 32*(6), 537–552. https://doi.org/10.1080/13543784.2023.2219387

Chimenti, M. S., Caso, F., Alivernini, S., De Martino, E., Costa, L., Tolusso, B., Triggianese, P., et al. (2019). Amplifying the concept of psoriatic arthritis: The role of autoimmunity in systemic psoriatic disease. *Autoimmunity Reviews, 18*(6), 565–575. https://doi.org/10.1016/j.autrev.2018.11.007

Cozzi, F., Ciprian, L., Carrara, M., Galozzi, P., Zanatta, E., Scanu, A., Sfriso, P., et al. (2018). Balneotherapy in chronic inflammatory rheumatic diseases—A narrative review. *International Journal of Biometeorology, 62*(12), 2065–2071. https://doi.org/10.1007/s00484-018-1618-z

Dantas, C., van Staalduinen, W., Jegundo, A., Ganzarain, J., Van der Mark, M., Rodrigues, F., Illario, M., & De Luca, V. (2019). Smart healthy age-friendly environments - Policy recommendations of the thematic network SHAFE. *Translational medicine @ UniSa, 19*, 103–108.

De Luca, V., Birov, S., Beyhan, O., Robinson, S., Sanchez-Nanclares, G., Acuña, M., Fernandes, A., Hammerschmidt, R., Annuzzi, G., Iaccarino, G., & Illario, M. (2019). European specifications for value-based pre-commercial procurement of innovative ICT for empowerment and self-management of diabetes mellitus patients. In *Proceedings of the 5th international conference on information and communication technologies for ageing well and e-health - ICT4AWE.*; ISBN 978-989-758-368-1; ISSN 2184-4992 (pp. 19–27). SciTePress. https://doi.org/10.5220/0007638700190027

De Macedo Antunes, J., Daher, D. V., De Araújo Giaretta, V. M., Ferrari, M. F. M., & Posso, M. B. S. (2019). Hydrotherapy and crenotherapy in the treatment of pain: Integrative review. *BrJP, 2*(2), 187. https://doi.org/10.5935/2595-0118.20190033

Delfino, M., Russo, N., Migliaccio, G., & Carraturo, N. (2003). Studio sperimentale sull'efficacia dei fanghi termali dell'isola di Ischia associati a balneoterapia nella cura della psoriasi volgare a placche. *La Clinica Terapeutica, 154*, 167–171.

Di Furia, L., Rusciano, M. R., Leonardini, L., Rossi, P., Giammarchi, C., Vittori, E., Tilocca, S., et al. (2016). A nutritional approach to the prevention of cancer: From assessment to personalized intervention. *Translational Medicine UniSa, 13*, 33–41.

Di Somma, C., Scarano, E., Barrea, L., Zhukouskaya, V. V., Savastano, S., Mele, C., Scacchi, M., et al. (2017). Vitamin D and neurological diseases: An endocrine view. *International Journal of Molecular Sciences, 18*(11), 2482. https://doi.org/10.3390/ijms18112482

Dodev, Y., Zhiyanski, M., Glushkova, M., Borisova, B., Semerdzhieva, L., Ihtimanski, I., Dimitrov, S., et al. (2021). An integrated approach to assess the potential of forest areas for therapy services. *Land, 10*(12), 1354. https://doi.org/10.3390/land10121354

Droli, M., Bašan, L., & Vassallo, F. G. (2022). Positioning climate therapy stays as a health tourism product: An evidence-based approach. *Emerging Science Journal, 6*(2), 256–272. https://doi.org/10.28991/esj-2022-06-02-04

Droli, M., Sigura, M., Vassallo, F. G., Droli, G., & Iseppi, L. (2022). Evaluating potential respiratory benefits of forest-based experiences: A regional scale approach. *Forests, 13*(3), 387. https://doi.org/10.3390/f13030387

European Union. (2022). Project - Health tourism skills building for regions and businesses. Available at: https://keep.eu/projects/18939/Trail-for-Health-Nor%20d-EN/.%20. Accessed 3 July 2024.

FAO. (2020). Forests for human health and well-being—Strengthening the forest–health–nutrition nexus. Forestry Working Paper No. 18. Available at: https://doi.org/10.4060/cb1468en. Accessed 3 July 2024.

Ferreira, L. S., Amaral, T. F. D., De Fátima Nunes Marucci, M., Nascimento, L. F. C., Lebrão, M. L., & De Oliveira Duarte, Y. A. (2011). Undernutrition as a major risk factor for death among older Brazilian adults in the community-dwelling setting: SABE survey. *Nutrition, 27*(10), 1017–1022. https://doi.org/10.1016/j.nut.2010.11.008

Fioravanti, A., Cantarini, L., Guidelli, G. M., & Galeazzi, M. (2010). Mechanisms of action of spa therapies in rheumatic diseases: What scientific evidence is there? *Rheumatology International, 31*(1), 1–8. https://doi.org/10.1007/s00296-010-1628-6

Forest Therapy Society (Japan). (2008). *Forest Therapy (official English page)*. Available at: https://www.fo-society.jp/en/. Accessed 5 November 2025.

Fornasini, S., Dianti, M., Bacchiega, A., Forti, S., & Conforti, D. (2020). Using geocaching to promote active aging: Qualitative study. *JMIR: Journal of Medical Internet Research/Journal of Medical Internet Research, 22*(6), e15339. https://doi.org/10.2196/15339

Garbicz, J., Całyniuk, B., Górski, M., Buczkowska, M., Piecuch, M., Kulik, A., & Rozentryt, P. (2021). Nutritional therapy in persons suffering from psoriasis. *Nutrients, 14*(1), 119. https://doi.org/10.3390/nu14010119

Garibaldi, R. (2022). Rapporto sul Turismo Enogastronomico Italiano 2019. Available at: https://www.robertagaribaldi.it/rapporto-sul-turismo-enogastronomico-italiano-2019-3/. Accessed 3 July 2024.

Gianfaldoni, S., Tchernev, G., Wollina, U., Roccia, M. G., Fioranelli, M., Gianfaldoni, R., & Lotti, T. (2017). History of the baths and thermal medicine. *Open Access Macedonian Journal of Medical Sciences, 5*(4), 566–568. https://doi.org/10.3889/oamjms.2017.126

Güleç, A. T. (2018). Natural thermal spa water versus hyperthermic tap water for treatment of recalcitrant hand warts in organ transplant recipients: A patient-blinded, comparative preliminary study. *Experimental and Clinical Transplantation, 16*(Suppl), 1. https://doi.org/10.6002/ect.tond-tdtd2017.p59

Gutenbrunner, C., Bender, T., Cantista, P., & Karagülle, Z. (2010). A proposal for a worldwide definition of health resort medicine, balneology, medical hydrology and climatology. *International Journal of Biometeorology, 54*(5), 495–507. https://doi.org/10.1007/s00484-010-0321-5

Hansen, M. M., Jones, R., & Tocchini, K. (2017). Shinrin-Yoku (forest bathing) and nature therapy: A state-of-the-art review. *International Journal of Environmental Research and Public Health, 14*(8), 851. https://doi.org/10.3390/ijerph14080851

Harzy, T., Ghani, N., Akasbi, N., Bono, W., & Nejjari, C. (2009). Short- and long-term therapeutic effects of thermal mineral waters in knee osteoarthritis: A systematic review of randomized controlled trials. *Clinical Rheumatology, 28*(5), 501–507. https://doi.org/10.1007/s10067-009-1114-2

Heyland, D. K. (2001). In search of the magic nutraceutical: Problems with current approaches. *The Journal of Nutrition, 131*(9), 2591S–2595S. https://doi.org/10.1093/jn/131.9.2591s

Huang, A., Seité, S., & Adar, T. (2018). The use of balneotherapy in dermatology. *Clinics in Dermatology, 36*(3), 363–368. https://doi.org/10.1016/j.clindermatol.2018.03.010

Illario, M., Maione, A. S., Rusciano, M. R., Goossens, E., Rauter, A., Braz, N., Jager-Wittenaar, H., et al. (2016). NutriLive: An integrated nutritional approach as a sustainable tool to prevent malnutrition in older people and promote Active and Healthy Ageing—The EIP-AHA Nutrition Action Group. *Advances in Public Health, 2016*, 1–9. https://doi.org/10.1155/2016/5678782

Johansson, Y., Bachrach-Lindström, M., Carstensen, J., & Ek, A. (2009). Malnutrition in a home-living older population: prevalence, incidence and risk factors. A prospective study. *Journal of Clinical Nursing, 18*(9), 1354–1364. https://doi.org/10.1111/j.1365-2702.2008.02552.x

Kamioka, H., Tsutani, K., Mutoh, Y., Honda, T., Shiozawa, N., Okada, S., Park, S.-J., et al. (2012). A systematic review of randomized controlled trials on curative and health enhancement effects of forest therapy. *Psychology Research and Behavior Management*, 85. https://doi.org/10.2147/prbm.s32402

Kazandjieva, J., Grozdev, I., Darlenski, R., & Tsankov, N. (2008). Climatotherapy of psoriasis. *Clinics in Dermatology, 26*(5), 477–485. https://doi.org/10.1016/j.clindermatol.2008.05.001

Kim, K.-I., Gollamudi, S. S., & Steinhubl, S. (2017). Digital technology to enable aging in place. *Experimental Gerontology, 88*, 25–31. https://doi.org/10.1016/j.exger.2016.11.013

Li, Q. (2022). Effects of forest environment (Shinrin-yoku/Forest bathing) on health promotion and disease prevention—The establishment of 'forest medicine'. *Environmental Health and Preventive Medicine, 27*(0), 43. https://doi.org/10.1265/ehpm.22-00160

Liang, J., Kang, D., Wang, Y., Yu, Y., Fan, J., & Takashi, E. (2015). Carbonate ion-enriched hot spring water promotes skin wound healing in nude rats. *PLoS One, 10*(2), e0117106. https://doi.org/10.1371/journal.pone.0117106

Lindner, S., Illing, K., Sommer, J., Krajnc-Nikolić, T., Harer, J., Kurre, C., Lautner, K., et al. (2021). Development of a binational framework for Active and Healthy Ageing (AHA) bridging Austria and Slovenia in a thermal spa region. *International Journal of Environmental Research and Public Health/International Journal of Environmental Research and Public Health, 18*(2), 639. https://doi.org/10.3390/ijerph18020639

Lubrano, E., Scriffignano, S., & Perrotta, F. M. (2020). Multimorbidity and comorbidity in psoriatic arthritis—A perspective. *Expert Review of Clinical Immunology, 16*(10), 963–972. https://doi.org/10.1080/1744666x.2021.1825941

Lubrano, E., Spadaro, A., Parsons, W. J., Atteno, M., & Ferrara, N. (2009). Rehabilitation in psoriatic arthritis. *Journal of Rheumatology. Supplement, 83*(0), 81–82. https://doi.org/10.3899/jrheum.09235

Mainil, T., Eijgelaar, E., Klijs, J., Nawijn, J., & Peeters, P. (2017). Research for TRAN Committee—Health tourism in the EU: A general investigation, European Parliament, Policy Department for Structural and Cohesion Policies. Available at: https://www.europarl.europa.eu/RegData/etudes/STUD/2017/601985/IPOL_STU(2017)601985_EN.pdf. Accessed 3 July 2024.

Mao, G.-X., Cao, Y.-B., Lan, X.-G., He, Z.-H., Chen, Z.-M., Wang, Y.-Z., Hu, X.-L., et al. (2012). Therapeutic effect of forest bathing on human hypertension in the elderly. *Journal of Cardiology, 60*(6), 495–502. https://doi.org/10.1016/j.jjcc.2012.08.003

Masiero, S. (2008). Thermal rehabilitation and osteoarticular diseases of the elderly. *Aging Clinical and Experimental Research, 20*(3), 189–194. https://doi.org/10.1007/bf03324772

Massimo, T., Blank, C., Strasser, B., & Schobersberger, W. (2013). Does climate therapy at moderate altitudes improve pulmonary function in asthma patients? A systematic review. *Sleep & Breathing, 18*(1), 195–206. https://doi.org/10.1007/s11325-013-0870-z

Matsumoto, S. (2018). Evaluation of the role of balneotherapy in rehabilitation medicine. *Journal of Nippon Medical School, 85*(4), 196–203. https://doi.org/10.1272/jnms.jnms.2018_85-30

Milne, A. C., Potter, J., Vivanti, A., & Avenell, A. (2009). Protein and energy supplementation in elderly people at risk from malnutrition. *Cochrane Library*. https://doi.org/10.1002/14651858.cd003288.pub3

Morer, C., Roques, C.-F., Françon, A., Forestier, R., & Maraver, F. (2017). The role of mineral elements and other chemical compounds used in balneology: Data from double-blind randomized clinical trials. *International Journal of Biometeorology, 61*(12), 2159–2173. https://doi.org/10.1007/s00484-017-1421-2

Morley, J. (1997). Anorexia of aging: Physiologic and pathologic. *The American Journal of Clinical Nutrition, 66*(4), 760–773. https://doi.org/10.1093/ajcn/66.4.760

Myers, J., Kokkinos, P., & Nyelin, E. (2019). Physical activity, cardiorespiratory fitness, and the metabolic syndrome. *Nutrients, 11*(7), 1652. https://doi.org/10.3390/nu11071652

Napolitano, M., Caso, F., Scarpa, R., Megna, M., Patrì, A., Balato, N., & Costa, L. (2016). Psoriatic arthritis and psoriasis: Differential diagnosis. *Clinical Rheumatology, 35*(8), 1893–1901. https://doi.org/10.1007/s10067-016-3295-9

Ochiai, H., Ikei, H., Song, C., Kobayashi, M., Miura, T., Kagawa, T., Li, Q., et al. (2015). Physiological and psychological effects of a forest therapy program on middle-aged females. *International Journal of Environmental Research and Public Health/International Journal of Environmental Research and Public Health, 12*(12), 15222–15232. https://doi.org/10.3390/ijerph121214984

OECD. (2010). *Improving health sector efficiency: The role of information and communication technologies*. OECD Publishing. https://doi.org/10.1787/9789264084612-en

Ohe, Y., Ikei, H., Song, C., & Miyazaki, Y. (2017). Evaluating the relaxation effects of emerging forest-therapy tourism: A multidisciplinary approach. *Tourism Management, 62*, 322–334. https://doi.org/10.1016/j.tourman.2017.04.010

Oyama, J.-I., Kudo, Y., Maeda, T., Node, K., & Makino, N. (2012). Hyperthermia by bathing in a hot spring improves cardiovascular functions and reduces the production of inflammatory cytokines in patients with chronic heart failure. *Heart and Vessels, 28*(2), 173–178. https://doi.org/10.1007/s00380-011-0220-7

Özkuk, K., Uysal, B., Ateş, Z., Ökmen, B. M., Sezer, R., & Dilek, G. (2018). The effects of inpatient versus outpatient spa therapy on pain, anxiety, and quality of life in elderly patients with generalized osteoarthritis: A pilot study. *International Journal of Biometeorology, 62*(10), 1823–1832. https://doi.org/10.1007/s00484-018-1584-5

Pascale, A. V., Finelli, R., Giannotti, R., Visco, V., Fabbricatore, D., Matula, I., Mazzeo, P., et al. (2018). Vitamin D, parathyroid hormone and cardiovascular risk. *Journal of Cardiovascular Medicine, 19*(2), 62–66. https://doi.org/10.2459/jcm.0000000000000614

Patel, A., Matsakas, L., Rova, U., & Christakopoulos, P. (2019). A perspective on biotechnological applications of thermophilic microalgae and cyanobacteria. *Bioresource Technology, 278*, 424–434. https://doi.org/10.1016/j.biortech.2019.01.063

Peroni, A., Gisondi, P., Zanoni, M., & Girolomoni, G. (2008). Balneotherapy for chronic plaque psoriasis at Comano Spa in Trentino, Italy. *Dermatologic Therapy, 21*, S31–S38. https://doi.org/10.1111/j.1529-8019.2008.00200.x

Polachek, A., Touma, Z., Anderson, M., & Eder, L. (2016). Risk of cardiovascular morbidity in patients with psoriatic arthritis: A meta-analysis of observational studies. *Arthritis Care & Research, 69*(1), 67–74. https://doi.org/10.1002/acr.22926

Porras, D. C., Siemonsma, P., Inzelberg, R., Zeilig, G., & Plotnik, M. (2018). Advantages of virtual reality in the rehabilitation of balance and gait. *Neurology, 90*(22), 1017–1025. https://doi.org/10.1212/wnl.0000000000005603

Presidency of the Council of Ministers. Decree of the President of the Council of Ministers of 12 January 2017: *Definition and update of the Essential Levels of Care pursuant to Article 1*(7) of Legislative Decree No. 502/1992. Official Gazette of the Italian Republic, General Series No. 65, 18 March 2017 (Ordinary Supplement No. 15). Available at: https://www.gazzettaufficiale.it/eli/id/2017/03/18/17A02015/sg

Prossegger, J., Huber, D., Grafetstätter, C., Pichler, C., Weisböck-Erdheim, R., Iglseder, B., Wewerka, G., et al. (2019). Effects of moderate mountain hiking and balneotherapy on community-dwelling older people: A randomized controlled trial. *Experimental Gerontology, 122*, 74–84. https://doi.org/10.1016/j.exger.2019.04.006

Quirino, N. (2016). *Wellness tourism e idroterapia. Riflessioni sulla documentazione statistica disponibile*. Federterme.

Rajoo, K. S., Karam, D. S., & Abdullah, M. Z. (2020). The physiological and psychosocial effects of forest therapy: A systematic review. *Urban Forestry & Urban Greening, 54*, 126744. https://doi.org/10.1016/j.ufug.2020.126744

Roberts, S. (2000). Regulation of energy intake in relation to metabolic state and nutritional status. *European Journal of Clinical Nutrition, 54*(S3), S64–S69. https://doi.org/10.1038/sj.ejcn.1601027

Roberts, S. B., Fuss, P., Heyman, M. B., Evans, W. J., Tsay, R., Rasmussen, H., Fiatarone, M., et al. (1994). Control of food intake in older men. *JAMA, 272*(20), 1601. https://doi.org/10.1001/jama.1994.03520200057036

Sachdeva, V., Roy, A., & Bharadvaja, N. (2020). Current prospects of nutraceuticals: *A review. Current Pharmaceutical Biotechnology, 21*(10), 884–896. https://doi.org/10.2174/1389201021666200130113441

Stephen, L., & De Felice, M. D. (2002). FIM rationale and proposed guidelines for the nutraceutical research & education act—NREA. Available at: https://fimdefelice.org/fim-rationale-and-proposed-guidelines-for-the-nutraceutical-research-education-act-nrea/. Accessed 3 July 2024.

Stratton, R. (2003). *Disease-related malnutrition: an evidence-based approach to treatment*. CABI eBooks. https://doi.org/10.1079/9780851996486.0000

Vega-Vázquez, M., Rodríguez-Serrano, M. Á., Castellanos-Verdugo, M., & Oviedo-García, M. Á. (2020). The impact of tourism on active and healthy ageing: Health-related quality of life. *Journal of Policy Research in Tourism, Leisure & Events/Journal of Policy Research in Tourism, Leisure and Events, 13*(3), 349–373. https://doi.org/10.1080/19407963.2020.1837844

Vimarlund, V., Borycki, E. M., Kushniruk, A. W., & Avenberg, K. (2021). Ambient assisted living: Identifying new challenges and needs for digital technologies and service innovation. *Yearbook of Medical Informatics, 30*(01), 141–149. https://doi.org/10.1055/s-0041-1726492

Viñas, B. R., Barba, L. R., Ngo, J., Gurinovic, M., Novakovic, R., Cavelaars, A., De Groot, L. C. P. G. M., et al. (2011). Projected prevalence of inadequate nutrient intakes in Europe. *Annals of Nutrition & Metabolism, 59*(2–4), 84–95. https://doi.org/10.1159/000332762

Vinnikov, D., Khafagy, A., Blanc, P. D., Brimkulov, N., & Steinmaus, C. (2016). High-altitude alpine therapy and lung function in asthma: Systematic review and meta-analysis. *ERJ Open Research, 2*(2), 00097–02015. https://doi.org/10.1183/23120541.00097-2015

Vuolo, L., Di Somma, C., Faggiano, A., & Colao, A. (2012). Vitamin D and cancer. *Frontiers in Endocrinology, 3*, 23546. https://doi.org/10.3389/fendo.2012.00058

Wang, S., Yeung, O., Johnston, K., & Callender, T. (2023). *Health, happiness, and the wellness economy: An empirical analysis*. Global Wellness Institute.

Westergren, A., Lindholm, C., Mattsson, A., & Ulander, K. (2009). Minimal eating observation form: Reliability and validity. *The Journal of Nutrition, Health & Aging, 13*(1), 6–11. https://doi.org/10.1007/s12603-009-0002-4

WHO. (2002). *Traditional medicine strategy 2002–2005*. World Health Organization.

Winters, M., Wagner, V., Patalano, R., Lindner, S., Alvino, S., Roller-Wirnsberger, R., Müller-Riedlhuber, H., et al. (2022). Chefs in future integrated healthcare—Current state and innovation needs: A first overview of the NECTAR project (AN EU curriculum for chef GASTRO-engineering in primary food care). *International Journal of Integrated Care, 22*(2), 7. https://doi.org/10.5334/ijic.6436

Wong, B. K. M., & Hazley, S. A. S. (2020). The future of health tourism in the industrial revolution 4.0 era. *Journal of Tourism Futures, 7*(2), 267–272. https://doi.org/10.1108/jtf-01-2020-0006

Zhao, S. S., Miller, N., Harrison, N., Duffield, S. J., Dey, M., & Goodson, N. J. (2019). Systematic review of mental health comorbidities in psoriatic arthritis. *Clinical Rheumatology, 39*(1), 217–225. https://doi.org/10.1007/s10067-019-04734-8

Designing for Longevity: Intersectoral Approach for Healthy Ageing Through the Built Environment

Mariangela Perillo, Erminia Attaianese, and Maddalena Illario

1 Introduction: The Interplay Between Built Environment and Public Health

Global challenges, driven by socio-demographic transformations, population ageing, the pervasive influence of digital technologies, and the systemic impacts of climate change, require innovative approaches to the design and organization of living environments. These approaches must be increasingly oriented toward health and well-being and capable of responding to the complex and evolving needs of citizens. In this context, conceptual frameworks such as "One Health" or "Planetary Health" highlight the urgency of adopting an ecological view of health, understood as a transactional concept. This perspective shifts the focus from the individual as an isolated entity to the dynamic interrelations between individuals and the multiple systems of which they are part, emphasizing the interdependence between human health and the broader ecosystem (Thompson et al., 2018). The built environment—defined as the ensemble of human-made surroundings that provide the setting for daily life at various spatial scales—plays a critical role in shaping health and well-being of people, influencing both individual functioning and longevity (Andalib et al., 2024; Antonovsky, 1979). Through direct and indirect mechanisms, buildings, neighbourhoods, and urban spaces impact individuals and communities across the life course. This influence is especially significant for older adults, whose quality of

M. Perillo (✉) · E. Attaianese
Department of Architecture, University of Naples Federico II, Naples, Italy
e-mail: mariangela.perillo@unina.it; erminia.attaianese@unina.it

M. Illario
Department of Public Health, University of Naples Federico II, Naples, Italy
e-mail: maddalena.illario@unina.it

A. Ricciardelli, L. Mercurio (eds.), *Building Innovation in Ageing and Health Policy*, Springer Series in Healthcare Management and Innovation,
https://doi.org/10.1007/978-3-032-09163-5_11

life may be either supported or compromised by the characteristics of their living spaces (Wister, 2005).

Vulnerable populations—particularly low-income and frail individuals—are disproportionately affected by poor-quality housing and degraded neighbourhoods, which increase exposure to environmental hazards. These conditions exacerbate the link between socio-environmental inequities and health disparities, representing a persistent and pressing public health challenge (Pagani et al., 2023). Despite the growing body of evidence connecting the built environment with health outcomes, these domains remain largely siloed in both policy and practice (Jackson et al., 2013). Collaboration between health professionals and experts in architecture, urban planning, and environmental design remains limited, and the health implications of spatial and infrastructural decisions are frequently overlooked in urban and territorial planning (Am et al., 2020). Aligned with the World Health Organization's recent definition of health—as the individual's capacity to adapt to their environment and maintain autonomy—there is a growing imperative to develop strategies that foster interdisciplinary and interprofessional collaboration between different sectors and fields. Such collaboration is essential to overcome current barriers and to leverage enabling factors for integrating environmental considerations into health-related policies and practices, particularly within the framework of the life course approach to population ageing.

2 Background: Bridging Health and Built Environment

In recent years, substantial progress has been made in understanding the complex interrelations among urban design, urban planning, governance, and their direct impacts on human health. Major global initiatives have underscored the crucial role of local urban policy decisions as fundamental public health interventions. Despite this growing recognition, integration of these linkages into effective policy implementation remains limited. The widely adopted "Health in All Policies" (HiAP) framework, supported by practical tools such as Health Impact Assessments (HIAs), offers promising pathways to advance the Sustainable Development Goals (SDGs) related to urban health (Ramirez-Rubio et al., 2019). The World Health Organization (WHO) acknowledges the vital influence of adequate indoor and outdoor living conditions on public health, with special attention to densely built urban contexts. Healthy environments that promote active lifestyles are essential, as individual and collective health are strongly shaped by environmental factors (McMichael, 2000). The built environment—encompassing all human-made indoor and outdoor living spaces—directly affects physical and social environments, thereby influencing people's health and quality of life. Environmental health, in its broadest sense, includes all health aspects determined or influenced by environmental factors, not only through direct pathological effects but also via the physical and social contexts such as housing, urban development, land use, transportation, industry, and agriculture (Srinivasan et al., 2003). Recent evidence increasingly links the built environment to diverse physical and mental health outcomes—ranging from anxiety, depression, and attention deficit disorder to asthma, heart disease, and obesity—often arising from poor urban planning and inadequate housing conditions (Raffestin & Lawrence, 1990). It is posited that each health profile is shaped by the surrounding built environment, which may exert both salutogenic (health-promoting) and pathogenic (health-damaging) effects. Furthermore, these effects interact dynamically over the life course with social environments and individual adaptive processes, highlighting the importance of qualitative dimensions as components of healthy life expectancy (Wister, 2005). Methodological advancements in measuring and analysing interactions among environmental, physical, and psychosocial factors are crucial to uncover the subtle yet powerful ways the built environment shapes healthy aging experiences. Addressing these complexities demands interdisciplinary collaboration among public health researchers, health professionals, architects, and urban planners, to develop indicators of sustainable communities and clarify their associations with environmental health outcomes. The scope of these challenges spans multiple spatial scales—from individual buildings to entire metropolitan regions—and a variety of health outcomes, including physical activity, mental health, respiratory conditions, and neurodevelopmental issues. Professionals such as urban planners, architects, and landscape architects, play essential roles in implementing change, supported by strong leadership and advocacy for integrating health considerations into building and redevelopment decisions (Jackson et al., 2013). Extensive research confirms a bidirectional relationship between the built environment and human well-being: while environmental conditions influence behaviours, experiences, and social practices, these practices, along with social inequalities, also play a crucial role in shaping environmental configurations. This complex interplay highlights the need for a holistic, interdisciplinary approach to understand how collective environmental factors impact health, reduce disparities, and inform prevention and intervention strategies (Andalib et al., 2024). Adopting a life course perspective, a strategic principle of the WHO's Health 2020 framework, is crucial to address how health advantages and disadvantages accumulate across generations (WHO, 2013). Figure 1 illustrates a public health framework for healthy ageing proposed by the World Health Organization (WHO, 2015).

Innovative models such as SHAFE (Smart, Healthy, Age-friendly Environments) exemplify this approach, promoting the integration of information and communication technologies (ICTs) into inclusive environmental design through collaborative, user-centred processes that engage diverse areas of expertise (Dantas et al., 2021). Recognizing that poor health is both a cause and consequence of deprivation, policy responses must transcend the health sector, engaging society at large. Early, timely, and coordinated action throughout the life course is fundamental to maximizing health and well-being and to fulfil global agendas such as the 2030 Sustainable Development Goals (Huber et al., 2016). Stakeholders across sectors emphasize the need for policy-relevant research that investigates the health impacts of built environment modifications—including assessing threshold effects among demographic groups and evaluating the economic implications of policy options—since generating such evidence is essential for developing solid evidence to support policy change (Fazli et al., 2017). The Ottawa Charter's strategy of creating supportive environments acknowledges the integral role of daily environments in health promotion.

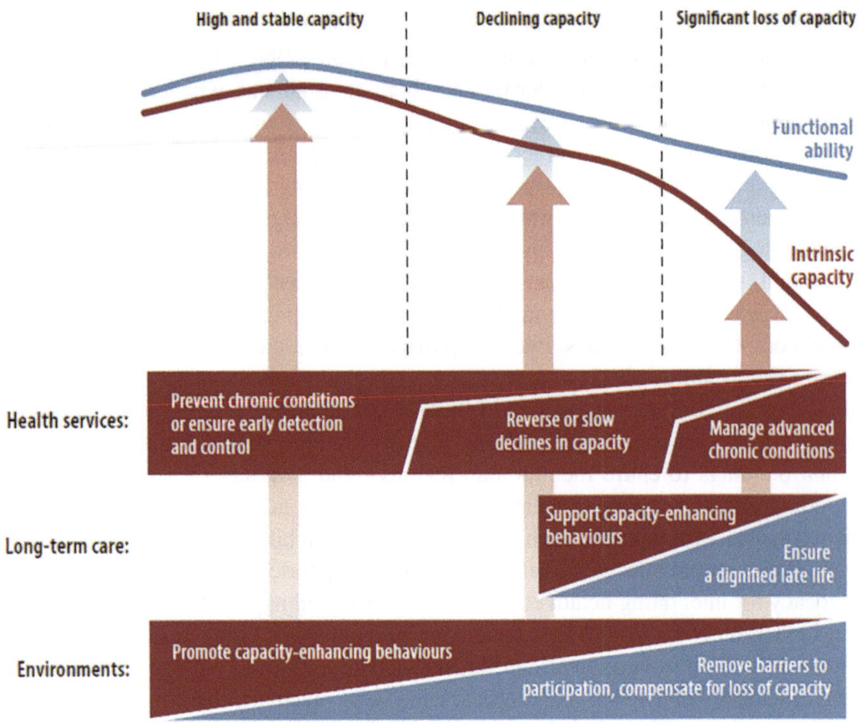

Fig. 1 A public-health framework for healthy ageing: opportunities for public-health action across the life course (from World Health Organization (2015). World report on ageing and health. Geneva: WHO)

This whole-systems approach has catalysed the emergence of health-promoting settings worldwide, fostering environments conducive to health (WHO, 1986). Today, urban environments exemplify a "public health paradox", while cities provide shelter and protection, promoting collective health, they also pose risks related to high energy consumption, pollution, and the urban heat island effect—exacerbated by rapid urbanization and loss of green spaces—leading to increased cardiovascular and pulmonary diseases (McMichael, 2000). Urbanization offers significant opportunities for public health promotion but also presents challenges that national health systems must address given the large urban populations involved. Since the Ottawa Charter and the advent of HiAP, the built environment and living spaces are increasingly recognized as complex social and political entities with significant health impacts. Addressing urban health challenges necessitates interdisciplinary and transdisciplinary approaches that integrate technical and medical expertise, while effective action depends on the collaborative engagement of both communities and professionals to comprehensively tackle contemporary health issues in urban environments (Capolongo et al., 2018).

3 Methods

The purpose of this study is to conduct a comprehensive analysis of the role of the built environment as a significant determinant of human health and well-being, particularly within the framework of the life-course approach to ageing. This research aims to identify and critically examine key initiatives and policies concerning the interrelationship between the healthcare sector and the environmental design of adaptable and responsive living spaces. This approach aims to highlight the potential of such spaces as strategic leverage points for designing indoor and outdoor environments that can positively influence user behaviour through the adoption of a life-course perspective. The methodology employed is structured in three phases: (i) scientific literature searching, (ii) critical selection of studies meeting predefined inclusion criteria, and (iii) synthesis of the collected data. The research strategy involved the use of the following keywords: Built Environment Design, Health and Longevity, Environmental Quality of Life, Intersectoral Policies and Practices, across the following databases: PubMed, Web of Science, and Google Scholar. The selection process encompassed studies examining the concept of the built environment, with particular attention to its convergences and divergences concerning human health within the healthcare field and the environmental design sector. Studies lacking direct references to the interaction between the built environment and human health were excluded. Overall, the research identified 35 studies, of which 31 were deemed eligible for inclusion.

4 Results

Intersectoral planning presents a complex challenge that requires balancing both qualitative and quantitative knowledge, as well as harmonizing instrumentally defined structures and tools with dialogue-based processes. Facilitating meeting points among municipal actors across departments and hierarchical levels is essential to foster a shared awareness (Strøm Synnevåg et al., 2018). In response to the fragmentation of existing approaches, Pagani et al. (2023) propose a transdisciplinary framework integrating six interconnected domains including environmental health, domestic architecture, building technologies, socio-economic inequalities, housing market dynamics, and urban planning. A core feature of this framework is the use of a Causal Loop Diagram (CLD) that visualizes systemic interdependencies and reinforcing feedback loops that perpetuate health inequities, particularly among socio-economically disadvantaged populations. Grounded in the European context and demonstrated through a case study in Geneva, the framework leverages spatio-temporal data to identify critical leverage points within the housing–street–health (HSH) nexus. By synthesizing data across disciplines, this model functions as both a diagnostic tool and a policy support mechanism, providing a structured foundation for evidence-informed, equity-oriented interventions in the built environment. In addition, Liu et al. (2022) employed structural equation modelling to elucidate the complex relationships between perceived neighbourhood environments and multiple health dimensions, including health-related behaviours, overall health status, and levels of life satisfaction. Their findings demonstrate that perceived neighbourhood quality significantly shapes individual health trajectories, with socio-demographic factors moderating these associations. These insights provide an empirical basis for context-sensitive public health strategies that address environmental determinants of health. Notably, the physical environment, integrated into daily life routines, emerges as a determinant not only of physical health but also of psychological well-being (Yang et al., 2023). A fundamental approach is the Health in All Policies (HiAP) framework, which underscores the importance of embedding health considerations into decision-making across all governance sectors, recognizing the living environment as a key determinant of population health, through intersectoral collaboration and coordinated professional networks. Municipalities are well-positioned to institutionalize sustainable, cross-sector strategies aimed at enhancing public health and advancing health equity (Quilling et al., 2022). Capacity building is pivotal in this process, encompassing efforts to strengthen local actors' competencies, promote intersectoral collaboration, and enable community participation. In this regard, Rütten et al. (2016) propose an innovative model grounded in interactive knowledge transfer, emphasizing collaborative concept development, participatory methodologies, and structured knowledge exchange as mechanisms for sustainably implementing evidence-based health promotion interventions. Lastly, the development of healthy longevity dashboards emerges as a promising strategic tool to monitor progress in addressing population ageing and the growing burden of non-communicable diseases. These dashboards facilitate the evaluation of policy effectiveness and the alignment of interventions over time. Anchored in a life-course perspective, they support integrated systems planning and foster multisectoral collaboration. Case studies demonstrate their adaptability across diverse demographic and data infrastructure contexts, highlighting their practical feasibility. Beyond their role as monitoring instruments, healthy longevity dashboards embody a strategic and forward-looking commitment to advancing health, productivity, and well-being through evidence-based, person-centred investment strategies (Haldane et al., 2023). Table 1 presents a summary of the objectives and findings of the analysed studies.

5 Discussion

Capacity development for health policy and systems research is as crucial as fostering supportive environments that sustain individuals' contributions (Tangcharoensathien et al., 2017). Urban health must be integrated from the earliest stages of urban planning, emphasizing a holistic, bottom-up approach to city development that serves as both prevention and collaboration in promoting health—a growing challenge for contemporary cities and their health systems (Capolongo et al., 2018). This necessitates a multidisciplinary framework that bridges the persistent divide between public health and built environment design, drawing from so many different fields (Hu & Roberts, 2020). A key call to action urges public health

Table 1 Summary of the objectives and main findings of the analysed studies

Author(s)	Year	Study design	Aim of the study	Main findings
Srinivasan et al.	2003	Research agenda	To examine the relationship between the built environment and public health, focusing on mediating and moderating factors, and to propose interdisciplinary research and policy recommendations for sustainable, health-promoting communities.	Poorly designed built environments are linked to adverse health outcomes and disparities. Sustainable communities may offer health benefits. Addressing these issues requires multilevel, interdisciplinary research, reliable metrics, interagency coordination, and improved community engagement to inform policy and practice.
Wister	2005	Narrative review	To synthesize interdisciplinary literature on how the built environment affects the health, functioning, and longevity of older adults, using ecological and person-environment models to identify salutogenic and pathogenic pathways.	The built environment influences health through complex, multilevel interactions across physical, social, and personal domains. It can act as both a health resource and a risk factor. Future research must adopt longitudinal, interdisciplinary approaches to capture direct and indirect pathways linking environment to well-being and healthy aging.
Jackson et al.	2013	Perspective	To reflect on a decade of progress in built environment and health research, identify remaining gaps, and propose future directions to integrate health considerations into planning, design, and policy.	Despite renewed interest, further research is needed across spatial scales and diverse health outcomes. Vulnerable populations remain underserved. Effective translation of evidence into practice, integration of health into design professions, support for interdisciplinary careers, and sustained leadership are critical for advancing healthy built environments.

(continued)

Table 1 (continued)

Author(s)	Year	Study design	Aim of the study	Main findings
Huber et al.	2016	Policy brief	To advocate for a life-course approach to health policy that addresses critical transitions and promotes early, timely, and intersectoral action to improve health, reduce inequalities, and support sustainable development.	Health is shaped by cumulative advantages and disadvantages across life stages and generations. Life-course policies that extend beyond the health sector and involve cross-sector collaboration can improve well-being, prevent intergenerational disadvantage, and support inclusive, equitable, and sustainable societal outcomes.
Fazli et al.	2017	Qualitative study	To identify knowledge gaps, barriers, and enabling mechanisms related to translating evidence on the built environment into effective policies that promote healthy, active living and reduce obesity-related illnesses, through multisectoral stakeholder engagement.	The study identified six key themes necessary for enabling built environment policy change: (1) the need for policy-informed and actionable research, including economic evaluations; (2) impactful, sector-specific communication strategies; (3) development of shared tools and metrics for monitoring changes; (4) strengthened intersectoral collaboration across government levels; (5) alignment of public and private sector priorities to build public support; and (6) implementation of tailored, solution-focused research to inform decision-making.
Tangcharoensathien et al.	2017	Perspective	To identify challenges, opportunities, and capacity-building needs for implementing effective multisectoral actions for health within complex governance systems, particularly in the context of sustainable development.	Effective multisectoral health actions are hindered by poor governance, corruption, weak institutional capacity, and industry interference. Opportunities exist through global and national frameworks (e.g. WHA/UNGA resolutions, Thailand National Health Assembly) that foster trust and collaboration. Key enablers include good governance (rule of law, transparency, accountability), active citizenship, and shared intersectoral visions. Capacity development at individual, institutional, and systemic levels, as well as regulatory measures and legal protections against corporate interference, are essential for sustained, health-promoting policies.

Thompson	2018	Perspective	To evaluate the influence of the World Health Organization's Ottawa Charter on UK health policy, with a specific focus on the strategies of creating supportive environments and reorienting health services, and to assess its continued relevance in addressing contemporary public health challenges and inequalities.	The Ottawa Charter remains a foundational framework for health promotion, yet its practical implementation in the UK has been limited. Health policy continues to prioritize individual behaviour change over addressing structural determinants of health. The settings-based approach inspired by the Charter (e.g. health-promoting schools, hospitals, workplaces) has gained international traction, but significant gaps persist in tackling health inequalities. A renewed application of the Charter's principles is advocated, emphasizing the redistribution of health services towards prevention, the development of supportive environments, and systemic strategies to reduce social and economic health disparities.
Capolongo et al.	2018	Policy framework	To update and expand the strategic objectives for achieving a "Healthy and Salutogenic City", building on previous work by the "Building and Environmental Hygiene" working group of the Italian Society of Hygiene and Preventive Medicine (SItI). The document aims to guide designers, local governments, policymakers, and health professionals in implementing urban planning and health policies that integrate environmental, social, and economic considerations to promote public health and well-being in urban contexts.	The study identifies ten strategic priorities for urban health, including climate change, land use, urban resilience, safety perception, green infrastructure, waste management, housing emergencies, energy planning, welfare networks, and participatory living. It emphasizes the interdependence between urban morphology and public health, highlighting cities' dual role as protectors and risk factors. Addressing challenges such as pollution, heat islands, and housing inequality requires integrated cross-sectoral strategies. Promoting salutogenic cities involves systemic shifts from individual interventions to co-designed housing, energy-efficient living, inclusive social housing, and community participation. A holistic, interdisciplinary approach engaging urban planners, health professionals, and communities is essential, aligning with frameworks like the Ottawa Charter and "Health in All Policies" for primary prevention.

(continued)

Table 1 (continued)

Author(s)	Year	Study design	Aim of the study	Main findings
Strøm Synnevåg et al.	2018	Qualitative case study	To examine how Norwegian municipalities use planning as a tool to implement the Health in All Policies (HiAP) approach, with a specific focus on understanding intersectoral processes through the lens of planning theory. The study addresses a gap in the literature by applying a planning perspective to explore the integration of public health considerations into municipal governance.	Norwegian municipalities face multiple dilemmas in implementing Health in All Policies (HiAP) through planning, including tensions between qualitative and quantitative knowledge, structural and processual procedures, and instrumental versus communicative approaches. A key challenge is balancing evidence-based, technocratic structures with participatory, dialogue-based processes across departments and hierarchies. Municipalities also struggle to either explicitly foreground public health—risking "health imperialism"—or to integrate it broadly into general planning language. The tension between bureaucratic, outcome-driven planning and political, consensus-building processes limits effective intersectoral action. These dilemmas highlight the challenge of reconciling top-down governance with collaborative participatory approaches needed for sustainable public health planning.
Nathan et al.	2018	Commentary	To advocate for enhanced collaboration between public health researchers, policymakers, and practitioners in order to better integrate built environment research into policy and practice. The article calls for a paradigm shift toward designing research that is policy-relevant, methodologically appropriate, and embedded in the real-world contexts of urban planning and governance.	Built environment research must be designed with an explicit understanding of the public policy context, employing relevant questions, methods, and outputs for policymakers and practitioners. Effective translation into policy requires multidisciplinary collaboration, inclusion of stakeholders, and tailored dissemination. Indicators and economic evaluations, though underused, are essential for actionable and credible research. Robust intervention-based and longitudinal studies are needed to strengthen evidence on cost-effectiveness and sustainability. Policy change is more likely when findings are clearly communicated, supported by case studies, linked to economic impacts, and aligned with stakeholder priorities. Addressing urban health challenges demands multisectoral partnerships across government and civil society. Researchers must navigate political and institutional networks to ensure evidence informs urban design, land use, transport, and housing policies promoting health equity and sustainability.

Steinmetz-Wood et al.	2019	Narrative review	To support researchers—particularly those with limited experience in mixed methods—in the planning and reporting of built environment and health studies by offering an overview of mixed methods research designs, integration strategies, and best practices. The paper aims to enhance methodological rigor and transparency in this interdisciplinary field.	Mixed methods research is well-suited to exploring the complex relationship between the built environment and health by combining quantitative precision with qualitative depth. The paper outlines core designs—convergent, explanatory, exploratory—and integration strategies such as comparison, connection, and assimilation. Clearly specifying design and integration enhances transparency, reproducibility, and interpretability. Integrated analysis clarifies reasoning, improving accessibility for policymakers and practitioners. An exploratory review found fewer than half of studies adequately report their mixed methods design or integration, risking research quality. The authors stress that better design and reporting can produce more robust evidence for health and planning policies.
Ramirez-Rubio et al.	2019	Research article	To develop a conceptual framework linking social determinants of health, environmental exposures, behaviours, health outcomes, and urban policies within the Sustainable Development Goals (SDGs) through a Health in All Policies (HiAP) lens; to critically analyse key components of HiAP as a mechanism for accelerating SDG implementation in urban and transport planning; and to examine lessons learned from Health Impact Assessments (HIAs) conducted in cities across Europe, Africa, and Latin America.	A comprehensive conceptual framework integrates urban health dimensions with 38 SDG targets across 15 goals, though key elements like physical activity, noise, social capital, and quality of life are missing from current SDGs. The SDG framework facilitates Health in All Policies (HiAP) implementation by promoting intersectoral collaboration, equity, stakeholder engagement, and policy coherence in urban health governance. Health Impact Assessments (HIAs) operationalize HiAP locally by quantifying health impacts and engaging communities. Barriers include data gaps, legal and institutional capacity, political will, and intersectoral coordination. Case studies from Barcelona and cities in Latin America and Africa illustrate effective health integration into urban planning through HIAs. The study underscores the need for disaggregated data, inclusive governance, and sustained collaboration among researchers, policymakers, and civil society for equitable, sustainable urban health development.

(continued)

Table 1 (continued)

Author(s)	Year	Study design	Aim of the study	Main findings
Hu and Roberts	2020	Scoping review	To examine the historical connections and current divergences between public health and built environment design disciplines, identify the primary health-related factors within the built environment, and propose an integrated, multidisciplinary framework to re-establish synergy between the two fields for improved population health outcomes.	Key factors through which the built environment impacts human health: physical, physiological, biological, and psychological. A disconnect exists between public health, focusing on macro-level issues, and built environment disciplines, centred on micro-level design. This divergence has limited collaboration despite shared goals. The study proposes a multidisciplinary, multilevel framework integrating human ecology, biology, psychology, and neurology to bridge the fields. Renewed collaboration is essential to mitigate negative impacts and enhance positive health outcomes. Three emerging research trends are identified to support future integrated approaches.
Cherbuin et al.	2021	Commentary	To advocate for and exemplify the role of international interdisciplinary research networks—specifically the IARU-ALH stream—in addressing the complex global challenges of ageing, by promoting healthy ageing, generating new scientific knowledge, and fostering science-informed societal change.	The ageing population poses global social, health, and economic challenges requiring coordinated international and interdisciplinary responses. The IARU-ALH network exemplifies collaboration across biology, medicine, public health, social sciences, policy, and demography to develop innovative, science-based solutions. Interdisciplinary research accelerates understanding of ageing and intervention potential but faces challenges including scepticism, disciplinary silos, funding limitations, and administrative complexity. Structural and operational barriers hinder progress, such as limited training pathways, coordination costs, and publication harmonization. Addressing these obstacles is vital to unlocking the network's potential for impactful, scalable, and sustainable healthy ageing solutions.

Ciraj et al.	2020	Short report	To describe the initiation, structure, and outcomes of a national interprofessional and intersectoral consultation conducted in India to evaluate the impact of the local built environment on public health, and to explore the potential of interprofessional collaboration in informing evidence-based, equity-oriented urban planning and policy reform.	The consultation engaged 108 academic professionals from healthcare, public health, architecture, engineering, and management to collaboratively assess the built environment's impact on health. It demonstrated that interprofessional approaches can generate actionable, context-specific recommendations addressing social determinants of health within a "Health in All Policies" framework. Thematic analysis informed local authorities, providing a model for policy engagement. Limitations included exclusion of citizens and policymakers, suggesting future broader stakeholder involvement. The initiative spurred new collaborative projects and capacity-building platforms like the Indian Interprofessional Education Network (IndIPEN), highlighting the role of higher education in preparing professionals for integrated public health and built environment planning.
Buffoli et al.	2020	Conference proceeding	To describe the development and dissemination of a qualitative-quantitative Health Impact Assessment (HIA) tool designed to evaluate the integration of Urban Health strategies into urban and environmental regeneration plans, with a particular focus on healthy ageing and equity. The study aims to support Local Health Agencies (LHAs) and policymakers by providing evidence-based criteria for promoting health-oriented urban planning.	A comprehensive HIA framework was developed, comprising 20 criteria across seven macro-areas: general criteria, environment, soil and subsoil, sustainability and hygiene of the built environment, urban and social development, mobility and transport, and outdoor spaces. Designed for use by local health authorities to assess urban plans and by architects/planners in early design stages, the tool evaluates public spaces through environmental and public health lenses to promote healthy lifestyles and reduce urban health inequities. The study calls for a paradigm shift from an individual-centred medical model to a social determinants model of health, advocating multidisciplinary collaboration. The tool offers a replicable, adaptable method to integrate health into urban redevelopment, fostering sustainable, inclusive, and health-promoting environments.

(continued)

Table 1 (continued)

Author(s)	Year	Study design	Aim of the study	Main findings
Garmany et al.	2021	Perspective	To highlight the pressing gap between increasing life expectancy and stagnating healthspan, and to outline emerging strategies—including biomedical, clinical, and societal approaches—for achieving disease-free longevity through integrative, multidimensional interventions that address chronic disease, frailty, and aging-related decline.	Despite rising global life expectancy, healthspan has not kept pace due to chronic diseases and frailty in older populations, creating a significant healthspan-lifespan gap that undermines quality of life. Key barriers include limited transdisciplinary collaboration, insufficient long-term resources, and difficulties translating science into equitable interventions. The authors call for an integrated approach combining public health, social engagement, and biomedical innovations—such as anti-senescent and regenerative therapies—to promote resilience and prevent age-related decline. The COVID-19 pandemic highlights vulnerabilities and scientific mobilization potential. The study urges enhanced decision-making and next-generation medical advances to close the healthspan-lifespan gap and protect the global longevity dividend.
Amri et al.	2022	Study protocol	To conduct an umbrella review of existing literature reviews to identify and synthesize facilitators and barriers to implementing intersectoral and multisectoral approaches—such as Health in All Policies (HiAP), Healthy Cities, and One Health—with the objective of enhancing the effective integration of social determinants of health (SDH) into policy and practice, and ultimately informing strategies for achieving health equity.	The study protocol highlights that health is significantly influenced by social determinants largely governed by sectors beyond traditional healthcare, such as education, housing, and labour. Intersectoral and multisectoral approaches are essential to address these determinants and achieve Sustainable Development Goals and health equity. The review identifies HiAP, Healthy Cities, and One Health as formal frameworks enabling cross-sector collaboration. Despite consensus, evidence on successful implementation and sustainability is limited. This umbrella review compiles insights from systematic reviews to guide policymakers in developing effective, context-sensitive multisectoral strategies. Multisectoral governance is critical for addressing inequities in low- and middle-income countries, with crises like COVID-19 underscoring the need for integrated policy. Findings emphasize coordinated policy action as a political imperative for advancing health and equity.

Lucantoni et al.	2022	Original research	To develop and apply, for the first time, a comprehensive model for producing policy recommendations on active ageing (AA) at the national level, addressing key challenges in operationalizing the AA concept in public policy. The study seeks to bridge the gap between the conceptual framework of AA and its practical implementation through policymaking, while promoting stakeholder engagement, a mainstreaming ageing approach, and multilevel governance.	The study identified persistent shortcomings in existing national AA strategies, none of which comprehensively addressed the main implementation challenges. In response, a novel model was developed and applied in Italy to guide policy formulation in this field. The model enables structured stakeholder participation, integrates international frameworks (e.g. MIPAA, SDGs), and adopts a life-course and equity-oriented perspective. While the recommendations are not yet legally binding, they offer a replicable approach adaptable to diverse national contexts. The pilot experience also underscored the importance of contextualization, sustainability, and political commitment for effective AA policy implementation.
Pineo and Moore	2022	Original research	To explore how the principles of healthy urbanism are operationalized in practice by built environment professionals, examining their experiences of implementing health considerations in new urban developments across six countries (Australia, China, England, the Netherlands, Sweden, and the USA), and to identify the drivers, barriers, and opportunities associated with integrating health into development processes.	The study identified three key themes influencing health integration into urban development: (1) managing risk, responsibility, and economic constraints, with adoption of healthy design linked to strong business cases and innovation opportunities; (2) pushing beyond business-as-usual via early engagement, champions, public awareness, and interprofessional communication; and (3) building knowledge and capacity, noting that financial and structural barriers often outweigh knowledge gaps. The findings highlight a gap between policy health goals and implementation, emphasizing the need for new incentives, better communication of health evidence, and deeper understanding of developers' motivations within policy and financial contexts.

(continued)

Table 1 (continued)

Author(s)	Year	Study design	Aim of the study	Main findings
Quilling et al.	2022	Scoping review	The aim of this scoping review was to provide an initial overview of theoretical models, approaches, and the extent to which evidence is integrated into overarching strategies for municipal health promotion. Specifically, it sought to identify which theoretical models and approaches are employed in the development of such strategies, and to what extent the concept of "evidence" is applicable and utilized in the design, implementation, and evaluation of municipal health promotion initiatives.	The review identified 15 relevant publications that emphasized three core strategic elements in municipal health promotion: capacity building, planning, and the establishment of health-promoting structures. The concept of capacity building encompassed actor competence development, intersectoral collaboration, and participatory processes. Planning was largely participatory and often evidence-informed, utilizing context-specific tools and participatory methods. The establishment of structures aimed to reduce access barriers and integrate hard-to-reach groups through localised and low-threshold services. Despite the use of evidence-based theoretical models, the review found no conclusive empirical evidence demonstrating effectiveness according to conventional medical standards. The findings underscore challenges in applying traditional evidence hierarchies to complex, multilevel community interventions and highlight the need for adapted research designs and participatory evaluation methods in this field.
Pagani et al.	2023	Original research	To develop a systemic, transdisciplinary, and spatio-temporal research framework to better understand the complex interactions between housing, street environments, and health (HSH), and to overcome disciplinary fragmentation in existing research on urban residential health.	The study proposes a causal loop diagram (CLD) integrating six perspectives—environmental health, architecture, building technology, socio-economic inequalities, housing prices, and urban planning—to map HSH interrelations. Applied to Geneva, the framework demonstrates how HSH interactions produce reinforcing feedback loops that perpetuate health and housing injustices. It supports coordinated interventions by enabling holistic diagnostics, fostering intersectoral collaboration, and guiding policy and urban design towards health equity.

Balis and Vincent	2023	Implementation study	To inform the development and refinement of implementation strategies by exploring delivery agents' perceptions of (1) built environment approaches for promoting physical activity, (2) the utility and content of a supporting implementation toolkit, and (3) additional support and resources needed for successful implementation in community settings.	Delivery agents expressed overall willingness to implement built environment approaches and held positive views of the toolkit. Key perceived barriers included lack of coalition-building guidance and funding. Findings informed the refinement of the toolkit and the creation of two additional implementation strategies: Coalition Coaching and Mini-Grants. These strategies aim to address identified barriers and support the translation of evidence-based built environment interventions into community practice.
Yang et al.	2023	Editorial	To introduce and synthesize the research contributions included in the special issue 'The Built Environment and Public Health: New Insights,' highlighting emerging evidence, methods, and challenges in studying the relationship between built environments and health.	The editorial summarizes 43 studies addressing the built environment–health nexus. It highlights methodological advancements such as the use of big data, spatial analysis, and non-linear modelling; growing attention to inequalities and contextual sensitivity; and the need for integrated, interdisciplinary approaches to inform public health planning and policy.
Browne and Pry	2023	Book chapter	To examine a multidisciplinary partnership between a local health district and a local government authority in New South Wales, Australia, aimed at embedding health considerations into land use planning processes. The study sought to explore how co-creation and reciprocal capacity building between public health and urban planning professionals can be operationalized to achieve healthier built environments and long-term improvements in population health and well-being.	The partnership successfully established mechanisms to integrate health into local planning policy, including the development of a high-level health policy, a health assessment framework, and a joint staff position. Capacity building outcomes were observed at the individual (e.g. upskilling through further education), organizational (e.g. policy revisions, co-investment), and systemic levels (e.g. new planning instruments and inter-agency collaboration). The implementation of the Social and Health Impact Assessment (SaHIA) process enabled health input into development applications, though its impact was constrained by the absence of enforceable planning standards. The study highlights the importance of a staged, integrated approach to policy change, which builds legal and institutional support for embedding health into urban planning systems.

(continued)

Table 1 (continued)

Author(s)	Year	Study design	Aim of the study	Main findings
Croffi et al.	2023	Research article	To develop a framework that identifies and quantifies building design aspects of the indoor environment that foster occupant well-being in high-rise, mixed-use developments, with the goal of integrating these metrics into digital design tools for early-stage evaluation.	The study establishes a tripartite framework—comfort, delight, and social dimensions—of quantifiable design aspects impacting satisfaction with the indoor environment and overall well-being. Using post-occupancy evaluations, environmental monitoring, and 3D modelling, the framework demonstrates how variables such as thermal comfort, daylight, views, space size, and access to green/social areas correlate with well-being outcomes. This approach enables the future development of a computational tool for predictive well-being assessment during the design phase, enhancing the social value of buildings.
World Health Organization	2023	Policy report	To present and conceptualize a new operational model for implementing and sustaining Health in All Policies (HiAP) approaches, with the goal of enhancing multisectoral collaboration to improve population health and health equity. The document aims to guide policy actors across various levels of government in applying HiAP principles by outlining key components, strategies, and contextual considerations.	The study introduces a new HiAP model structured around four operational pillars that emphasize synergy across government sectors while addressing potential conflicts of interest. HiAP approaches are shown to be context-dependent, iterative, and reliant on a balance of technical expertise and political acumen. The model supports both comprehensive health equity agendas and targeted initiatives (e.g. non-communicable diseases, child health), promoting sustained intersectoral collaboration. Key findings highlight that successful implementation requires tailoring to local governance structures, fostering a web of HiAP actors, and integrating scientific evidence on the social determinants of health into cross-sector policymaking.
Haldane et al.	2023	Technical report	To propose a harmonized framework for the development of national healthy longevity dashboards, enabling countries to consolidate multisectoral data to monitor progress, inform strategic planning, and guide investments aimed at promoting health and human capital across the life course.	A healthy longevity dashboard enables countries to monitor ageing preparedness and non-communicable disease management by integrating multisectoral data to support life course–oriented interventions. Case studies demonstrate feasibility across diverse demographic and data contexts. Beyond monitoring, these dashboards serve as strategic tools to align health, productivity, and well-being priorities with targeted policy actions.

Andalib et al.	2024	Scoping review	To provide a comprehensive scoping review of the complex and multidirectional relationships between the built environment, health, and well-being, with the aim of identifying key environmental determinants and informing evidence-based strategies for healthier urban development.	The review identified key built environment elements—such as green/blue spaces, social areas, neighbourhood quality, architecture, safety, accessibility, amenities, aesthetics, lighting, and dwelling characteristics—that significantly influence physical, mental, and social health and well-being. These factors exhibit bidirectional associations with health outcomes including cardiovascular disease, cancer, stress, depression, and happiness. Methodological triangulation combining statistical and physiological measures is crucial to understanding these complex relations. The review provides theoretical and practical insights for urban planning and public health, highlighting gaps in research on specific design features and non-residential settings.
Walker et al.	2024	Study protocol	To evaluate the feasibility, acceptability, and short-term impact of a novel policy formation approach—Policy Co-design—that integrates coproduction and co-design methods to address implementation barriers in adolescent substance use disorder (SUD) prevention and treatment. The study aims to assess the method's ability to improve multisector collaboration, uptake of research evidence, alignment of political and organizational will, and resource coordination. It also explores the replicability of the approach among behavioural health policy stakeholders and intermediary organizations across the United States.	Preliminary findings suggest that Policy Co-design is a feasible and acceptable method for engaging cross-sector stakeholders in behavioural health policy development. Previous applications of the model have led to rapid implementation of evidence-informed initiatives (e.g. MOUD in jails), demonstrated strong stakeholder engagement, and attracted interest from policy professionals and intermediary organizations. The current study contributes to closing knowledge gaps in policy-focused implementation science by systematically testing participatory, design-informed strategies that anticipate downstream policy implementation challenges.

(continued)

Table 1 (continued)

Author(s)	Year	Study design	Aim of the study	Main findings
Suoheimo et al.	2025	Book chapter	To integrate systems thinking into service design by providing a comprehensive, transdisciplinary framework that equips designers, policymakers, and stakeholders with the tools and knowledge to create sustainable, equitable, and contextually appropriate services. The study aims to address the complexity of contemporary service systems by bridging theoretical foundations and practical case studies, emphasizing systemic responsibility and cross-disciplinary collaboration in diverse socio-economic, political, and technological contexts.	Service design is shifting from user touchpoints to a systemic, transdisciplinary practice engaging designers, clinicians, engineers, and policymakers. The book underscores integrating systems theories (sociology, ecology, economics, psychology) with practical tools—such as co-design, evidence-based design, and ecosystem mapping—to address complex challenges. It highlights risks of systemic oppression and proposes methods inspired by Theatre of the Oppressed and intersectional feminism to decentralize design authority. Case studies illustrate successful healthcare and built environment interventions emphasizing resilience, sustainability, measurable health outcomes, and responsibility-centred design addressing ethical, social, and cultural considerations.
Cacciatore et al.	2025	Narrative review	To examine the intersection between urbanization, health inequities, and disease patterns by identifying both traditional and emerging risk factors, with the objective of outlining strategies to promote healthier, more equitable urban environments across the lifespan.	Urbanization intensifies health disparities through its influence on social determinants of health, environmental exposures, and healthcare access. Rapid urban growth, especially in low- and middle-income countries, contributes to multimorbidity and rising non-communicable diseases. The review highlights the need for integrated, multisectoral policies—such as green infrastructure, improved urban mobility, and expanded mental health care—that promote equity, sustainability, and population well-being. Participatory governance and intersectoral collaboration are essential for building resilient, inclusive cities capable of mitigating both traditional and emerging urban health risks.

researchers and policymakers, to deepen their understanding of the built environment's impact on health by fostering collaboration with stakeholders beyond the health sector (Giles-Corti et al., 2015). Mixed methods research, combining quantitative and qualitative approaches, is particularly suited to capturing the complexity of this field (Mertens et al., 2016; Steinmetz-Wood et al., 2019). Despite longstanding recognition of the connections between the built environment and health, a persistent gap remains in translating this knowledge into practice. Urban planners have recently expanded their focus to include active living, environmental exposure, and physical and mental health, while architects and engineers have enhanced local environments through detailed design solutions. Nevertheless, the fragmentation between disciplines demands integrated approaches and renewed collaboration between environmental design professionals and public health practitioners, as advocated by the International Alliance of Research Universities—Ageing, Longevity and Health (IARU–ALH) (Cherbuin et al., 2021). Thus, the evolving public health paradigm requires a shift from a predominantly medical model focused on individuals to a broader social model, recognizing health as the outcome of complex socio-economic, cultural, and environmental interactions. Achieving this demands the engagement of diverse stakeholders to ensure evidence-based, feasible, and policy-relevant interventions (Buffoli et al., 2020). Formalized intersectoral and multisectoral collaboration frameworks, such as Health in All Policies (HiAP), are vital for addressing complex health challenges and promoting equity by integrating health considerations across governance domains (Guglielmin et al., 2018; Baum et al., 2014). In this scenario, capacity building emerges as a cornerstone for sustainable public health outcomes, enhancing individual and organizational skills while fostering community involvement and creating supportive environments conducive to health-promoting behaviours (Browne & Pry, 2023). Furthermore, innovations in evaluation, such as Croffi et al.'s measurable indoor environmental factors linked to physical and emotional well-being, align with broader efforts to embed the health value into design practices, informing inclusive, well-being-oriented architecture (Croffi et al., 2023). Finally, addressing "wicked problems" in health and urban development necessitates systems-thinking and real-world design interventions that transcend disciplinary boundaries. Service design has evolved into a systemic practice bridging stakeholders, from health professionals and architectural and urban experts to policymakers, employing participatory and evidence-based approaches. Initiatives discussed by Suoheimo et al. (2025) demonstrate how interdisciplinary collaboration fosters resilient and adaptable healthcare infrastructures informed by empirical health data and validated through practice.

6 Conclusion

Architecture plays a central role in promoting health and well-being, as the built environment profoundly shapes people's lives across the entire life course. Designing with awareness involves creating spaces that address individuals' physical, psychological, and social needs, thereby fostering healthy, active, and inclusive lifestyles.

Achieving these objectives requires continuous, structured dialogue among diverse professional figures to develop multidisciplinary projects capable of addressing complex challenges and leveraging the opportunities presented by innovation. A particularly relevant example is the SHAFE (Smart, Healthy, Age-Friendly Environments) model, which promotes intelligent and inclusive solutions that support independent living through a life-course perspective. This approach values diversity—in age, gender, ability, culture, and personal choices—and emphasizes the joint optimization of physical and social environments, supported by digital tools and services. The SHAFE model exemplifies how integrating diverse competencies can foster authentic co-design processes aimed at enhancing individuals' physical and psychological well-being. In urban contexts, characterized by ongoing transformation and increasingly urgent demographic and health challenges, this integrated and participatory vision offers a concrete pathway toward sustainable, resilient, and truly human-centred environments. Interdisciplinary research holds great promise to accelerate our understanding of human ageing and to generate innovative and more effective solutions to this complex and pressing issue. However, realizing these potentials demands focused, strategic efforts and investments to maximize benefits for both individuals and societies. Promoting healthier built environments is a shared responsibility that must be collectively addressed to ensure the well-being of present and future generations. This requires a multilevel and collaborative approach targeting communities, policy frameworks, systems and structures to create environments conducive to health throughout the lifespan, from childhood through older adulthood. The progress of health-promoting environments depends on sustained, coordinated collaboration among researchers, communities, policymakers, and health promotion practitioners, reinforcing the essential role of cross-sectoral partnerships in advancing health and well-being through the built environment.

Acknowledgements This article is based upon work from the Italian Ministry of University and Research's Enlarged Partnership 8 "A novel public-private alliance to generate socioeconomic, biomedical and technological solutions for an inclusive Italian ageing society" (Project number: PE0000015), supported by the Italian National Recovery and Resilience Plan, financed by Next Generation Europe programme.

References

Amri, M., Chatur, A., & O'Campo, P. (2022). Intersectoral and multisectoral approaches to health policy: An umbrella review protocol. *Health Research Policy and Systems, 20*, 21. https://doi.org/10.1186/s12961-022-00826-1

Andalib, E., Temeljotov-Salaj, A., Steinert, M., Johansen, A., Aalto, P., & Lohne, J. (2024). The interplay between the built environment, health, and well-being—A scoping review. *Urban Science, 8*(4), 184. https://doi.org/10.3390/urbansci8040184

Antonovsky, A. (1979). Health, stress, and coping. In *New perspectives on mental and physical well-being* (pp. 12–37).

Balis, L. E., & Vincent, J. (2023). Implementation strategies to support built environment approaches in community settings. *Health Promotion Practice, 24*(3), 502–513. https://doi.org/10.1177/15248399221081835

Baum, F., Lawless, A., Delany, T., MacDougall, C., Williams, C., Broderick, D., Harris, E., McDermott, D., & Popay, J. (2014). Evaluation of Health in All Policies: Concept, theory and application. *Health Promotion International, 29*(Suppl 1), i130–i142. https://doi.org/10.1093/heapro/dau032

Browne, C., & Pry, J. (2023). A case study: An intersectoral partnership approach to embedding health in land use planning. In N. Biloria, G. Sebag, & H. Robertson (Eds.), *The empathic city. S.M.A.R.T. environments* (pp. 161–176). Springer. https://doi.org/10.1007/978-3-031-32840-4_13

Buffoli, M., Rebecchi, A., Dell'Ovo, M., Oppio, A., & Capolongo, S. (2020). Transforming the built environment through healthy-design strategies. In C. Bevilacqua, F. Calabrò, & L. Della Spina (Eds.), *New metropolitan perspectives* (pp. 247–257). Springer. https://doi.org/10.1007/978-3-030-52869-0_16

Cacciatore, S., Mao, S., Nuñez, M. V., Baeriswyl, S., Bolleter, J., Lawrence, R. & Rossi, G. (2025). Urban health inequities and healthy longevity: Traditional and emerging risk factors across the cities and policy implications. *Aging Clinical and Experimental Research, 37*, 143. https://doi.org/10.1007/s40520-025-03052-1

Capolongo, S., Rebecchi, A., Dettori, M., Appolloni, L., Azara, A., Buffoli, M., et al. (2018). Healthy design and urban planning strategies, actions, and policy to achieve salutogenic cities. *International Journal of Environmental Research and Public Health, 15*(12), 2698. https://doi.org/10.3390/ijerph15122698

Cherbuin, N., Iijima, K., Kalula, S., Malhotra, R., Rasmussen, L. J., Chan, A., et al. (2021). Societal need for interdisciplinary ageing research: An international alliance of research universities "Ageing, Longevity and Health" stream (IARU-ALH) position statement. *Biomedicine Hub, 6*(1), 42–47. https://doi.org/10.1159/000513513

Ciraj, A. M., Godinho, M. A., Murthy, S., Manapure, N. H., Ramadevi, N., Kinjawadekar, A., et al. (2020). The built environment and health: Fostering interprofessional collaboration for better policy recommendations. *Journal of Interprofessional Care, 34*(3), 414–417. https://doi.org/10.1080/13561820.2019.1650009

Croffi, J., Kroll, D., Soebarto, V., Barrie, H., & McDougall, K. (2023). Wellbeing fostered by design: A framework for evaluating indoor environment performance. *Buildings Cities, 4*(1), 507–523. https://doi.org/10.5334/bc.336

Dantas, C., Willeke, V., Van Staalduinen, W., Illario, M., & Spiru, L. (2021). Smart and inclusive environments for all – SHAFE explained. T*echnium Social Sciences Journal, 25*, 630–638. https://doi.org/10.47577/tssj.v25i1.4844

European Observatory on Health Systems and Policies, Huber, M., Galea, G., Lazdane, G., & Kosinska, M. (2016). Implementation of the life-course approach through strengthened intersectoral action. *Eurohealth, 22*(3), 25–28. Available from: https://iris.who.int/handle/10665/332691

Fazli, G. S., Creatore, M. I., Matheson, F. I., Guilcher, S. J. T., Kaufman-Shriqui, V., Manson, H., et al. (2017). Identifying mechanisms for facilitating knowledge to action strategies targeting the built environment. *BMC Public Health, 17*(1), 1. https://doi.org/10.1186/s12889-016-3954-4

Garmany, A., Yamada, S., & Terzic, A. (2021). Longevity leap: Mind the healthspan gap. *NPJ Regenerative Medicine, 6*, 57. https://doi.org/10.1038/s41536-021-00169-5

Giles-Corti, B., Sallis, J. F., Sugiyama, T., Frank, L. D., Lowe, M., & Owen, N. (2015). Translating active living research into policy and practice: One important pathway to chronic disease prevention. *Journal of Public Health Policy, 36*(2), 231–243. https://doi.org/10.1057/jphp.2014.53

Guglielmin, M., Muntaner, C., O'Campo, P., & Shankardass, K. (2018). A scoping review of the implementation of Health in All Policies at the local level. *Health Policy, 122*(3), 284–292. https://doi.org/10.1016/j.healthpol.2017.12.005

Haldane, V., Garcia, G. M., Bockarie, T., Wu, D., Herrera, C. A., Castro, M. L. L., et al. (2023). Healthy longevity initiative: A performance dashboard for decision-making in low- and middle-income countries. In *Unlocking the power of healthy longevity: Compendium of research for the healthy longevity initiative*. Washington, D.C. Available from: http://documents.worldbank.org/curated/en/099091024171528878

Hu, M., & Roberts, J. D. (2020). Connections and divergence between public health and built environment—A scoping review. *Urban Science, 4*(1), 12. https://doi.org/10.3390/urbansci4010012

Jackson, R. J., Dannenberg, A. L., & Frumkin, H. (2013). Health and the built environment: 10 years after. *American Journal of Public Health, 103*(9), 1542–1544. https://doi.org/10.2105/AJPH.2013.301482

Liu, J., Tian, Z., Liu, H., Kong, H., Du, X., & Xue, Q. (2022). Perceived neighbourhood environment impacts on health behaviour, multi-dimensional health and life satisfaction: Evidence from China. *International Journal of Environmental Research and Public Health, 19*(7), 4163. https://doi.org/10.3390/ijerph19074163

Lucantoni, D., Principi, A., Socci, M., Zannella, M., & Barbabella, F. (2022). Active ageing in Italy: An evidence-based model to provide recommendations for policy making and policy implementation. *International Journal of Environmental Research and Public Health, 19*(5), 2746. https://doi.org/10.3390/ijerph19052746

McMichael, A. J. (2000). The urban environment and health in a world of increasing globalization: Issues for developing countries. *Bulletin of the World Health Organization, 78*(9), 1117–1126.

Mertens, D. M., Bazeley, P., Bowleg, L., Fielding, N., Maxwell, J. F., Molina-Azorin, J. F., & Niglas, K. (2016). Expanding thinking through a kaleidoscopic look into the future: Implications of the Mixed Methods International Research Association's Task Force report on the future of mixed methods. *Journal of Mixed Methods Research, 10*(3), 221–227. https://doi.org/10.1177/1558689816649719

Nathan, A., Villanueva, K., Rozek, J., Davern, M., Gunn, L., Trapp, G., et al. (2018). The role of the built environment on health across the life course: A call for collaborACTION. *American Journal of Health Promotion, 32*(6), 1460–1468. https://doi.org/10.1177/0890117118779463a

Pagani, A., Christie, D., Bourdon, V., Wall Gago, C., Joost, S., Licina, D., et al. (2023). Housing, street and health: A new systemic research framework. *Buildings Cities, 4*(1), 629–649. https://doi.org/10.5334/bc.298

Pineo, H., & Moore, G. (2022). Built environment stakeholders' experiences of implementing healthy urban development: An exploratory study. *Cities Health, 6*(5), 922–936. https://doi.org/10.1080/23748834.2021.1876376

Quilling, E., Mielenbrink, V., Osterhoff, A., et al. (2022). State of evidence on municipal strategies for health promotion and prevention: a literature and database research (scoping review). *BMC Public Health, 22*, 301. https://doi.org/10.1186/s12889-022-12607-0

Raffestin, C., & Lawrence, R. (1990). An ecological perspective on housing, health and wellbeing. *Journal of Sociology and Social Welfare, 17*, 143–160.

Ramirez-Rubio, O., Daher, C., Fanjul, G., et al. (2019). Urban health: An example of a "health in all policies" approach in the context of SDGs implementation. *Globalization and Health, 15*, 87. https://doi.org/10.1186/s12992-019-0529-z

Rütten, A., Wolff, A., & Streber, A. (2016). Interaktiver Wissenstransfer in der Gesundheitsförderung: das GESTALT-Projekt. Erste Ergebnisse der Erprobung eines Ansatzes zur nachhaltigen Implementierung evidenzbasierter Bewegungsprogramme. *Das Gesundheitswesen, 78*(06), 359–366. https://doi.org/10.1055/s-00000022, https://doi.org/10.1055/s-006-31942, https://doi.org/10.1055/s-0035-1548882

Srinivasan, S., O'Fallon, L. R., & Dearry, A. (2003). Creating healthy communities, healthy homes, healthy people: Initiating a research agenda on the built environment and public health. *American Journal of Public Health, 93*(9), 1446–1450. https://doi.org/10.2105/AJPH.93.9.1446

Steinmetz-Wood, M., Pluye, P., & Ross, N. A. (2019). The planning and reporting of mixed methods studies on the built environment and health. *Preventive Medicine, 126*, 105752. https://doi.org/10.1016/j.ypmed.2019.105752

Strøm Synnevåg, E., Amdam, R., & Fosse, E. (2018). Intersectoral planning for public health: Dilemmas and challenges. *International Journal of Health Policy and Management, 7*(11), 982–992. https://doi.org/10.15171/ijhpm.2018.59

Suoheimo, M., Jones, P., Lee, S.-H., & Sevaldson, B. (Eds.). (2025). *Systemic Service Design* (1st ed.). Routledge. https://doi.org/10.4324/9781003501039

Tangcharoensathien, V., Srisookwatana, O., Pinprateep, P., Posayanonda, T., & Patcharanarumol, W. (2017). Multisectoral actions for health: Challenges and opportunities in complex policy environments. *International Journal of Health Policy and Management, 6*(7), 359–363. https://doi.org/10.15171/ijhpm.2017.61

Thompson, S. R., Watson, M. C., & Tilford, S. (2018). The Ottawa charter 30 years on: Still an important standard for health promotion. *International Journal of Health Promotion and Education, 56*(2), 73–84. https://doi.org/10.1080/14635240.2017.1415765

Walker, S. C., Ahrens, K. R., Owens, M. D., et al. (2024). Using policy codesign to achieve multi-sector alignment in adolescent behavioral health: A study protocol. *Implementation Science Communications, 5*, 54. https://doi.org/10.1186/s43058-024-00583-y

Wister, A. V. (2005). The built environment, health, and longevity. *Journal of Housing for the Elderly, 19*(2), 49–70. https://doi.org/10.1300/J081v19n02_04

World Health Organization. (1986). Ottawa Charter for Health Promotion. Geneva: World Health Organization. Retrieved from https://www.who.int/publications/i/item/ottawa-charter-for-health-promotion

World Health Organization. (2015). World report on ageing and health. Geneva: World Health Organization.

World Health Organization. (2023). *Working together for equity and healthier populations: sustainable multisectoral collaboration based on health in all policies approaches*. WHO. Licence: CC BY-NC-SA3.0 IGO.

World Health Organization Regional Office for Europe. (2013). *Health 2020: A European policy framework and strategy for the 21st century*. WHO. Available from: https://iris.who.int/handle/10665/326386

Yang, L., Wang, R., He, B., Ye, Y., & Ao, Y. (2023). Editorial: the built environment and public health: New insights. *Frontiers in Public Health, 10*, 1079182. https://doi.org/10.3389/fpubh.2022.1079182

Digital Work and Aging: An Empirical Study on Age-Dependent Effects of Work-from-Home, Gender, and Work-Life Balance on Self-Reported Mental Well-Being

Alberto Varone and Francesco Bolici

1 Introduction

Work is undergoing a profound transformation, driven by the dual forces of demographic shifts and digital transformation (Komp-Leukkunen, 2023; OECD, 2020). Populations across developed nations are aging, leading to increasingly multigenerational workforces where older individuals represent a growing share of employees (OECD, 2020). Simultaneously, digitalization is reshaping industries, processes, and the very nature of job tasks, demanding new skills and altering established work patterns (Belbase & Chen, 2019; Komp-Leukkunen, 2023). Within this evolving landscape, distributed work models, particularly work-from-home (WFH), have moved from niche arrangements to mainstream practice, a trend significantly accelerated by the global response to the COVID-19 pandemic (Dingel & Neiman, 2020; Jansen et al., 2024; Pit et al., 2021). While estimates suggest a significant portion of jobs, especially knowledge-based roles, can be performed remotely (Dingel & Neiman, 2020; Ng et al., 2022; Varone & Bolici, 2025), the widespread adoption of these models presents both opportunities and challenges for workers and organizations.

The potential benefits of remote work, such as increased flexibility and autonomy, are often highlighted (Ng et al., 2022; Sousa et al., 2023). However, research also points to potential downsides, including risks to psychological well-being

A. Varone (✉)
University of Cassino and Southern Lazio, Cassino, Italy

Syracuse University (iSchool), Syracuse, NY, USA
e-mail: alberto.varone@unicas.it

F. Bolici
University of Cassino and Southern Lazio, Cassino, Italy
e-mail: f.bolici@unicas.it

A. Ricciardelli, L. Mercurio (eds.), *Building Innovation in Ageing and Health Policy*, Springer Series in Healthcare Management and Innovation,
https://doi.org/10.1007/978-3-032-09163-5_12

stemming from factors like social isolation, blurred work-life boundaries, increased stress, and loneliness (Araújo & Lua, 2021; Galanti et al., 2021; Miyake et al., 2022; Toscano et al., 2022). Critically, the impact of distributed work is unlikely to be monolithic. Emerging evidence suggests that outcomes like stress, engagement, satisfaction, and performance can vary significantly based on individual, organizational, and technological factors (Galanti et al., 2021; Ng et al., 2022; Toscano et al., 2022). Yet, significant gaps remain in our understanding of the specific effects of remote work, particularly in relation to frequency (i.e., the balance between work days from home vs. employer's premises), on key outcomes like workers' psychological well-being (Fan & Moen, 2025; Ng et al., 2022; Shimura et al., 2021). This gap becomes particularly critical when considering the aging workforce. As digitalization progresses, older workers face unique pressures, navigating choices between upskilling and retirement, potentially exacerbating existing inequalities (Hecker et al., 2021; Komp-Leukkunen, 2023). Concerns about digital fluency, often fueled by age stereotypes, can impact older workers' confidence and integration into digitally mediated work (Hampel & Kunze, 2023; Hecker et al., 2021). While some research indicates older workers can successfully work from home (Chen & Munnell, 2020) and may even experience benefits like reduced psychological demands in remote settings (Fan & Moen, 2025), other studies suggest they might perceive remote work less positively or face specific strains related to technology use (Schellaert & Derous, 2024; Toscano et al., 2022). However, although the benefits of age-inclusive workplaces are recognized (OECD, 2020) and the need for research to inform supportive policies is clear (Pit et al., 2021; Ribeiro et al., 2024), there is insufficient empirical evidence on the age-specific psychosocial consequences of varying WFH frequencies. This knowledge is crucial for developing effective, age-sensitive organizational policies that promote well-being and leverage the potential of a multigenerational workforce in the modern era (Komp-Leukkunen, 2023; OECD, 2020).

In response to this gap, this study investigates the differential impact of distributed work arrangements on psychological well-being across age groups. Specifically, we aim to examine how the frequency of WFH, when controlled for gender and work-life balance, influences self-reported well-being scores across the age spectrum (16–24, 25–34, 35–44, 45–55, 56+). By employing an age-stratified analytical approach using large-scale European data (EWCTS 2021), this research seeks to uncover generational differences potentially masked in studies examining the workforce as a whole. Our work supports answering the following research question: How does the frequency of WFH impact psychological well-being across various workers' age cohorts within digitally enabled work contexts?

This research is significant as it directly addresses the call for a more nuanced, age-sensitive understanding of work in the digital age (Fan & Moen, 2025; Komp-Leukkunen, 2023). It moves beyond feasibility questions (Chen & Munnell, 2020) to examine the psychosocial outcomes of distributed work across the life course. The findings promise to contribute evidence for designing digital work policies that are not only efficient but also equitable and supportive of worker well-being at all ages, fostering environments where employees can live, learn, and earn longer and healthier lives (OECD, 2020; Ranasinghe et al., 2024).

2 Theoretical Background

This study is situated at the intersection of several key theoretical streams: the transformation of work through digitalization and distributed models, the determinants of psychological well-being in the workplace, and the life-course perspective applied to an aging workforce. Understanding how these streams converge is essential for analyzing and interpreting the differential impact of work-from-home (WFH) frequency on well-being across age groups.

2.1 The Evolving World of Work: Digitalization and Distributed Work Models

Contemporary workplaces are fundamentally shaped by ongoing digital transformation (Bolici et al., 2025b; Komp-Leukkunen et al., 2022). This involves more than just adopting new tools; it entails the integration of digital technologies into core processes, the rise of data-driven decision-making, and the increasing use of intelligent automation systems like artificial intelligence (Crowston & Bolici, 2019, 2025; Zhao & Xie, 2023). This digitalization impacts job tasks, required competencies, communication patterns, and organizational structures (Belbase & Chen, 2019; Bolici et al., 2025a). While offering potential for efficiency gains, it also necessitates continuous adaptation and learning from employees, particularly concerning digital skills and fluency (Hecker et al., 2021; Ranasinghe et al., 2024). The risk of job substitution through automation can also be a source of occupational stress, potentially moderated by factors like remote work engagement (Zhao & Xie, 2023). One major consequence of digitalization, combined with external pressures like the COVID-19 pandemic, has been the normalization of distributed work, especially WFH (Jansen et al., 2024; Ng et al., 2022). The capacity for jobs to be performed remotely varies significantly by occupation and industry (Dingel & Neiman, 2020), and access to remote work opportunities during crises like the pandemic was not equitable, often influenced by factors like ethnicity, education, and pre-existing job roles (Andrea et al., 2022; Settels, 2023). The effectiveness of remote work often depends on a confluence of factors within the Technology-Organization-Environment (TOE) framework, including technological competence, organizational support (like work flexibility), and enabling environmental factors (like government support) (Ng et al., 2022). As organizations increasingly adopt remote or hybrid models, understanding their impact becomes crucial.

2.2 Psychological Well-Being in the Work Context

Psychological well-being in the workplace encompasses subjective experiences of satisfaction, positive affect, engagement, and the absence of excessive stress or burnout (Galanti et al., 2021; Shimura et al., 2021). This study utilizes the WHO-5 Well-Being Index, a widely validated measure capturing positive mood, vitality, and general interest over a recent period, providing a concise assessment of subjective psychological health. Worker well-being is influenced by a complex interplay of job demands and resources (Kanfer et al., 2020). Key factors include job control or autonomy (Galanti et al., 2021; Sousa et al., 2023), social support from colleagues and supervisors (Hampel & Kunze, 2023; Miyake et al., 2022; Schellaert & Derous, 2024), manageable workload, and clear expectations. Crucially, the ability to balance work responsibilities with personal life demands (work-life balance) is consistently linked to well-being (Galanti et al., 2021; Komp-Leukkunen, 2023; Toscano et al., 2022). The blurring of boundaries between work and home, often exacerbated by remote work, can significantly challenge this balance and impact well-being (Araújo & Lua, 2021). Gender differences in well-being are also frequently observed, potentially reflecting differing work experiences, societal roles, or reporting patterns (Araújo & Lua, 2021; Toscano et al., 2022).

Distributed work arrangements, particularly WFH, fundamentally alter the work context and can therefore have significant psychosocial consequences. WFH can enhance perceived autonomy and flexibility, allowing employees greater control over their work schedule and environment (Ng et al., 2022; Sousa et al., 2023). This autonomy can contribute positively to job satisfaction (Sousa et al., 2023). Some research suggests remote work can be associated with reduced psychological and physical stress responses, potentially due to greater control or reduced exposure to office stressors (Shimura et al., 2021). Despite the benefits, WFH carries significant risks. Social isolation due to reduced face-to-face interaction with colleagues is a primary concern, negatively impacting engagement and potentially increasing loneliness (Galanti et al., 2021; Miyake et al., 2022). The erosion of boundaries between professional and personal life can lead to increased family-work conflict and make it difficult to psychologically detach from work (Araújo & Lua, 2021; Galanti et al., 2021). This can intensify workload perceptions and contribute to stress and exhaustion (Ng et al., 2022; Toscano et al., 2022). Furthermore, full-time remote work may increase presenteeism (working while unwell), potentially harming long-term health and productivity (Shimura et al., 2021). Inadequate technological infrastructure, lack of technical support, or insufficient protection within existing labor frameworks can also create stress and disadvantage remote workers (Ng et al., 2022; Rajevska et al., 2022). Physical health issues, like back pain, have also been associated with potentially suboptimal home working conditions (Saes-Silva et al., 2023).

The amount of time spent working from home likely matters. Occasional remote work might offer flexibility benefits without triggering significant isolation, while full-time WFH could maximize risks like loneliness and presenteeism (Miyake et al., 2022; Shimura et al., 2021). Hybrid models may offer a balance, but require careful management to ensure equitable experiences. Therefore, examining well-being across different WFH frequencies (from never to always) is crucial for understanding dose-response relationships.

2.3 The Age Dimension: A Life-Course Perspective

Applying a life-course perspective suggests that individuals' experiences and adaptation to work arrangements like WFH are shaped by their age, accumulated experiences, life stage, and the socio-historical context (Komp-Leukkunen, 2023; OECD, 2020).

OECD countries face significant workforce aging, necessitating policies that support longer working lives and leverage the skills of older employees (OECD, 2020). Ageism remains a barrier, potentially affecting opportunities and perceptions (Hampel & Kunze, 2023; OECD, 2020). While stereotypes persist about older workers and technology, many possess valuable experience and can adapt effectively, especially with adequate support and training (OECD, 2020; Ranasinghe et al., 2024). Digitalization presents both challenges (need for upskilling, potential ICT strain) and opportunities (flexible work potentially extending careers) (Hecker et al., 2021; Komp-Leukkunen, 2023; Schellaert & Derous, 2024). The ability and preference for WFH among older workers is an area of active inquiry (Chen & Munnell, 2020; Settels, 2023).

Several factors suggest that WFH frequency might affect well-being differently across age groups. First, younger workers, often earlier in their careers, may rely more heavily on the physical workplace for building social networks and mentorship, making them potentially more vulnerable to isolation from extensive WFH (Kłopotek, 2017; Miyake et al., 2022). Older workers might have more established external social networks but still benefit from workplace support systems (Schellaert & Derous, 2024). Second, different age groups face distinct work-life demands (e.g., young children for mid-career workers, potentially fewer dependents or different care responsibilities for older workers). How WFH interacts with these varying demands will influence work-life balance and resulting well-being (Araújo & Lua, 2021; Komp-Leukkunen, 2023). Third, older workers may possess greater experience in navigating work challenges and established coping mechanisms, potentially leading to greater resilience when facing the stressors of remote work or ICT strain (Fan & Moen, 2025; Schellaert & Derous, 2024). Fourth, while digital fluency varies within all age groups, older cohorts might experience higher average ICT-related strain if adequate support or training is lacking, potentially mediating the relationship between telework intensity and outcomes (Hampel & Kunze, 2023; Schellaert & Derous, 2024). Lastly, proximity to retirement and differing career goals might influence how older workers perceive and value the flexibility or challenges of WFH (Parfenova, 2023; Schellaert & Derous, 2024). Some studies find higher job satisfaction among older remote workers (Sousa et al., 2023), while others find they perceive the experience less positively overall (Toscano et al., 2022).

Accordingly, the literature suggests that psychological well-being in distributed work settings is significantly influenced by the work arrangement itself (WFH frequency), the resources and demands inherent in it (autonomy, isolation, boundary management), and individual characteristics and resources (age, gender, work-life balance capability). By applying a life-course lens, our work shows that the net effect of WFH frequency on well-being will vary systematically across age cohorts, possibly attributable to differences in social needs, life stage demands, technological adaptation, and accumulated coping resources, as previously suggested in the literature. This study seeks to empirically analyze these differential impacts within today's digitally enabled European work context.

3 Methods

3.1 Data Source and Sample

This study utilized data from the European Working Conditions Telephone Survey (EWCTS) 2021, the seventh edition of this large-scale, cross-sectional survey conducted by the European Foundation for the Improvement of Living and Working Conditions (Eurofound) (Eurofound, 2023). The EWCTS aims to provide a comprehensive overview of the working lives of employees and self-employed individuals across Europe. Data collection for the 2021 wave occurred between March and November 2021 via computer-assisted telephone interviews (CATI), covering 36 European countries. The survey employs a rigorous methodology involving stratified random sampling within countries to ensure representativeness of the target working population (Rodriguez et al., 2024). The use of this dataset is advantageous due to its large sample size, broad geographical coverage, and detailed information on work arrangements, psychosocial factors, and well-being, particularly relevant in the context of the widespread adoption of remote work following the COVID-19 pandemic.

For the present analysis, specific inclusion criteria were applied to focus the sample on the population most relevant to the research question concerning distributed work in digitally enabled contexts. First, only respondents currently active in the labor market were included. Second, to ensure the sample consisted of individuals whose jobs are potentially amenable to remote work, we restricted the analysis to those in occupations classified as ICT-related and teleworkable according to the framework developed by Sostero et al. (2020). This filtering approach aims to isolate the effects of WFH frequency within a population where such arrangements are feasible and increasingly adopted.

After applying these criteria, the final analytical sample comprised 46,426 individuals. Table 1 presents the distribution of the sample across the five age cohorts used in the stratified analysis.

Table 1 Descriptive statistics for the analyzed sample

Group	Number of observations	Mean WHO-5	Std. deviation (SD)
16–24	2897	16.28	4.97
25–34	11,224	15.68	4.93
35–44	12,970	15.58	5.02
45–55	12,396	16.08	5.02
56+	6939	16.83	4.87

3.2 Measures

The primary outcome measure was psychological well-being, assessed using the World Health Organization's Five Well-Being Index (WHO-5). The WHO-5 is a positively worded scale widely recognized for its validity and reliability in measuring subjective psychological well-being across diverse populations and contexts (Topp et al., 2015). It consists of five items evaluating the frequency of positive feelings over the preceding 2 weeks: feeling cheerful and in good spirits (cheerful), feeling calm and relaxed (relaxed), feeling active and vigorous (active), waking up feeling fresh and rested (rested), and finding daily life filled with things that interest the respondent (interesting).

Each item was rated on a 6-point Likert scale (original coding: 1 = "All of the time" to 6 = "At no time"). Following standard practice to ensure higher scores reflect better well-being (Topp et al., 2015), the items were reverse-coded (0 = "At no time", to 5 = "All of the time"). The raw sum score was then computed by summing the reverse-coded responses, yielding a total score ranging from 0 to 25. This raw sum score was used as the dependent variable in the regression analyses, as it maintains the original interval properties of the summed scale and allows for direct interpretation of the magnitude of regression coefficients. Higher scores on this scale indicate higher levels of psychological well-being. Table 1 provides descriptive statistics for the mean and standard deviation of the WHO-5 score by age cohort.

For the regression analyses, the independent and control variables were operationalized as follows:

Work-from-Home (WFH) Frequency: This was measured using the survey item asking respondents about the frequency of working from home. Responses were treated as a categorical variable with five levels: "Never" (original code 1), "Rarely" (2), "Sometimes" (3), "Often" (4), and "Always" (5). For the regression analysis, this was entered as a factor variable, with "Never" serving as the reference category against which other frequencies were compared.

Age Cohorts: Respondents were assigned to one of five mutually exclusive age groups based on their declared age in the dataset: 16–24 years, 25–34 years, 35–44 years, 45–55 years, and 56+ years.

Gender: Included as a dichotomous variable distinguishing between male and female.

Table 2 GVIF resulting from all the regression models

Age cohort	Remote-work cat	Gender	Work-life balance
16–24 years old	1.0023	1.0009	1.0028
25–34 years old	1.0022	1.0020	1.0024
35–44 years old	1.0019	1.0038	1.0017
45–55 years old	1.0010	1.0011	1.0011
56+ years old	1.0017	1.0016	1.0019

Values are rounded to four decimal places
All GVIFs are ≈ 1, indicating negligible multicollinearity in all models

Work-life balance: It indicates a self-reported assessment of the quality of work-life balance. This is expressed in a 4-point Likert scale with a baseline of "Not at all well" at a maximum of "Very well."

3.3 Statistical Analysis

To investigate the differential impact of WFH frequency on psychological well-being across age groups, we employed Ordinary Least Squares (OLS) regression analysis (Weisberg, 2005). The primary analytical strategy involved constructing five separate regression models, one for each age cohort (16–24, 25–34, 35–44, 45–55, 56+). In each model, the WHO-5 raw sum score was the dependent variable. The independent variables included the categorical measure of WFH frequency (with "Never" as the reference), gender (with "Male" as the reference), and the categorical measure of work-life balance (with "Not at all well" as the reference). This stratified approach allowed for a direct comparison of the regression coefficients (β) associated with WFH frequency, gender, and work-life balance across the different age groups, revealing how the relationships between these factors and well-being vary with age.

To assess potential multicollinearity among predictors, Variance Inflation Factors (VIFs) were examined. For categorical predictors with multiple levels, such as WFH frequency and work-life balance, Generalized VIFs (GVIF) were calculated to ensure comparability with standard VIF thresholds (Fox, 2016; Fox & Monette, 1992). The resulting values across all models were very close to 1 (see Table 2), indicating that multicollinearity was not a concern and ensuring the stability of the coefficient estimates (Hair et al., 2006; Neter et al., 1989). Statistical significance for the regression coefficients was assessed using p-values, with a conventional threshold of $p < 0.05$. All analyses were conducted using the RStudio software.

4 Results

Our analysis revealed an age-dependent pattern in how the frequency of WFH affects self-reported psychological well-being (see Tables 3, 4, 5, 6 and 7).

Table 3 Regression results for the age cohort 16–24 years old

Variable	Estimate	Std. error	t	p-value
Intercept	12.686	0.452	28.094	< 0.001 ***
WFH frequency: Rarely	−0.386	0.310	−1.245	0.213
WFH frequency: Sometimes	−0.531	0.302	−1.757	0.079
WFH frequency: Often	−0.709	0.259	−2.735	0.006 **
WFH frequency: Always	−1.551	0.265	−5.856	< 0.001 ***
Gender: Female	−1.459	0.174	−8.403	< 0.001 ***
Work-life balance: Not very well	2.256	0.507	4.447	< 0.001 ***
Work-life balance: Well	4.424	0.460	9.622	< 0.001 ***
Work-life balance: Very well	6.186	0.463	13.370	< 0.001 ***

Residual SE: 4.658 (df = 2877)
Multiple R^2: 0.126; Adjusted R^2: 0.123
F-statistic: 51.72 (df = 8, 2877) $p < 0.001$

Table 4 Regression results for the age cohort 25–34 years old

Variable	Estimate	Std. error	t	p-value
Intercept	12.596	0.214	58.838	< 0.001 ***
WFH frequency: Rarely	−0.789	0.150	−5.250	< 0.001 ***
WFH frequency: Sometimes	−0.728	0.137	−5.326	< 0.001 ***
WFH frequency: Often	−1.323	0.119	−11.123	< 0.001 ***
WFH frequency: Always	−1.817	0.129	−14.084	< 0.001 ***
Gender: Female	−0.821	0.087	−9.387	< 0.001 ***
Work-life balance: Not very well	1.890	0.239	7.895	< 0.001 ***
Work-life balance: Well	4.076	0.217	18.800	< 0.001 ***
Work-life balance: Very well	5.920	0.219	26.982	< 0.001 ***

Residual SE: 4.615 (df = 11,173)
Multiple R^2: 0.123; Adjusted R^2: 0.122
F-statistic: 195.9 (df = 8, 11,173), $p < 0.001$

Table 5 Regression results for the age cohort 35–44 years old

Variable	Estimate	Std. error	t	p-value
Intercept	12.800	0.206	62.064	< 0.001 ***
WFH frequency: Rarely	−0.705	0.148	−4.763	< 0.001 ***
WFH frequency: Sometimes	−0.779	0.129	−6.060	< 0.001 ***
WFH frequency: Often	−1.252	0.112	−11.174	< 0.001 ***
WFH frequency: Always	−1.571	0.125	−12.517	< 0.001 ***
Gender: Female	−0.909	0.083	−10.885	< 0.001 ***
Work-life balance: Not very well	1.624	0.227	7.163	< 0.001 ***
Work-life balance: Well	3.942	0.207	19.059	< 0.001 ***
Work-life balance: Very well	5.677	0.211	26.969	< 0.001 ***

Residual SE: 4.722 (df = 12,890)
Multiple R^2: 0.114; Adjusted R^2: 0.114
F-statistic: 208.2 (df = 8, 12,890) $p < 0.001$

Table 6 Regression results for the age cohort 45–55 years old

Variable	Estimate	Std. error	*t*	*p*-value
Intercept	12.744	0.232	54.881	< 0.001 ***
WFH frequency: Rarely	−0.449	0.152	−2.952	0.003 **
WFH frequency: Sometimes	−0.595	0.128	−4.646	< 0.001 ***
WFH frequency: Often	−0.989	0.113	−8.782	< 0.001 ***
WFH frequency: Always	−1.169	0.130	−8.984	< 0.001 ***
Gender: Female	−1.026	0.085	−12.061	< 0.001 ***
Work-life balance: Not very well	1.758	0.254	6.922	< 0.001 ***
Work-life balance: Well	4.240	0.232	18.283	< 0.001 ***
Work-life balance: Very well	6.163	0.235	26.242	< 0.001 ***

Residual SE: 4.702 (df = 12,324)
Multiple R^2: 0.121; Adjusted R^2: 0.120
F-statistic: 211.5 (df = 8, 12,324) $p < 0.001$

Table 7 Regression results for the age cohort 56+ years old

Variable	Estimate	Std. error	*t*	*p*-value
Intercept	12.973	0.352	36.811	< 0.001 ***
WFH frequency: Rarely	−0.292	0.199	−1.471	0.141
WFH frequency: Sometimes	−0.326	0.174	−1.873	0.061
WFH frequency: Often	−0.566	0.148	−3.835	< 0.001 ***
WFH frequency: Always	−0.406	0.165	−2.458	0.014 *
Gender: Female	−1.181	0.111	−10.625	< 0.001 ***
Work-life balance: Not very well	2.283	0.387	5.899	< 0.001 ***
Work-life balance: Well	4.313	0.354	12.171	< 0.001 ***
Work-life balance: Very well	6.229	0.357	17.463	< 0.001 ***

Residual SE: 4.605 (df = 6894)
Multiple R^2: 0.105; Adjusted R^2: 0.104
F-statistic: 101.2 (df = 8, 6894) $p < 0.001$

The association between WFH frequency and well-being displayed a clear !age-related gradient, particularly for high levels of remote work, when compared to the reference category of "Never" working from home. Individuals working from home "Always" reported significantly lower well-being scores across most age groups. This negative association was strongest in the 25–34 cohort (β = −1.817), followed by the 35–44 cohort (β = −1.571) and the 16–24 cohort (β = −1.551). The effect diminished notably for the 45–55 group (β = −1.169) and was substantially smaller for the 56+ group (β = −0.406). A similar, though less pronounced, age-dependent pattern emerged for working from home "Often." The negative association compared to "Never" was largest for the 25–34 cohort (β = −1.323) and the 35–44 cohort (β = −1.252), decreasing for the 45–55 group (β = −0.989) and the 56+ group (β = −0.566). For the youngest cohort (16–24), the coefficient was also negative (β = −0.709). The coefficients for "Sometimes" and "Rarely" working from home (compared to "Never") were generally smaller in magnitude and less consistent across age groups. For instance, "Rarely" showed coefficients near zero for the 16–24 and 56+ cohorts, while being negative for the 25–34 ($\beta = -0.789$), 35–44 ($\beta = -0.705$), and 45–55 ($\beta = -0.449$) cohorts. "Sometimes" showed a similar pattern, with coefficients near zero for the youngest and oldest groups, and negative values for the middle age groups (25–34: $\beta = -0.728$; 35–44: $\beta = -0.779$; 45–55: $\beta = -0.595$).

A consistent gender difference in reported well-being was observed across all age cohorts. Females reported significantly lower WHO-5 scores compared to males (the reference category), even after controlling for WFH frequency and work-life balance. The magnitude of this negative association varied somewhat by age: $\beta = -1.458$ (16–24), $\beta = -0.821$ (25–34), $\beta = -0.909$ (35–44), $\beta = -1.026$ (45–55), and $\beta = -1.180$ (56+).

Work-life balance emerged as a substantial predictor of psychological well-being, demonstrating a strong positive association across all age groups compared to the reference category ("Not at all well"). Reporting "Very well" work-life balance was associated with the largest increase in WHO-5 scores. The coefficients were remarkably consistent and large across cohorts: $\beta = 6.186$ (16–24), $\beta = 5.920$ (25–34), $\beta = 5.677$ (35–44), $\beta = 6.163$ (45–55), and $\beta = 6.229$ (56+). Reporting "Well" work-life balance also showed a strong positive association with well-being in all age groups: $\beta = 4.423$ (16–24), $\beta = 4.076$ (25–34), $\beta = 3.942$ (35–44), $\beta = 4.240$ (45–55), and $\beta = 4.313$ (56+). Even reporting "Not very well" work-life balance was associated with significantly higher well-being compared to "Not at all well," although the effect was smaller than for "Well" or "Very well": $\beta = 2.256$ (16–24), $\beta = 1.890$ (25–34), $\beta = 1.624$ (35–44), $\beta = 1.758$ (45–55), and $\beta = 2.283$ (56+).

Considering these findings, the regression analyses highlight that the negative association between high-frequency WFH and well-being diminishes with age. Conversely, female gender is consistently associated with lower well-being across the age spectrum, while positive work-life balance shows a uniformly strong, positive association with well-being irrespective of age group. Therefore, while extensive remote work may pose well-being challenges, particularly for younger workers, older workers appear comparatively more resilient to these effects, whereas the importance of achieving a good work-life balance for well-being transcends age.

5 Discussion and Implications

This study identified an age-dependent relationship between digital work arrangements, specifically WFH frequency, and psychological well-being, while also considering the influence of gender and work-life balance.

The observed age-graded impact of WFH on well-being, where extensive WFH is associated with lower well-being most pronouncedly in younger to mid-career cohorts (16–44 years) but significantly attenuated in older workers (56+), resonates strongly with life-course theories. These theories posit that aging is a lifelong process, and adult functioning, including resilience, is shaped by accumulated biological capital and lifetime trajectories of capability (Kuh, 2007). Older workers may have developed more effective coping mechanisms or possess different social and professional needs at their career stage (Fan & Moen, 2025), reflecting diverse adaptation styles rooted in long-term experiences (Crosnoe & Glen, 2002). In contrast, younger workers, who are often navigating earlier career and life stages, might find that extensive WFH disrupts crucial opportunities for social integration, mentorship, and professional identity formation (Miyake et al., 2022). This aligns with life course epidemiology concepts suggesting that certain developmental periods may be more sensitive to specific environmental exposures like reduced workplace interaction (Berkman et al., 2011).

The finding that females report lower well-being across all age cohorts, even after controlling for WFH frequency and work-life balance, points to enduring systemic issues. This disparity suggests that factors beyond current work arrangements, potentially rooted in cumulative disadvantages or differing social trajectories shaped by gender (Berkman et al., 2011; Stowe & Cooney, 2015), contribute significantly to well-being. The often-cited "double burden" (Araújo & Lua, 2021) may not be fully alleviated by remote work and can reflect broader societal and structural challenges, such as the reconciliation of work and family, that continue to disproportionately affect women throughout their life course (Bovenberg, 2008). Life course perspectives indeed emphasize how social structures, including gender, intricately shape individual experiences and outcomes over time (Stowe & Cooney, 2015).

Furthermore, work-life balance emerged as the most substantial positive predictor of psychological well-being across all age groups, highlighting that the capacity to effectively manage the interface between professional responsibilities and personal life is crucial for employee well-being, irrespective of age or the extent of remote work. This finding strongly supports policy arguments advocating for systemic support for work-family reconciliation across the entire life course, rather than focusing on isolated life stages or benefits (Bovenberg, 2008). The life course principle of "linked lives" (Stowe & Cooney, 2015) also underscores this, as well-being is inextricably tied to the quality of an individual's roles and relationships both within and outside the formal work domain, making effective boundary management a critical skill and organizational support for it essential.

5.1 Implications and Future Research Directions

The findings and their interpretation offer several implications for organizational policy, practice, and future research.

Organizations should recognize the differential impact of WFH on various age groups. This calls for developing age-sensitive WFH policies that may include tailoring the extent of remote work offered or providing specific support mechanisms based on career stage and associated developmental needs. For younger employees, who appear more vulnerable to the potential downsides of high-frequency WFH, organizations should consider designing hybrid models that explicitly ensure adequate social connection, networking opportunities, and robust mentorship. For older workers, policies could focus on leveraging their adaptability while ensuring continued engagement and knowledge transfer.

To address the persistent gender gap in well-being, organizations must move beyond flexible work arrangements alone and tackle underlying systemic gender biases. This includes fostering an equitable environment that genuinely supports women's career progression and work-life balance across their entire life course, potentially involving proactive policies aimed at mitigating the "double burden" (Bovenberg, 2008).

Given the profound impact of work-life balance on well-being for all employees, organizations should elevate their support to a core strategic priority. This involves designing work structures, cultivating managerial competencies, and promoting workplace cultures that empower employees of all ages to achieve and maintain a healthy work-life interface. This could include implementing policies focused on workload management, schedule flexibility, and fostering an environment where employees feel comfortable utilizing such provisions.

Future research should aim to further investigate the specific mechanisms behind the observed age-related resilience to WFH. Indeed, investigating whether this stems from better-established social networks, different job characteristics, specific coping strategies, or altered work motivations near retirement (Parfenova, 2023) would provide a valuable contribution with strong practical impact on workers' well-being. Moreover, longitudinal studies are needed to track how WFH impacts well-being trajectories over longer periods and across different life transitions (Kuh, 2007).

6 Conclusion

This study analyzed the age-dependent effects of WFH frequency on psychological well-being, considering the roles of gender and work-life balance within Europe's digitally enabled workforce. By employing an age-stratified analysis of the EWCTS 2021 data, we found that high-frequency WFH is associated with diminished self-reported mental well-being, with this effect being most acute for younger and mid-career professionals and notably less pronounced for older workers. Moreover, our findings confirmed a persistent well-being gap for female employees across all age cohorts and underscored the importance of positive work-life balance as a powerful determinant of higher well-being.

These insights contribute age-sensitive evidence for improving workers' well-being in the evolving domain of digital work. Understanding both differential impacts and universal needs is vital for organizations aiming to design equitable, supportive, and effective distributed work policies. Such policies are essential not only for optimizing productivity but also for fostering environments where a multi-generational workforce can thrive in an era of profound work transformation (OECD, 2020; Ranasinghe et al., 2024).

This study has some limitations. The cross-sectional nature of the EWCTS 2021 dataset precludes the inference of causal relationships between WFH arrangements and well-being. Self-reported measures of well-being may also be subject to inherent biases. Additionally, the data were collected in 2021, during the immediate aftermath of the COVID-19 pandemic. Consequently, pandemic-related stressors, shifts in workplace norms, and the transitional nature of many remote work policies at that time might have influenced respondents' perceptions and experiences, potentially affecting the generalizability of findings to a more stable post-pandemic work environment.

References

Andrea, S. B., Eisenberg-Guyot, J., Blaikie, K. J., Owens, S., Oddo, V. M., Peckham, T., Minh, A., & Hajat, A. (2022). The inequitable burden of the COVID-19 pandemic among marginalized older workers in the United States: An intersectional approach. *The Journals of Gerontology: Series B, 77*(10), 1928–1937. https://doi.org/10.1093/geronb/gbac095

Araújo, T. M. d., & Lua, I. (2021). Work has moved home: Remote work in the context of the COVID-19 pandemic. *Revista Brasileira de Saúde Ocupacional, 46*, e27. https://doi.org/10.1590/2317-6369000030720

Belbase, A., & Chen, A. (2019). *How did computerization since the 1980s affect older workers?* (Issues in Brief) [Working paper]. Center for Retirement Research. https://EconPapers.repec.org/RePEc:crr:issbrf:ib2019-19

Berkman, L. F., Ertel, K. A., & Glymour, M. M. (2011). Chapter 24 - Aging and social intervention: Life course perspectives. In R. H. Binstock & L. K. George (Eds.), *Handbook of aging and the social sciences* (7th ed., pp. 337–351). Academic Press. https://doi.org/10.1016/B978-0-12-380880-6.00024-1

Bolici, F., Varone, A., & Diana, G. (2025a). Beyond AI automation: How replace, reinforce, reveal, and orchestrate modes align task interdependence and organizational design for effective AI implementation. In *Proceedings of theorizing data & AI 2025*. Theorizing Data & AI 2025.

Bolici, F., Varone, A., & Diana, G. (2025b). Innovating workspaces: The evolution of distributed work from telecommute to remote work. *ECIS 2025 proceedings*. https://aisel.aisnet.org/ecis2025/general_track/general_track/9

Bovenberg, A. L. (2008). The life-course perspective and social policies: An overview of the issues. *CESifo Economic Studies, 54*(4), 593–641. https://doi.org/10.1093/cesifo/ifn029

Chen, A., & Munnell, A. H. (2020). *Can older workers work from home?* http://dlib.bc.edu/islandora/object/bc-ir:108904

Crosnoe, R., & Glen, E. (2002). Successful adaptation in the later years: A life course approach to aging. *Social Psychology Quarterly, 65*(4), 309. https://doi.org/10.2307/3090105

Crowston, K., & Bolici, F. (2019). Impacts of machine learning on work. In *Proceedings of the 52nd Hawaii international conference on system sciences*.

Crowston, K., & Bolici, F. (2025). *Deskilling and upskilling with generative AI systems*. Proceedings of the iConference, iConference.

Dingel, J. I., & Neiman, B. (2020). How many jobs can be done at home? *Journal of Public Economics, 189*, 104235. https://doi.org/10.1016/j.jpubeco.2020.104235

Eurofound. (2023). *European Working Conditions Telephone Survey 2021 | European Foundation for the Improvement of Living and Working Conditions*. https://www.eurofound.europa.eu/en/data-catalogue/european-working-conditions-telephone-survey-2021-0

Fan, W., & Moen, P. (2025). The future(s) of work? Disparities around changing job conditions when remote/hybrid or returning to working at work. *Work and Occupations, 52*(1), 91–129. https://doi.org/10.1177/07308884231203668

Fox, J. (2016). *Applied regression analysis and generalized linear models* (3rd ed.). Sage.

Fox, J., & Monette, G. (1992). Generalized collinearity diagnostics. *Journal of the American Statistical Association, 87*(417), 178–183. https://doi.org/10.1080/01621459.1992.10475190

Galanti, T., Guidetti, G., Mazzei, E., Zappalà, S., & Toscano, F. (2021). Work from home during the COVID-19 outbreak: The impact on employees' remote work productivity, engagement, and stress. *Journal of Occupational and Environmental Medicine, 63*(7), e426. https://doi.org/10.1097/JOM.0000000000002236

Hair, J. F., Black, W. C., Babin, B. J., & Anderson, R. E. (Eds.). (2006). *Multivariate data analysis* (6th ed.). Pearson/Prentice Hall.

Hampel, K., & Kunze, F. (2023). The older, the less digitally fluent? The role of age stereotypes and supervisor support. *Work, Aging and Retirement, 9*(4), 393–398. https://doi.org/10.1093/workar/waad001

Hecker, I., Spaulding, S., & Kuehn, D. (2021). *Digital skills and older workers: Supporting success in training and employment in a digital world.* Urban Institute. https://eric.ed.gov/?id=ED616367

Jansen, T., Ascani, A., Faggian, A., & Palma, A. (2024). Remote work and location preferences: A study of post-pandemic trends in Italy. *The Annals of Regional Science, 73*(3), 897–944. https://doi.org/10.1007/s00168-024-01295-w

Kanfer, R., Lyndgaard, S. F., & Tatel, C. E. (2020). For whom the pandemic tolls: A person-centric analysis of older workers. *Work, Aging and Retirement, 6*(4), 238–241. https://doi.org/10.1093/workar/waaa014

Kłopotek, M. (2017). The advantages and disadvantages of remote working from the perspective of young employees. *Organizacja i Zarządzanie: Kwartalnik Naukowy, 4*, 39. https://doi.org/10.29119/1899-6116.2017.40.3

Komp-Leukkunen, K. (2023). A life-course perspective on older workers in workplaces undergoing transformative digitalization. *The Gerontologist, 63*(9), 1413–1418. https://doi.org/10.1093/geront/gnac181

Komp-Leukkunen, K., Poli, A., Hellevik, T., Herlofson, K., Heuer, A., Norum, R., Solem, P. E., Khan, J., Rantanen, V., & Motel Klingebiel, A. (2022). Older workers in digitalizing workplaces: A systematic literature review. *The Journal of Aging and Social Change, 12*(2), 37–59. https://doi.org/10.18848/2576-5310/CGP/v12i02/37-59

Kuh, D. (2007). A life course approach to healthy aging, frailty, and capability. *The Journals of Gerontology Series A: Biological Sciences and Medical Sciences, 62*(7), 717–721. https://doi.org/10.1093/gerona/62.7.717

Miyake, F., Odgerel, C.-O., Hino, A., Ikegami, K., Nagata, T., Tateishi, S., Tsuji, M., Matsuda, S., & Ishimaru, T. (2022). Job stress and loneliness among desk workers during the COVID-19 pandemic in Japan: Focus on remote working. *Environmental Health and Preventive Medicine, 27*, 33–33. https://doi.org/10.1265/ehpm.22-00107

Neter, J., Wasserman, W., & Kutner, M. H. (1989). *Applied linear regression models* (2nd ed.). Irwin.

Ng, P. M. L., Lit, K. K., & Cheung, C. T. Y. (2022). Remote work as a new normal? The technology-organization-environment (TOE) context. *Technology in Society, 70*, 102022. https://doi.org/10.1016/j.techsoc.2022.102022

OECD. (2020). *Promoting an age-inclusive workforce: Living, learning and earning longer.* OECD. https://doi.org/10.1787/59752153-en

Parfenova, O. A. (2023). Paths of extended employment among intellectual and creative workers aged 60 and above. *The Journal of Social Policy Studies, 21*(3), 539–550. https://doi.org/10.17323/727-0634-2023-21-3-539-550

Pit, S., Fisk, M., Freihaut, W., Akintunde, F., Aloko, B., Berge, B., Burmeister, A., Ciacâru, A., Deller, J., Dulmage, R., Han, T. H., Hao, Q., Honeyman, P., Huber, P. C., Linner, T., Lundberg, S., Nwamara, M., Punpuing, K., Schramm, J., et al. (2021). COVID-19 and the ageing workforce: Global perspectives on needs and solutions across 15 countries. *International Journal for Equity in Health, 20*(1), 221. https://doi.org/10.1186/s12939-021-01552-w

Rajevska, O., Reine, A., & Baltmane, D. (2022). Impact of the first wave of COVID-19 on the employment of older people in Latvia, the Baltic States and Europe. *SHS Web of Conferences, 131*, 01005. https://doi.org/10.1051/shsconf/202213101005

Ranasinghe, T., Grosse, E. H., Glock, C. H., & Jaber, M. Y. (2024). Never too late to learn: Unlocking the potential of aging workforce in manufacturing and service industries. *International Journal of Production Economics, 270*, 109193. https://doi.org/10.1016/j.ijpe.2024.109193

Ribeiro, J., da Silva, F. P., & Vieira, P. R. (2024). Remote workers' well-being: Are innovative organizations really concerned? A bibliometrics analysis. *Journal of Innovation & Knowledge, 9*(4), 100595. https://doi.org/10.1016/j.jik.2024.100595

Rodriguez, J. L., García, M. del M. R., Rodríguez, B. C., Ferri-García, R., Moreno, L. N., Chorne, L. D., Navarro, M. C., & Suárez-Lledo, V. (2024). *European working conditions telephone survey 2021: Data quality assessment*. https://policycommons.net/artifacts/14523254/european-working-conditions-telephone-survey-2021/15422983/

Saes-Silva, E., Saes, M. d. O., Meucci, R. D., Meller, F. d. O., Schäfer, A. A., & Dumith, S. C. (2023). Remote work and back pain during the COVID-19 pandemic in adults and older population in South Brazil. *Ciência & Saúde Coletiva, 28*, 731–738. https://doi.org/10.1590/1413-81232023283.14362022

Schellaert, M., & Derous, E. (2024). Retirement decisions in times of COVID-19: The role of telework, ICT-related strain and social support on older workers' intentions to continue working. *Personnel Review, 53*(8), 1950–1973. https://doi.org/10.1108/PR-04-2023-0286

Settels, J. (2023). Conditional on the environment? The contextual embeddedness of age, health, and socioeconomic status as predictors of remote work among older Europeans through the COVID-19 pandemic. *Sociological Perspectives, 66*(4), 609–639. https://doi.org/10.1177/07311214231167171

Shimura, A., Yokoi, K., Ishibashi, Y., Akatsuka, Y., & Inoue, T. (2021). Remote work decreases psychological and physical stress responses, but full-remote work increases presenteeism. *Frontiers in Psychology, 12*, 730969. https://doi.org/10.3389/fpsyg.2021.730969

Sostero, M., Milasi, S., Hurley, J., Fernández-Macías, E., & Bisello, M. (2020). *Teleworkability and the COVID-19 crisis: A new digital divide?* (JRC working papers series on labour, education and technology no. 2020/05; issue 2020/05). European Commission, Joint Research Centre (JRC). http://hdl.handle.net/10419/231337

Sousa, M., Mendes, A., Almeida, D., & Rocha, Á. (2023). Digital remote work influencing public administration employees satisfaction in public health complex contexts. *Computer Science and Information Systems, 20*(4), 1569–1589. https://doi.org/10.2298/CSIS230110060S

Stowe, J. D., & Cooney, T. M. (2015). Examining Rowe and Kahn's concept of successful aging: Importance of taking a life course perspective. *The Gerontologist, 55*(1), 43–50. https://doi.org/10.1093/geront/gnu055

Topp, C. W., Østergaard, S. D., Søndergaard, S., & Bech, P. (2015). The WHO-5 well-being index: A systematic review of the literature. *Psychotherapy and Psychosomatics, 84*(3), 167–176. https://doi.org/10.1159/000376585

Toscano, F., Bigliardi, E., Polevaya, M. V., Kamneva, E. V., & Zappalà, S. (2022). Working remotely during the COVID-19 pandemic: Work-related psychosocial factors, work satisfaction, and job performance among Russian employees. *Psychology in Russia: State of the Art, 15*(1), 3–19. https://doi.org/10.11621/pir.2022.0101

Varone, A., & Bolici, F. (2025). From speculation to implementation: A systematic review of return-to-office research and its impact for organizations. *Proceedings of WOA2025*. WOA2025, Pescara, Italy.

Weisberg, S. (2005). *Applied linear regression*. John Wiley & Sons.

Zhao, H., & Xie, H. (2023). Workplace intelligent technology use and health of older remote workers. *Journal of Occupational and Environmental Medicine*. https://doi.org/10.1097/JOM.0000000000003402

MIX
Papier aus verantwortungsvollen Quellen
Paper from responsible sources
FSC® C105338

If you have any concerns about our products,
you can contact us on
ProductSafety@springernature.com

In case Publisher is established outside the EU,
the EU authorized representative is:
Springer Nature Customer Service Center GmbH
Europaplatz 3, 69115 Heidelberg, Germany

Printed by Libri Plureos GmbH
in Hamburg, Germany